WON'T LOSE
THIS DREAM

ALSO BY ANDREW GUMBEL

*Down for the Count: Dirty Elections
and the Rotten History of Democracy in America*

*Oklahoma City: What the Investigation Missed—
and Why It Still Matters*

WON'T LOSE THIS DREAM

How an Upstart Urban University Rewrote the Rules of a Broken System

ANDREW GUMBEL

NEW YORK
LONDON

Requests for permission to reproduce selections from this book should be made through our website: https://thenewpress.com/contact.

Published in the United States by The New Press, New York, 2020
Distributed by Two Rivers Distribution

ISBN 978-1-62097-470-4 (hc)
ISBN 978-1-62097-471-1 (ebook)
CIP data is available.

The New Press publishes books that promote and enrich public discussion and understanding of the issues vital to our democracy and to a more equitable world. These books are made possible by the enthusiasm of our readers; the support of a committed group of donors, large and small; the collaboration of our many partners in the independent media and the not-for-profit sector; booksellers, who often hand-sell New Press books; librarians; and above all by our authors.

www.thenewpress.com

Composition by dix!
This book was set in Garamond Premier Pro

Printed in the United States of America

10 9 8 7 6 5 4 3 2 1

To the students of Georgia State—
the ones who made it when the odds were stacked
against them and the ones who haven't, yet.

Our nation cannot afford to waste the human talent, the cultural and social richness, represented by those currently underrepresented in our society. If we do not create a nation that mobilizes the talents of all our citizens, we are destined for a diminished role in the global community and increased social turbulence. Most tragically, we will have failed to fulfill the promise of democracy upon which this nation was founded.

—James J. Duderstadt, *A University for the 21st Century*

We must view the movement to transform our schools as just as vital to our twenty-first century humanity as the civil rights movement was to our twentieth-century humanity. That is how we must approach our investment in the future. That is how we must demonstrate our love for young people and their creative capacities.

—Grace Lee Boggs, *The Next American Revolution*

CONTENTS

Introduction: The Difference with Those Harvard Kids   3

1: Fishing Village   19

2: Admit Them   39

3: Who Are We? Where Are We Going?   58

4: The Path to Destruction   76

5: Multidimensional Chess   96

6: Moneyball on Campus   113

7: This Is Not a Scam, Do Not Hang Up   134

8: A Well-Managed Plantation   151

9: Birth of an Idea   168

10: The Feeling Is Mutual   182

11: A Hundred Years from Now   198

12: Rogue Cows   213

13: Secure the Bag   232

14: Reproducibility   248

Acknowledgments   265

Notes   271

Selected Bibliography   295

Index   299

WON'T LOSE
THIS DREAM

INTRODUCTION:
THE DIFFERENCE WITH
THOSE HARVARD KIDS

Where Princeton Nelson came from, a college education wasn't just at the outer edges of possibility, it was beyond imagination. Yet here he was, a proud member of the class of 2018 at Georgia State University, a computer science major with a cap and gown and a more than respectable 3.3 GPA, taking his place at a crowded indoor commencement ceremony along with the Atlanta Fife Band and professors in gowns of many colors and a cascade of balloons in Panther blue and white that tumbled from the ceiling like confetti.

He, too, got to shake hands with the university president, Mark Becker, whose welcoming remarks had invoked "the magical power of thinking big." He, too, got to hug his fellow graduates, many of them seven or eight years younger than him, many sporting homemade slogans on their caps thanking God, or their mothers, or joking that "the tassel was worth the hassle." He, too, could bask in the pride of his relatives, none more amazed or delighted than the grandmother who had thrown him out as a teenager because he'd been too unruly to handle, or the aunt who had thrown him out all over again as a young adult because she didn't like the company he was keeping.

Nelson came from nothing, and he understood at an early age that it would be up to him to carve a path to something better, because nobody else was going to do it for him. Even when he slipped—and he slipped a lot—he knew the choices he made could mean the difference between life and death. He was born in an Iowa prison, the child of two parents convicted of drug dealing at the height of the crack cocaine epidemic, and within days he was in foster care, along with three older siblings. His mother stayed behind bars until he was three, and his father remained so conspicuously absent that Nelson didn't learn his name until the age of fourteen. Mostly, he was raised by his grandmother, Loretta, who brought all four children home and did her best to raise them on an assembly worker's salary in a small red house in suburban Chicago.

Nelson's mother was in no state to take him even when she got out of prison. She fell back into the drug underworld and, months after her release, was found shot to death in an abandoned building on Chicago's South Side. Nelson remembers seeing her body laid in an open casket at the funeral and remembers, too, how everyone looked at him, the poor homeless child with no mom or dad. "I don't think mom is going to wake up," he whispered to an uncle. And in that moment he intuited that his childhood, his age of innocence and wide-eyed wonder, was over already.

Loretta moved Princeton and his siblings to Atlanta for a fresh start, but there was little she could do to make up for what he had lost—or never had. By sixth grade, he was attending an institution for children with severe emotional and behavioral problems. By tenth grade, his grandmother found him so unruly she sent him to live with his older brother, now back in Chicago, where he was soon running with gang members and carrying a pistol to class in his school bag. Nelson's saving grace was that he was a good student, but his natural intelligence never offered more than a temporary reprieve from the storm raging in his head. Back in Atlanta, he was caught smoking weed in a high school bathroom and arrested, the first of three occasions during his wild teenage years when he wound up in police custody and Loretta had to bail him out. His grades yo-yoed, he bounced in and out of special schools, and he barely graduated high school.

Turning himself around was a long and painful process. For

years, he worked in warehouses and smoked weed and gave little thought to where his life was going. Still, he hated the feeling that he was a disappointment to his grandmother. He could never quite forget how his brother in Chicago had told him he was smart enough for college, so he signed himself up at Atlanta Technical College, thinking at first that he'd train to be a barber. Then it dawned on him that as long as he was taking out loans he'd be better off working toward an academic degree, not just a trade qualification. As it happened, there was a community college, Atlanta Metropolitan, right across the street, and he wandered over one day to enroll as a music major. He'd always enjoyed creating music beats on his grandmother's computer. Why not see where it could take him?

As he stood in line to register, he noticed a chart listing the professional fields expected to be most in demand in the Atlanta area by 2020, and his eyes fell on the words "computer science." "What did I have next to me in my grandmother's house this whole time?" he said. "A computer!" It wasn't just music beats that he'd created. He'd also worked on MySpace pages and video games, never thinking there could be a future in it. But now, apparently, there was. "It was a flash of light," he said, "I'm thinking, I'm a computer science major. That's my calling."

Nelson's grades were strong enough to earn him an associate's degree in computer science in two years. But his life, like that of almost every lower-income college student, remained precarious at best, a constant battle for time and money. When his aunt and uncle bought the house where he and his grandmother were living, one of the first things they did was evict him, saying they were concerned about his pot use and the shortcuts they suspected he was taking to make ends meet. They didn't do it the gentle way, either. A sheriff's deputy rapped at the door one morning and ordered Nelson to grab his things right away.

Before he could think of pursuing his studies further, he had to deal with the realities of homelessness. For two weeks he slept on the concrete floor of a bus station so he could bump up his savings from a job flipping burgers and buy himself a car. Once he had his Volkswagen Jetta, he signed on as an Uber driver. Soon he had a third job, as a security guard. Three days a week he stayed in a hotel to enjoy a bed and a hot shower; the other four days he parked overnight at a twenty-four-hour gas station or outside a Kroger's supermarket where the lights and security cameras made it less likely he'd be robbed, or worse.

He was still homeless when he started at Georgia State in the fall of 2016, and that presented a new problem: he couldn't hope to succeed with three jobs on top of a full course load and nowhere to rest his head. Still, he plowed ahead because he was afraid that the federal Pell grants he'd been relying on to subsidize his studies would run out if he delayed too long, and he didn't want to lose his one and only shot at a full university degree. He didn't want to throw himself on anyone's mercy. He didn't even want to *talk* about his predicament, because he'd done that once at the burger joint and his fellow kitchen workers had laughed at him. Once classes started, he quit that job to free up some hours in his schedule in the hope that something else would turn up. His grandmother had always taught him to stay positive.

And something *did* turn up. Starting in his second year, he joined forces with two of his fellow computer science majors and started designing websites as a side gig. That made him hopeful enough to move out of his car and put all his savings into a deposit for an apartment in Castleberry Hill, less than two miles from campus. The apartment became his touchstone; as long as he could hold on to it, he felt his life was on track. And losing it became his biggest fear. "I can't be one of those people who say, *I almost had it*," he told himself. It was touch and go, at first, because the freelance design work didn't come in as quickly as hoped and he had to take a full-time job as a cell phone technician for two weeks to make what he needed for the next month's rent. He never told his professors what was going on. He just skipped class and let his grades suffer, calculating that he could catch up on the coursework later. And he did.

To many eyes, Nelson might not have looked like college material at all. Georgia State, though, was starting to enjoy a national reputation for its pioneering work in retaining and graduating large numbers of students much like him—poor, black, and struggling to make it as the first in their family to attend college. The university understood his need for extra support. When Nelson was caught smoking weed on campus his first year, the authorities went easy on him. When it became apparent he was depressed because of the financial pressures, he was encouraged to see a campus therapist, the first counselor he'd ever talked to. When he told the director of academic assistance that he'd grown up an orphan and had nobody to depend on but himself, she gave him a part-time job on her help desk. Twice when his money was running dangerously low, the university awarded him grants to help him reach the finish line.

Academics were never Nelson's problem. Next to what he'd been through, a challenging course in math or programming held no terrors. Rather, he became fascinated by what it meant to live a normal, middle-class life and was determined to learn how to lead one himself. He'd spend hours sitting in coffee shops, just observing: how people sat, how they picked up their spoon and sipped their coffee, how they talked and listened and kept their negative emotions in check. "You don't want to be judged. Not when you've been judged all your life and told you ain't gonna be shit when you grow up," he said. "I'm always thinking about where I came from. And I still feel like I'm dumb, like I'm still competing with all these college students and falling short."

It's a feeling that did not go away even after he graduated and headed toward his first full-time job as a software engineer for Infosys. "That's the difference between me and those Harvard kids," he said. "If people like me fail, we're going to fail *our life*."

Nelson was far from the only member of Georgia State's class of 2018 with a tale of adversity and triumph. Greyson Walldorff, who had been forced to give up an athletic scholarship in his sophomore year because of a concussion, stayed afloat and completed a business degree by starting a landscaping company that grew over time to five employees and more than a hundred clients. Larry Felton Johnson completed a journalism degree on his fourth try, forty-nine years after he first enrolled, thanks to a state program that offered free tuition to students over the age of sixty-two. Then there was Savannah Torrance, who had almost dropped out in her freshman year because she was commuting sixty miles each way from her mother's house, working long shifts at a supermarket, and absolutely hating the chemistry class she thought she needed to build a career in the medical field. Thanks to some timely guidance from Georgia State's advising center, though, she switched to speech communications, which required no chemistry, won a state merit scholarship she'd narrowly missed out of high school, and was soon thriving both in her studies and as a student orientation leader, university ambassador, and member of the student government association.

Georgia State boasts almost no success story that doesn't include at least one moment where everything was in danger of crumbling to dust. At a school where close to 60 percent of undergraduates are poor enough to qualify for the federal Pell grant, that is just the nature of things. Most students don't get to dwell in the heady realm of intellectual pursuit and personal self-discovery without also having to work twenty or thirty hours a week, scrimping for every last dollar to stay enrolled in class, bearing the responsibility of friends or family members in trouble, battling the Atlanta traffic in a battered car that may or may not start, and struggling to snatch even the semblance of a full night's sleep. The students who walk this sort of tightrope tend to be people of uncommon determination and strength of spirit, and often it takes no more than a gentle nudge to reinforce their self-belief and keep them on track.

That nudge might come from a trusted professor who expresses faith in their abilities, or from an advisor suggesting a course rearrangement to save a semester, or from the scholarship office pointing to free money for the taking. At the same time, the pressure is unrelenting. One botched exam, one misjudged decision, one personal crisis or skipped paycheck: any of these can be enough to crush the dream of a university education forever.

What is remarkable about Georgia State students is that despite the precariousness of many of their lives, they still graduate in extraordinary numbers. In 2018, more than seven thousand crossed the commencement stage, five thousand of them to pick up a bachelor's degree and the rest an associate's degree from one of the university's five community college campuses scattered around the Atlanta suburbs. That translated to a six-year graduation rate of close to 60 percent, significantly above the national average. Eight years earlier, when Georgia State was just beginning to develop a systematic approach to improving student outcomes, the number completing bachelor's degrees was a little over four thousand. Seven years before *that*, in 2003, it was under three thousand—a graduation rate of less than one-third of those admitted.

Imagine a panoramic photograph of the 2018 festivities: crowds of people waving and cheering in their caps and gowns, brimming with hope for what life has to offer. Now imagine airbrushing out one-fifth of the faces. That's how many people, eight years earlier, whose lives were *not* transformed, who were *not* offered the opportunity to break into the middle class, *not* given the chance to justify the cost of loading themselves and their families with debt at the start of their college careers. Rather, they dropped out before reaching the finish line. Now imagine going through the exercise again and airbrushing out *one quarter* of those remaining to shrink the crowd to the 2003 level. We're talking about thousands of people—tens of thousands, over the years—whose stories might have started out much like Princeton Nelson's or Savannah

Torrance's, but who were unable to fulfill their potential, unable to break the cycle of generational poverty, unable to defy the gaping inequalities of modern American society.

Now put all those missing faces back into the picture, and Georgia State's achievement becomes clear: a *74 percent increase* in the graduation rate over fifteen years. This is not just about the lives of a few unusually tenacious and talented individuals. We are talking about a fundamental transformation, a real-time experiment in social mobility that the university has learned to perform consistently, and at scale.

How did Georgia State do it? Not by resting on its glorious reputation, because until recently it had no such thing. To the extent that anyone had heard of Georgia State—most outside Georgia had not—people regarded it as the red-headed stepchild of the state university system, too large to ignore but too humdrum to care much about, a fall-back choice for students who had been rejected from the University of Georgia, ninety minutes' drive away in Athens, and couldn't afford private school or out-of-state tuition. Georgia State didn't have a sports team as fabled or as beloved as the UGA Bulldogs. It hadn't given birth to a generation-defining music scene, as the Athens campus had with R.E.M. and the B-52s. It had played little role in the formation of famous alumni like Ludacris (who stayed one year) or Julia Roberts (who left without graduating). It couldn't even get much love from the state legislature, whose offices were just a couple of blocks from the heart of campus.

The lackluster reputation was not entirely deserved, because the university boasted a strong faculty and had played an important role in diversifying and internationalizing Atlanta as the city asserted itself as the economic capital of the New South. Still, its core mission was a workaday one, and it occurred to nobody that fighting for students without the advantages of wealth or strong family support could be remotely glamorous or groundbreaking.

That changed in a hurry in the wake of the 2008 recession when a new leadership team at Georgia State, acting out of economic necessity as well as moral conviction, determined that there was nothing inevitable about the failure of students who were poor, or nonwhite, or whose parents had never attended college. Rather, what held them back were barriers erected by the university itself and by the broader academic culture. Georgia State developed data to understand those barriers and to identify the inflection points where students most commonly came to a crossroads between success and failure.

This was no side project: the university reengineered its leadership and its entire institutional culture to give students the tools to fulfill their potential. It took considerable risks in doubling its enrollment of lower-income students (now almost 60 percent) and in vastly increasing the number of minority students (now more than 70 percent). Yet retention and graduation rates went up dramatically. Not only did lower-income students, African Americans, and Latinos stop lagging behind their peers, as they do at almost every other institution in the country; they started graduating in slightly *higher* numbers than the university average.

This was mind-boggling, gravity-defying stuff. The received wisdom had always been that students born poor or otherwise disadvantaged were doomed to fail in large numbers—that demographics was destiny, and there was nothing a university, no matter how dedicated or enlightened, could do about it. Was it really possible that Georgia State had erased all achievement gaps, without lowering its standards or misinterpreting or falsifying the results? In the early years, few in higher education wanted to believe it, and Georgia State itself had a handful of internal critics who yearned for the more conventional prestige of an Emory or a Berkeley. Still, the data was overwhelming and soon became impossible to refute. The staggering fact is that a student like Princeton Nelson—poor, black, and parentless—is now no more or less likely to graduate than the heir to a long line of college-educated multimillionaires. For years, Georgia State has graduated more

African Americans than any other university in the country—not by tailoring special programs to them but by treating them like everyone else and providing support where they need it, regardless of wealth, or skin color, or any other consideration. This is the wonder of Georgia State, and it rests on a simple idea: that if students are good enough to be admitted, they deserve an environment in which they can nurture their talents regardless of personal circumstances.

The university has become so adept at turning out graduates that it has often struggled to find a venue big enough for its commencement festivities. For a decade it borrowed the Georgia Dome, home of the Atlanta Falcons, until it was demolished in 2017. Then it had to ask Georgia Tech, its crosstown rival, for permission to use McCamish Pavilion, its unusually large basketball arena. Even there, Georgia State has had to spread the occasion over two days, sometimes more, so attendees don't wait for hours while every last student name is read out. The longer-term goal is to move into a brand-new custom facility, an $80 million convocation center being erected near the old Atlanta Braves baseball stadium south of downtown. The stadium, previously known as Turner Field, has itself become a Georgia State facility, the home of the Panthers football team, and it, too, hosts occasional commencement ceremonies—but only in the spring, and only when the notoriously fickle Atlanta weather permits.

The time could not be riper for universities to push back against four decades of inequality, exclusionary policy-making, and skyrocketing costs that have worn away at the very core of their mission and the meritocratic promise of the American Dream. From the end of the World War II until the late 1970s, broad access to higher education was widely acknowledged to be a vital part of America's economic health, a spur to innovation and growth that gave the country an enduring competitive edge over Europe and the Far East. The halcyon days of the GI Bill and the rapid university expansion of the 1950s and 1960s are long gone, however. While the children of the rich and the very rich continue to enjoy expanding opportunities to pursue a university education, the prospects for everyone else have either stagnated or narrowed dramatically.

Once, student success was thought to be a simple combination of academic promise and hard work. Now even the pretense of that egalitarianism is gone; it's all about money and whether your parents went to college. A study by the National Center for Education Statistics from 2000—when things were better than they have become—found that a student in the top income quartile with at least one college-educated parent had a 68 percent chance of graduating before the age of twenty-six, whereas a student in the bottom quartile whose parents did not go to college had a 9 percent chance. Universities may still want to be champions of enlightenment and social progress, but in reality they have become places where inequalities are magnified, not addressed—"the main mechanism," as Richard Reeves writes in his sobering book *Dream Hoarders*, "for the reproduction of upper-middle-class status across generations."

This is not a sustainable trajectory. We live in a post-industrial society and demand for university graduates is soaring, not only in well-established fields like medicine, engineering, mathematics, and the humanities, but also in newer ones like computer science, health informatics, and biotech. Soon, according to Georgetown University's Center on Education and the Workforce, fully two-thirds of the jobs in America will require some form of post-secondary training. Where are so many graduates supposed to come from? While a handful of well-heeled, well-connected students and their parents seek to cajole or even bribe their way into the Ivy League or prestigious regional schools like the University of Southern California, much of the rest of the country faces the prospect of sinking tens of thousands of dollars into debt just for a shot at *any* university degree. The proportion of high school graduates defined as low income—currently around 50 percent, and higher still in the South and West—keeps going up, while the sources of available funding for higher education keep shrinking. Pell grants, the federal funding stream for low-income students introduced in 1972, used to cover more than 80 percent of the average cost of public university, and the entire cost of community college. Now Pell covers less than one-third of the cost at four-year institutions, and barely 60 percent at community colleges. State grants have gone in a very similar direction.

It's not that these staggering problems have gone unnoticed. Mostly, institutions have been at a loss to address them. Many prefer to keep their focus elsewhere—on graduate programs, on research, or on cultivating an elite class of undergraduates from that golden upper quartile. Some like to point fingers: at the shortcomings of the K–12 education system, at budget-cutting state legislatures, at a political culture that loves to hate academia and questions why students don't invest in their own futures instead of relying on the public purse for financial aid. It has become fashionable for elite institutions to brag about the lower-income students they champion and finance, but they do this at a scale entirely dwarfed by a public university like Georgia State, which has three times as many Pell-eligible students *as the entire Ivy League.*

It has taken more than twenty years to come up with a more durable answer to the problem and to push back against a higher education culture that too often serves the interests of everyone *but* the students. The first stirrings came at a handful of public universities in Florida, Georgia, Tennessee, and Arizona—states with rapidly growing urban populations and a hunger for economic growth that exceeded any appetite to hold back historically suppressed racial minorities. Why, administrators in these states started asking, should faculty members get to decide when to teach classes if it means students have to wait extra semesters to take courses essential to their majors? Why should students with no family history of negotiating an undergraduate degree have to figure out for themselves which classes to take, in which order? Starting in the mid-1990s, these campuses rewrote course maps, rethought student advising, grouped freshmen together by subject area, lifted registration holds for petty library fines, and found a variety of other ways to ease the students' path through the campus bureaucracy.

After 2008, Georgia State was able to take these ideas and turbocharge them with the analytical powers of emerging new data technologies. The incoming president, Mark Becker, was a statistician by training who understood the power of creating successful models and scaling them across tens of thousands of students. His student success guru, Tim Renick, was a religious studies professor, not a scientist, but he had spent the first twenty years of his career using data to defend and grow a program that many of his colleagues in the College of Arts and Sciences, particularly the philosophers, regarded with deep suspicion. Renick had been a singularly gifted classroom teacher and needed no persuading that lower-income and first-generation students were worth believing in, because he'd seen over and over how they responded to his teaching and thrived.

Soon, Georgia State was partnering with private vendors to develop new forms of data analytics and online technology: an academic advising platform that could predict outcomes based on student performance as early as the first semester of freshman year, or an artificial intelligence chatbot to guide high school graduates through the thicket of financial aid forms they needed to fill out before their first day on campus. The university also fundamentally redefined the relationship between the central administration and the deans and faculty, so Renick was able to institute wide-ranging reforms without the usual pushback from colleges and department heads who thought they knew better.

For Renick, in particular, the issue was moral as much as technocratic. He couldn't stomach a system that knowingly sold students a bill of goods, inducing them to load themselves up with

debt for a degree that at least half of them stood no chance of getting. The moral imperative was particularly potent in the context
of Atlanta and the legacy of Martin Luther King Jr., whose grave
lies just a few blocks from Georgia State outside the Ebenezer
Baptist Church. King understood not only how intolerable and
unsustainable racial discrimination was in a world growing ever
smaller because of advances in technology; to him, inequality of
any kind was a threat to an increasingly interconnected world.
"Every society has its protectors of the status quo and its fraternities of the indifferent who are notorious for sleeping through revo-
lutions," King wrote in his late essay, "The World House," "But
today our very survival depends on our ability to stay awake, to
adjust to new ideas, to remain vigilant and face the challenge of
change. The large house in which we live demands that we transform this worldwide neighborhood into a worldwide brother-
hood. Together we must learn to live as brothers or together we
will be forced to perish as fools."

More than fifty years later, Georgia State is very much awake
and implementing the sort of changes he was writing about. To
be sure, Atlanta is a radically different city from the one Dr. King
knew. The Sweet Auburn neighborhood of his childhood, once
home to a thriving black business community, did not rise with
the civil rights movement but fell into a long decline triggered by
the advent of the interstate system and the displacement of thousands of downtown residents. Downtown suffered a second slump
a couple of decades later as banks, law firms, shops, and restaurants decamped to Midtown and points north. If the area is reviving now, it is in large part thanks to the expansion of Georgia
State's downtown footprint. Many of the old bank and law buildings now belong to the university, and the once-blighted east side
of Downtown has seen a frenzy of new construction, mostly of
student residences. The issue is no longer whether Atlanta is "too
busy to hate," as the slogan used at the ugly tail-end of the segregation era had it, but rather whether the city can bridge the

socioeconomic divides that have opened up in the half-century since. "Civil rights is run and done. We're not dealing with race anymore. It's far more class than race," the civil rights leader and former Atlanta mayor Andrew Young said in an interview for this book. "Education, democracy and freedom . . . it is becoming a reality. And what's pushing us are institutions like Georgia State."

In other words: it's no longer just about higher education, it's about wholesale societal change for the next generation. What started as a moral imperative to graduate large numbers of traditionally underserved students has become a national rallying cry, a challenge to other institutions to ditch the old excuses and follow Georgia State's lead.

There is nothing simple, of course, about upending and redirecting a university the size of Georgia State. With more than 50,000 students spread across seven physical campuses, and more than 15,000 faculty members, administrators, support staff, and part-time employees, it is truly a behemoth. And while it is tempting to think that the men and women responsible for developing Georgia State as a national model for undergraduate education simply dreamed up their ideas in high office towers and rolled them out in one long, triumphal procession, the reality has been a lot more fraught and complicated.

Yes, there have been flashes of true brilliance and laser-focused leadership. But Georgia State has also gone through bouts of hesitation and internal disagreement. It has made false starts and false turns, struggled to shake its own ingrained bad habits, and pushed mightily against skeptics and naysayers. It has run up against staggering instances of imaginative blindness that have, at times, led to heartbreaking lost opportunities. To this day, Renick and his collaborators regularly hear *horror stories*, as they call them, and rush to rescue students who continue to be poorly advised and needlessly discouraged.

The point, though, is that Georgia State has established a

system alert to these lapses and given its administrators the confidence that in almost every case the problems can and will be fixed. If success has done one thing to the university, it is to have scattered the clouds of fatalism, that mournful skepticism prevalent in so much of academia about the likelihood of meaningful change, because people have seen the transformation for themselves and feel its effects every day.

By now, Georgia State's pioneering innovations have been written up in the *New York Times* and discussed with fervor at hundreds of education conferences. Public universities nationally are in broad agreement that the revolution in downtown Atlanta points the way to all their futures. What has not yet been told is *how* these breakthroughs came about: the battles that needed to be fought, the constituencies that needed to be won over, the points of resistance, the rules of the game that were rewritten or discarded; the interactions of those who willingly threw themselves into the work and stuck with it despite long hours and modest compensation, because they couldn't imagine doing anything more meaningful with their lives; and of course the role played by the students, whose tenacious example and unbreakable will either inspired important changes or exemplified their life-changing benefits or, often, a bit of both. This book is that story.

1

FISHING VILLAGE

Mark Becker had been president of Georgia State University for just over a year when he stood before his top administrators and faculty leaders on a crisp February morning in 2010 and told them that together they were going to do something amazing.

The catch was, he wasn't sure yet what that something would be. Becker knew he wanted to create a world-class urban research university to rival NYU or UCLA. He knew, too, that he wanted Georgia State to be a national model for graduating students of all backgrounds. He knew, above all, that he wanted to make a *statement*. But he hadn't worked out the details. One big reason he was taking the stage of the four-hundred-seat speaker's auditorium in the student center was to inspire his colleagues to develop the vision with him. His colleagues, though, weren't at all sure they wanted to go along for the ride.

Nobody doubted that Becker had big dreams; they'd heard him speak before and his ambition and drive were unmistakable. What concerned the deans and the other top administrators was his sincerity. They worried, on the one hand, that he was all for show—that the fine speeches he'd been giving were a warm-up to prepare him for a bigger job at a more prestigious university just as soon as he could land one. And they worried, too, about the opposite, that he was all *too* sincere in his desire for sweeping change right where he was, and that they would be the targets.

In other words, a tough crowd.

Becker kicked off his presentation with the celebrated 1997

Apple ad, "Think Different," with its paean to "the crazy ones, the misfits, the rebels, the troublemakers, the round pegs in the square holes, the ones who see things differently." He followed that with slides of two *BusinessWeek* covers about Apple: the first, from 1996, a premature corporate obituary titled "The Fall of an American Icon," and the second, from eight years later, a love letter to Steve Jobs and his visionary leadership. Next, Becker showed pictures of Shenzhen, the first when it was little more than a Chinese fishing village, and the second in its present-day incarnation as a megalopolis of more than 12 million people. Finally, he showed New Orleans Saints fans, first as they donned homemade paper-bag costumes to mourn their losing season in 1999–2000, and then as they exploded with joy on winning the Super Bowl a decade later.

Becker's message came across loud and clear: that change can come faster than you would ever think possible. But not everyone in the audience was buying it. Did Becker see Georgia State as a *fishing village*, a hick-filled backwater he was going to have to civilize? What was he implying with the line in the Apple ad about rule breakers with "no respect for the status quo"? Michael Eriksen, the head of the university's public health program, remembered liking the disruptive quality of Becker's presentation, but worrying the president had blurred the way an individual might see the world and the implications for a large institution that needed rules and procedures of some kind just to function. "How do you move forward without disparaging the present?" Eriksen asked. "People were getting the message, 'you're not good enough, you haven't been successful, and that needs to change.' That's not necessarily well received. It's threatening."

This was Becker's first major address at Georgia State without a formal script, just a set of PowerPoint slides, and for all his outward self-confidence he was a relatively unpolished public speaker at this juncture. That made him not only hard to warm to, but also hard to read. He came across as brash *and* reserved, sweepingly ambitious *and* maddeningly vague, and many people had no idea what to make of it. "They didn't have a good sense of him," said Allison Calhoun-Brown, one of the architects of the student success mission that was just getting started. "He was completely unknown, and on top of that, he seemed to have a huge ego. Rightly or wrongly, that was the perception."

Becker himself sensed a disconnect between the loftiness of his vision and his ability to convey it, but he had no immediate answer to the problem except to have faith that, in time, people would see what he was seeking to achieve and come around. He knew his public persona leaned a little too much toward the statistics professor he had once been and not enough toward the inspirational leader he was aiming to become. Even in his "think different" presentation, he hadn't been able to resist pointing out the perfect symmetry between the Saints' 3–13 losing season and their 13–3 record a decade later. He had a rectitude and a fearless work ethic that had always served him well, but he was also uneasy being at the center of attention. In a job as visible as a university presidency, that was easy to misinterpret as standoffish, or haughty, or self-serving. "It's hard in that first year," Becker acknowledged. "Everyone wants your vision. You're drinking from a fire hose, and at the same time you're trying to find your voice and be authentic to who you are. It gets easier later on, because you have accomplishments to talk about. At the beginning, it's all promise and process. And I'm not good at bullshit."

Becker was far from a blank slate, of course. Before coming to Georgia State, he'd been provost—chief academic officer—at the University of South Carolina, and before that dean of public health at the University of Minnesota. But he'd always preferred to fly under the radar because he felt he could accomplish more that way. He never thought much of peacock administrators who preened and strutted all over campus. If he had an opinion to express or a tough call to make, he preferred to do it in the appropriate forum; he saw no need to seek public credit for his actions, or to defend himself if people complained. "He wasn't someone who needed to be anyone's buddy," his friend and fellow public health luminary Harris Pastides said. "He moved fast. He got the job done, and he moved on."

What had drawn Becker to Georgia State was not in fact its backwardness but the opposite, its promise as a vital urban institution in one of the most dynamic cities in America. Becker was a fan of the urban theorist Richard Florida, who argued that the engines of twenty-first-century prosperity were no longer going to be cities but large urban corridors like the one that ran from Charlotte to Atlanta—"Char-Lanta," as he called it—whose economy was as large as South Korea's. These corridors were where industries and large companies would want to cluster, and where the brightest and best educated would want to live. That prospect presented an alluring set of opportunities to a well-located university, as Becker explained to the Georgia State search committee at his job interview. "I made two bets," he recalled saying. "One, that the recession wouldn't last forever. Atlanta would come back strong. And two, I bet on the future of sunbelt cities."

As president, he arrived thinking that he would build on what was already a strong faculty and prepare students and researchers for opportunities in cutting-edge new disciplines and cross-disciplines—in the sciences, in information technology, in health care and entertainment. He also wanted to integrate the university more deeply into Atlanta's urban fabric through partnerships and research grants. As he said in his inaugural State of the University speech in April 2009: "The opportunity to be both bigger and better is staring us in the face."

It was not, at the outset, an agenda focused on lower-income undergraduates racing against time and limited resources to get through their coursework and earn a degree. This was hardly surprising, given the standards of mainstream academic thinking at the time. Really, Georgia State was a university with two separate identities: on the one hand, a top-tier research institution with un-tapped potential to perform at the level of its powerhouse neigh-bors, Emory and Georgia Tech; and, on the other hand, a typical second-tier urban education machine, accepting large numbers of B-average students from across the state (and beyond) in the hope that half of them, maybe, would make it to the graduation stage. The research piece would seem naturally exciting to a career ad-ministrator. The important but more mundane education piece— not so much.

Becker certainly did not disregard Georgia State's teaching mission when he arrived, but he had only loosely formed ideas about what he wanted to do with it. He talked in general terms about celebrating the diversity of the students and making the university more attractive to the best and the brightest. Any other incoming president might have taken a similar stance. And yet Becker was *not* any other incoming president. For all the brilliance of his academic credentials—a PhD in statistics from Penn State University, plus stints at Cornell, the University of Florida, the University of Washington (as a National Institutes of Health fel-low), and the University of Michigan—perhaps the most distinc-tive thing about him was that, like a significant percentage of the Georgia State undergraduate population, he was the first in his family to go to college.

Becker knew from personal experience what it was like to won-der if he truly belonged in the university environment. He knew what it was like to deal with faculty and administrators who were not only untroubled by high attrition rates but who saw students as the educational equivalent of cannon fodder. *Look to your left and look to your right,* he remembered hearing as a freshman, *and in four years, one of you won't be here.* It was a mantra heard all over the country, but it hadn't sat well with him at the time, and it didn't sit well with him now. He knew, too, how powerful it could be for a professor to put a hand on a student's shoulder and suggest a path forward that had never previously seemed possible.

He'd had a couple of mentors like that himself, and without them he might never have applied to grad school and embarked on an academic career.

Little wonder, then, if Becker's new colleagues at Georgia State weren't sure if he was one of them—because, in a crucial sense, he wasn't. He'd grown up as an army brat in northern Maryland assuming that he would follow his father into military service. He had no familiarity with the rituals and traditions of campus life or academic discourse. Havre de Grace, where he was raised, was a depressed former canning town just a few miles from the Aberdeen Proving Ground, where his father served as an ordnance warrant officer. As a child, he was steeped in military history and the ethos of "duty, honor, country" as espoused by General Douglas MacArthur in his famous farewell address to the cadets at West Point. It was an ethos that would stick with him and, at times, give him an oddly old-fashioned aura in the university context. The military itself, though, started to lose its charm as a career option when, at the age of seventeen, he realized he wasn't good at taking orders.

Becker enrolled at nearby Harford Community College, largely because he didn't know what else to do. If he gravitated toward the military after all, he'd need a college degree, because his parents were insisting that he join the officer corps and he wouldn't qualify without one. If he preferred to go in a different direction, the classes he was taking might point the way.

And they did. Becker discovered a passion for physics and math and soon transferred to Towson, where he graduated magna cum laude in mathematics. His parents hoped he'd accept a high-paying offer to work as an army statistician at the Ballistic Research Laboratory, also based at the Aberdeen Proving Ground, but he chose the relative penury of grad school instead and with it an entirely different sort of life.

Becker worked his way swiftly up the academic ladder, first as a statistics professor, then as a public health specialist, and ultimately, after he had been at the University of Michigan for a few years, as an administrator. By then it was the 1990s, a time when state funding for higher education across the country had been on the wane for a while and seemed unlikely to recover since Democrats and Republicans now agreed that the era of big government was over. A key figure for Becker in this period was the long-serving University of Michigan president, James Duderstadt, who believed it was up to universities to find their own alternative funding and push for the values they cared about, or else they risked surrendering their independence to the self-interested logic of the marketplace. Academic freedom and the pursuit of truth were high up on that list of values. So was social mobility.

Becker took Duderstadt's lessons to heart when, as dean of public health at Minnesota and again as provost at South Carolina, he was forced to institute cuts of his own. The way he saw it, he had to figure out a way to master the budgetary constraints and use them to point the institution in a more positive direction; he couldn't let the constraints master *him*. In other words, he was determined to use the administrative tools available to him to spark new ideas and creative thinking. A drop in state appropriations didn't have to be a tragedy if it spurred grant writers to develop relationships with philanthropic foundations and other external funding sources. And it didn't have to be a tragedy if it meant making smarter, more innovative decisions about student enrollment and shaping the next generation of college graduates.

Changing institutions for the better became Becker's passion, the driver of his ambition. Why else go into administration at all? "Change is what I do. It's what I'm good at," he reflected years later. "Maintaining the status quo would kill me." As his ambitions grew, he paid particular attention to Frank Rhodes, a former president of Cornell, who shared Duderstadt's concern that universities risked selling out their values to the marketplace and believed that higher education urgently needed to adapt if it was to survive. To run a university, Rhodes wrote, was to "dream the institution into something new, to challenge it to greatness, to el-evate its hopes and extend its reach, to energize it to new levels of success and galvanize it to higher levels in every area."

Becker determined that if he ever got to run a university of his own, this was how he wanted to go about it.

It was Becker's friend Harris Pastides who first told him about Georgia State. In early 2008, both of them held senior positions at the University of South Carolina—Pastides as vice president of research, Becker as provost—and both were in the market for a university presidency. Becker imagined, at first, that he'd return to the Midwest where he'd been for most of his career, and he spent considerable time and energy going through the application process at the University of Iowa. Pastides, meanwhile, not only applied to Georgia State but was offered the job before Becker was ever in contention. Pastides hadn't put in his application with high expectations, but as he went through the interview process he was pleasantly surprised both by the university and by Atlanta's potential as a world-class city. He would have gladly taken the job, too, until family reasons precluded the move at the last minute. (He ended up becoming president at South Carolina instead.) Over scotch one evening, Pastides encouraged Becker to consider Georgia State himself. It might not have the prestige of a Big Ten school, he said, but that wasn't a reason to overlook it.

Becker knew, at this stage, that he needed to find somewhere that genuinely excited him. He'd flubbed his interview at the University of Iowa because they asked him repeatedly if he would be willing to stay in the job for ten years, and he couldn't bring himself to say yes. It was a question he had been expecting and an answer he knew they wanted, but when push came to shove his old-fashioned sense of honor and, perhaps, some deeper misgiving about the position stopped him from saying something he didn't mean.

By the time he faced the Atlanta search committee, though, he was ready. Lehman Brothers, a seemingly untouchable Wall Street powerhouse, had gone under a few days earlier, and the prognosis for the rest of the financial system seemed downright apocalyptic. Becker remained undaunted. He expressed his faith that Atlanta would bounce back soon enough from the economic hardships that loomed. He talked about the recession not as a body blow threatening the university's survival, but rather as an opportunity to shape a more vital and dynamic institution going forward.

It was exactly what his interviewers had hoped to hear. They didn't want someone to manage them into decline; they wanted a visionary, a president with energy and ideas—"someone bright, quick, creative, and collegial," as Erroll Davis, then the chancellor of Georgia's university system, put it, "but not so collegial that they can't get anything done." Becker seemed to have it all. "He was obviously a passionate city person," Paul Alberto, then the chair of Georgia State University's senate executive committee, recalled. "It wasn't just an interview line. He and his family clearly wanted to be part of a big city that was growing . . . He had the leadership style and the vision. And then he threw in, 'Oh, by the way, I can manage budget cuts because I've been provost up in South Carolina.'"

Becker's interviewers didn't just approve. They showered him with applause.

Georgia State, much like Mark Becker, had a history of moving quickly. The president Becker was appointed to succeed, Carl Patton, had wrested the university from the clutches of a white Southern good-ol'-boy network and transformed it, over an eventful sixteen-year tenure, from a white-majority commuter school focused principally on part-time professional training for business executives, accountants, and lawyers into a large, diverse, internationally minded residential campus with top-tier research status and a full panoply of liberal arts and science degree offerings.

That upward trajectory had slowed, however. Research funding was now stagnant, and the university could not match the increase in student diversity with consistent progress in retention and graduation rates. The leadership culture was growing a little stale, too. Patton had spent much of his tenure undoing the good-ol'-boy ethos of top-down decision-making, but in so doing had tilted the university so far in the direction of collegiality that the administration now found itself deferring to deans and faculty chairs on all manner of executive decisions and ran into heavy resistance any time it pressed for change that one campus group or another found threatening. Even a process as fundamental as budgeting was subject to scrutiny by a faculty committee that not only offered its opinions but actively moved numbers from column to column on a spreadsheet until its members were satisfied with the outcome.

The recession threatened not only to exacerbate this slowdown in momentum but to put Georgia State on a path to more permanent decline. The Georgia legislature suddenly had a $2.2 billion budget hole to fill, and it was clear to one and all that universities were going to be first in the firing line. Higher education loomed so large in Georgia politics that it was often referred to as "the fourth branch of government"—not a compliment—and legislators, particularly the Republicans who had taken control of the Georgia House in 2005, reserved a special resentment for a system they believed had taken too much for granted for too long. It did not help that the chair of the House higher education subcommittee, a colorful and loquacious former real estate agent named Bob Smith, was perpetually at loggerheads with Erroll Davis, the chancellor of the Georgia University system. Georgia State could only watch the two of them go at it and wait for the inevitable hammer to come down.

As a small-government conservative, Smith was naturally suspicious of intellectuals who, in his words, "tend to have a little more upper edge as a human than they probably should," and he found Davis's way of asking for money to be haughty and disrespectful—or, as he liked to say, "perfunctory," a word he pronounced with an *n* so soft it sounded like an obscenity. Davis, for his part, was painfully conscious of being an outsider—and not only because he was the first black chancellor in Georgia history. He had spent much of his career as an energy executive in Wisconsin and neither knew his way around Georgia politics nor found it easy to make the right connections. Davis saw himself as a man of the world, a pragmatist who liked to call things by their name, and he was repeatedly dismayed to see Smith's subcommittee mistake his directness for arrogance, or worse. "People don't like confrontation here," he observed. "They don't like the candid conversations that people such as I are trained to have."

Instead, he and Smith resorted to a different kind of candid conversation. When Davis suggested the system could find ways to absorb a certain amount of pain, Smith took it as an indication that the cuts weren't deep enough and he demanded more. When Davis warned that deeper cuts would force him to raise tuition, as a matter of basic mathematics, Smith became enraged because the sons and daughters of his constituents were enrolled in state universities and he didn't want to have to listen to them complaining about the extra money coming out of their pockets.

None of this was good news for universities. "We were being cut, cut, cut . . . and we were losing the argument," recalled Tom Lewis, Georgia State's head of government affairs. "What they wanted to hear was how we were going to do better with less. They needed to see blood in the streets. If they didn't see us in pain, it wasn't to our benefit."

If anyone could have mollified the legislature, it was Lewis, because he was the consummate political operative, a former governor's chief of staff who had been dealing with headstrong committee chairs and their budgetary fixations his whole career. The way he would typically tame a Bob Smith was to charm him, go to breakfast with him at some simple diner in his district, and above all hear him out and let him know he was being taken seriously.

"You've got to be able to say, 'how's yer momma?'" Lewis said. "You need to know their wives' names, their kids' names, what they are majoring in."

It did no harm that Lewis was born and raised in a rural county eighty miles east of Atlanta and possessed not a lick of pretension; the Georgia in him was so thick it all but dripped off his lips. In the midst of a generational economic crisis, though, even he was limited in what he could do. First, the system called for the legislature to allocate a lump sum to the university system, leaving it up to the board of regents to divide it up. And second, despite Lewis's best efforts, Georgia State was far from beloved in government circles. Most legislators were alumni of the University of Georgia or Georgia Tech and gave strikingly little thought to the urban campus that many of them could—but rarely chose to—see out of the state capitol office windows. "These politicians try to reward people they are close to," Carl Patton, the former president, said. "And Bob Smith was a UGA guy. He didn't have a soft spot in his heart for Georgia State."

Smith's committee held its hard line with the regents, and the regents informed Georgia State that its share of the cutbacks for the 2009–10 financial year would be $52 million, a cut of more than 20 percent. The university wasn't just looking at layoffs and fat-trimming here and there. There was a chance it would no longer be able to carry out its fundamental functions—teaching classes, conducting research, even keeping its buildings cleaned and heated.

Fortunately, help was at hand, starting with the American Recovery and Reinvestment Act, the federal bailout that spread emergency funding around the country and provided Georgia State with a $32 million windfall. The regents agreed to an additional annual fee of $200 per student, generating $13 million for the university in the first year. Georgia State's finance chief, Jerry Rackliffe, then came up with a voluntary separation policy for retirement-eligible faculty members that allowed him to move several million dollars more off the books. Rackliffe knew that public institutions in Georgia were not generally authorized to offer early retirement or buyouts in the conventional sense, but the beauty of the separation policy as he formulated it was that it stayed strictly within state and system rules while also giving Georgia State a leeway more commonly associated with the private sector. In short, the university offered qualifying employees six months' salary up front if they agreed to leave right away. That opened up a variety of options: to eliminate or downgrade their positions, or to refill them after a six-month delay, by which time a new fiscal year would have rolled around and the new hires would be part of a fresh budgetary round. The operation required some delicacy, because nobody wanted the legislature or the media asking why Georgia State was paying people to leave in the middle of a recession. But Rackliffe was a known quantity, a veteran of the system with a reputation for finding creative solutions to seemingly intractable problems, and the plan won the regents' approval two years in a row, by which time 159 employees, roughly half those eligible, had taken the offer.

Nothing about this recessionary process was painless. Georgia State had to lay off about 150 people, and the tuition and fee increases piled pressure on lower-income students already scrabbling for every last dollar. People were fearful and angry, rocked by the uncertainty of what the cuts meant and of others that might still be to come. Becker wasn't happy about any of that. But he also understood that the constraints presented him with choices, and those didn't have to be all bad. There was a way to make the cuts uniformly demoralizing and self-defeating—if, say, the university simply replaced experienced faculty members with younger, less-impressive professors in the same field. But they could also be wielded to repopulate and reorganize the university more broadly in anticipation of a brighter future. Becker opted for the latter.

————

Conventional wisdom suggested that the smartest thing a large public university could do in a recession was to become more selective about the students it enrolled. The logic was that since jobs were scarce and more people were turning to college as an alternative to full-time employment, universities had an opportunity to be pickier about admissions in the hope of enhancing their overall reputation and emerging from the recession further up the *U.S. News & World Report* rankings than they had been before.

When Mark Becker arrived at Georgia State, it did not occur to him to buck that conventional wisdom. Indeed, when he gave his inaugural State of the University address in 2009, he was proud to say that average SAT scores were on the rise and about to hit record heights. He was proud, too, that the university had its first ever waiting list of prospective freshmen. Even if he didn't think of it quite in these terms, the upshot was that Georgia State was turning more students away. And, that, in the mainstream way of thinking, was a good thing.

In reality, large public universities have two fundamental choices when it comes to enrolling students in a down economy. They can become more restrictive, as the conventional wisdom has it, and as almost every one of them chose to do after 2008. Or they can make up for the shortfall in state revenues by *boosting* enrollment and finding ways to retain and graduate as many of those extra students as possible.

For a flagship university that already has a highly selective admissions process—a University of North Carolina, say, or a Berkeley, or one of the Big Ten schools where Becker spent much of his career—focusing on student quality is easier to justify, not least because some other institution in the state system can almost certainly be counted on to pick up the rejected applicants and give them a decent education anyway. The issue becomes more complicated at a place like Georgia State, which has a broader mandate and a large number of students for whom admission can spell the difference between a continuing cycle of generational poverty and breaking through to the middle class.

As Becker began his presidency, there were conflicting views on this question, and those views sharpened considerably after he made his first consequential hire. Risa Palm, who became Georgia State's provost in the summer of 2009, had a long résumé as an administrator at top institutions—the University of Colorado, the University of Oregon, the University of North Carolina, Louisiana State University, and SUNY, the New York state university system—but next to no experience with lower-income and first-generation college students, other than a short community college stint at the very start of her career. It occurred to nobody before she arrived that her pedigree could work against the needs of Georgia State's student population. On the contrary, the university felt lucky to have her. She was a widely respected urban geographer who had come of age in the 1970s in an era of severely restricted opportunities for women and was reputed to be formidable, sharp-witted, and highly disciplined. She was, according to Michael Eriksen, who was on her search committee, an easy pick, "head and shoulders above the other candidates."

Palm herself was altogether less effusive; mostly, she was happy just to have a job. Twice in a row, at LSU in 2003 and again at SUNY in 2006, she had been hired as provost only to have the legs kicked out from under her because the administrator who selected and championed her had left. If the price of those unfortunate experiences was to end up at this "unsung sort of place," as she saw her new place of employment, so be it. "I felt cursed," she recalled years later. "I saw the job at Georgia State and thought, that seems reasonable." She had no more positive word.

She knew Becker because they'd both been provosts in the Southeastern Conference—she at LSU and he at South Carolina—and her hope was that together they would find ways to turn Georgia State around. "Like venture capitalists," as Michael

Eriksen later characterized it, "going somewhere that's not at the peak of reputation and coming together to achieve something that requires some vision and realization of risks and potential reward." Palm had heard Becker's first State of the University speech while she was interviewing for the job and found it inspiring. Still, she worried that Becker would follow the pattern set by her previous bosses and disappear within a year or two.

Unfortunately, her mixed feelings showed, and that colored a lot of what followed. "Her affect gave us a real sense that she thought she had moved down by coming to Georgia State," said Lauren Adamson, who was dean of the College and Arts and Sciences at the time. "She was always talking about her work at more eminent schools, in more demanding roles. We tried to explain the institution she was joining, but it took her a while. There were people she was publicly quite rude to. She would make fun of them in meetings and roll her eyes when they talked. It was just nasty, interpersonal stuff, and it was unnecessary."

Some of the friction may have been inevitable, given the signals she and Becker were sending about major change at the university. The very fact that she didn't think the old way of doing things was working was bound to sit badly with some of the old guard. Hugh Hudson, then the history department chair and state head of the American Association of University Professors, was more attached than most to the Patton-era ethos of shared governance and could not hide his distress at what he saw as a more corporatist, top-down leadership style. "For twenty years we'd worked very hard to create a model in which people actually participated and discussed issues and tried to come up with appropriate solutions," Hudson said. "That was the opposite of what Risa believed."

Some of the friction, though, was a byproduct of Palm's personality. A number of her new colleagues appreciated her bluntness— her willingness, as one put it, to overturn an apple cart that needed overturning. But she could also be curt and hard-edged with those who had not yet won her confidence, and some inevitably found this uncomfortable. Hudson was particularly taken aback when, early in her tenure, Palm told him and other members of the budget committee that she had a low opinion of a number of the deans and did not expect them to last. (Palm questioned but did not outright refute his account.) "I don't think Risa appreciated she had talented people who wished the best for the university and its students," Hudson said. "It was a talent pool she simply didn't have any interest in using." He resigned from his administrative positions soon thereafter.

The question of student enrollments erupted a few months into Palm's tenure when she took exception to the latest *U.S. News & World Report* list of national universities. Georgia State ranked 217th. That wasn't much lower or higher than where the university had been for years, a reflection of the students it served more than the quality of its teaching. But Palm saw it as her mandate to say: *enough*. "I'd never been at a university ranked below 200," she explained. "As far as I was concerned it was something we needed to fix."

At one unusually testy meeting of faculty and administrators, she let her emotions boil over. "Is that really how you see yourself?" several participants remembered her saying. "Do you really want the number 217 branded on your forehead? Because that's how people perceive you." And she laid out what was essentially the agenda of improvement through exclusion: choosing students with higher SAT scores and encouraging departments to jump through a number of other hoops, like reducing class size, that *U.S. News* defined as marks of quality.

Several people in attendance took offense at her tone and, more importantly, felt she was flat wrong on the merits. A number of them had spent years in the classroom and had watched time and again as students from the toughest backgrounds came into their own and thrived academically for reasons unconnected to SAT scores or any of the other criteria lauded by *U.S. News*. Academic performance, in their experience, had little to do with why so many students dropped out before completing their degrees. They left, usually, because they ran out of funds to keep paying for classes and struggled to navigate a university bureaucracy ill-equipped to give them the support they needed. Insisting on higher SAT scores was unlikely to do anything for retention or graduation rates. Rather, it would discriminate against those students—the ones without money or a family history of attending college—who needed a Georgia State education the most.

Palm was not the only person to view student quality as the primary issue. The powerful dean of the business school, a forthright and physically imposing man named Fenwick Huss, had been frustrated for years by what he saw as a large pool of underperforming undergraduates who would enroll as business majors only to fall short of the minimum grade-point average to complete his programs—if they passed the introductory math and accounting classes at all. "My view was, we were doing them a disservice by admitting them in the first place," he said. Huss saw the business school as Georgia State's flagship, the one part of the university with a track record and a half-decent national reputation, and his priority was to make sure it stayed that way. Helping potentially talented students who had no family background in higher education, or who had attended less-than-stellar high schools, was of little interest to him. As far as he was concerned, the best would rise to the top regardless (especially if they had strong SAT scores to prove their bona fides), and the rest were being deluded into thinking they had a chance at all. The bulk of his attention was not on undergraduates or even on Downtown, where most of them lived and studied. Rather, he focused on graduate students and a new teaching facility he'd established for them seven miles to the north in leafy Buckhead, the redoubt of Atlanta's white business elite, where in Tom Wolfe's memorable description "the lawns rose from the street like big green breasts, and at the top of each breast was a house big enough to be called a mansion." Buckhead was further from the corporate towers of Midtown—the

banks, law firms, and Fortune 500 companies like Coca Cola
and Equifax—but it was cleaner, clubbier, and more conducive to
networking. "The people I knew wouldn't go downtown, wouldn't
want to be downtown," Huss said. "It wasn't the place to be. We
were running a bigger engine."

Becker largely stayed out of the debate at this stage. In his
speeches, he gave the impression that he wanted both quality *and*
quantity. "We anticipate that the incoming freshman class will
be both the largest in history and the best prepared," he'd said in
April 2009, a few months before Palm's arrival. Later that year,
he gave another speech making clear he wanted to recruit "a student body that reflects the demographic profile of our state and
nation"—in other words, one that maintained or even increased
campus diversity. From such incompletely formed thoughts a policy was ultimately crafted. Palm instructed the admissions office
to work toward raising the SAT scores of incoming students, but
without shrinking—or growing—their overall number. Accordingly, the fall intake remained broadly stable from 2009 to 2011,
despite an increase in applications, and the average SAT score
crept up from 1090 to 1109.

The person least happy about this turn of events was a relatively new senior administrator yet to win either Becker's or
Palm's full confidence. His name was Tim Renick, a career professor of religious studies who now bore the title of associate provost for academic progress. It was an experimental position that
Palm's predecessor had created a few months before the start of
the Becker presidency to expand the traditional portfolio of a
university enrollment manager. The idea was to synchronize different pieces of the university—academic, administrative, and
financial—to identify and remove obstacles that were tripping up
students who otherwise showed the drive and the talent to succeed. Renick didn't have anything too definitive to show for his
work at this early stage, but he knew that controlling for SAT
scores was a mistake because it meant paying less attention to high

school grade-point average, a far more reliable predictor of student outcomes, particularly at the lower end of the income scale.

Making the case for this was far from easy, not least because Palm had doubts about the job Renick had been given and his suitability for it. "Tim had no experience," she explained years later. "He wasn't at the level he's at now." She tolerated him largely because Ron Henry, the previous provost, had asked her as a parting request to give his appointee a chance. So Renick bided his time, waiting until he had the evidence and the credibility to make his counterarguments, trusting that he would survive in his job long enough to do so.

2

ADMIT THEM

Tim Renick knew exactly what it was to be a lower-income student, juggling multiple jobs with a full course load and working furiously to graduate on time, because he'd been one himself. His experience was not at a large urban school like Georgia State, where shift work is a normal part of students' daily routine and worry over every dollar a widely shared burden, but at Dartmouth College, the Ivy League. That certainly spoke to his academic pedigree—he was marked for brilliance from an early age. But in a class of students where the norm ranged from upper-middle-class comfort to extreme wealth, it also made him an outsider and a bit of an oddball. One of his jobs at Dartmouth was to work the breakfast shift in the cafeteria and he'd often find himself scraping leftover eggs off the plates of his classmates. Sometimes his richer, better-fed peers would scrawl messages to him on their paper napkins. The gesture wasn't ill-intentioned, necessarily, but it reinforced a fundamental difference.

Renick had grown up around wealth, on the same fabled stretch of Long Island where Nick Carraway, in *The Great Gatsby*, reveled in the "consoling proximity of millionaires." It was a consolation Renick never yearned for himself. His father was a career military officer stationed at the U.S. Merchant Marine Academy in Kings Point, geographically a hop and a skip from the grand north shore mansions of Great Neck, but culturally a world away. The family lived just off Steamboat Road, in a modest neighborhood that was home to much of the local African American population and remained largely invisible to the majority of Renick's classmates. "I was used to being in a position where I didn't feel I was one of the crowd," he recalled. "Most people I grew up with didn't get it. They were oblivious to the working class."

Renick attended a high-achieving local high school where graduates were routinely groomed for the Ivy League, and after finishing as class valedictorian it came as a surprise to nobody that he ended up at Dartmouth. Still, he was never going to experience college the way the kids from Exeter or Choate could—nor would he have wanted to. He felt less commonality with peers talking excitedly about their spring break trips to Europe or the Caribbean than he did with his workmates in the cafeteria kitchen, many of whom were struggling to survive as the recession of the early 1980s gripped the mills and factories of the Connecticut River valley. Over time, he was promoted to cafeteria manager and learned to supervise entire meal shifts, a testament to his nascent organizational skills as well as his ability to inspire confidence in the people around him. He also had a paid position as a teaching assistant and another as a tutor in the composition lab.

Renick majored in political science and was thinking about law school and a career in public affairs when he spent a summer in Washington, DC, interning for a New Hampshire congressman, and came to realize politics was not for him. What had most captivated him in his studies was political ethics, a burning topic in the wake of the Watergate scandal that had consumed Richard Nixon's presidency six years earlier. When he got to Capitol Hill, though, he was dismayed to find people obsessing over the vagaries of power for power's sake, with little, if any thought for the public good. So he switched gears, to a double major in religion and government, then continued his religious studies as a grad student at Princeton.

It took him just four years to complete a master's and a doctorate and land his first job in the fledgling religious studies program at Georgia State. Atlanta was a destination that chose him as much as he chose it. It was now 1986, and he felt fortunate to find employment of any kind in a tight academic labor market. But it wasn't long before he saw that this was a place where his passion for teaching and for social justice could find full expression. "It was clear from the first semester that teaching here was more meaningful," he said. "There were all sorts of people at Dartmouth and Princeton who did brilliantly and would go on to run companies and earn millions of dollars. But they might do that whether I was there or not. In fact, they might do that whether *Princeton* was there or not . . . Here, I was teaching people from families who earned less than $25,000 a year, people to whom the university system was entirely foreign and who in many cases were receiving no help from home. My operating assumption was that while they hadn't been given the same opportunities, they were no less capable."

Renick had his hands full from the outset, because the professor he expected to be his boss quit before he started, and the chair of the philosophy department who had championed the idea of developing a religious studies program was elevated to an associate deanship. Not only was Renick left to build a brand-new program on his own; he was also at the mercy of a philosophy department deeply split on the question of whether religious studies belonged in their curriculum at all. The department leadership had no compunction about loading him up with five classes a day ("hour after hour, like high school"), many of them mainstream philosophy classes for which Renick felt only peripherally qualified. "They saw me as the Antichrist," he said. "Not everyone was against me being there, but some were horrified. They saw me as an affront to their autonomy, undermining the very nature of philosophy as an objective field of study based on rational principles. To them this was the end of the world."

Nevertheless, Renick rose to the challenge, showing remarkable grace under what was by any standards ridiculous pressure for a neophyte professor still in his mid-twenties. Within his first year, he not only had to shoulder his teaching load but also write a detailed proposal for a religious studies major and begin the process of hiring a second faculty member. Somehow, he managed to do all that and still keep his focus where he felt it belonged—on the students. He set high standards, getting his classes to read lengthy passages from Saint Augustine and Thomas Aquinas regardless of their educational background and their familiarity with handling such ostensibly difficult primary source materials. He imposed equally high expectations on himself, making sure he returned all essays and tests fully marked and annotated by the next class. He wouldn't just skim-read the assignments, either; students came to expect that whatever space they left unfilled on their last page would be packed with handwritten comments.

This was all but unheard of at a large public university, and an insane amount of extra work for Renick to pile on an already overloaded work schedule. But Renick understood that feedback was crucial for students who might otherwise question if they belonged at Georgia State, especially in the crowded, impersonal intro classes that could make or break them within the first couple of semesters. "Tim always thought of teaching as a moral enterprise," said Stephen Prothero, Renick's first faculty hire who later moved on to Boston University. "It does not surprise me that he has turned administration into a moral enterprise, too . . . It was all right there, in his utter dedication to help students learn in a way that best fit their needs."

Renick's students were effusive, too. Within a couple of years they were buzzing about the young teacher with a penchant for Doc Martens and skinny ties, and they enrolled as religious studies majors in numbers that equaled or even eclipsed the rest of the philosophy department. He had a light touch, an impish sense of humor, and a keen ability to relate medieval doctrinal philosophy—or anything else—to present-day moral concerns and dilemmas. One of his extended classroom riffs on Aquinas's argumentative structure was a spoof theological inquiry into the merits of smooth versus chunky peanut butter, complete with objections, responses, and citations of classic authorities (Plato, he reasoned, is a chunky butter guy because "a thing is more perfect as it more closely approaches its original form"). "Tim had this capacity to bring the very best work out of people and inspire them to be interested in things they had no idea they could be interested in," said Matt Lyons, who studied under Renick in the 2000s. "He could give a lecture on dishwashing that would change your life, that would give you a window into larger lessons on how to think and how to lead a healthy and productive life. He exuded tremendous kindness and did everything he could to create an environment where students were engaged and wanting to learn."

Renick's teaching philosophy was simple: challenge students, and they will respond. That didn't mean engaging them solely in the classroom. Often it meant helping them outside of class, too, taking an interest in their lives and offering them support where possible to work through money problems, family problems, or anything else that troubled them. Many, when they came to him, were working multiple jobs and squeezing in classes where they could; Georgia State, in those days, was still exclusively a commuter school, and almost none had backgrounds that inclined them naturally to a subject as cerebral and arcane as religious studies.

Matt Hinton, for example, had been a disaffected rocker in high school—"a young Morrissey in the making"—more often to be found at some bar waiting to go onstage than in the library hitting the books. Half the essays he wrote still smelled of smoke when he turned them in. Yet he was so taken by Renick's classes that he was invited, as a freshman, to do graduate-level work and ended up becoming a religion professor himself—alongside many other career pursuits spanning music, documentary film, and a popular chain of burrito restaurants. Another protégé, Anthony Petro, had gone through the hell of being gay in a one-stop rural town an hour north of Atlanta and came to Georgia State as an unconfident, first-generation student with a bad stutter. He switched from anthropology to religious studies under Renick's influence and went on to a glittering academic career of his own, including stints at the University of Chicago and Princeton.

It wasn't long before Renick began to win broad recognition for his talents. As a fourth-year professor, he won the college of arts and sciences' teaching award. In 2002, he was named the best teacher in Georgia's research university system, and in 2004 the American Academy of Religion recognized him as their outstanding teacher nationally. Yet he came close to being swallowed up by the philosophy department's turf battles and ideological disputes—not just once, but on multiple occasions. When he came up for tenure in 1992, the objectivists in the department who found religious studies inherently suspect used a point system to assess his worthiness, only to declare him to be a crucial half-point short. The chair of the tenure committee, one of Renick's most dogged antagonists, explained in a letter that the numbers spoke for themselves and there was nothing he could do, but in Renick's mind this was a hollow excuse for something altogether more premeditated. The only recourse was to appeal to the dean of arts and sciences, and it was Renick's good fortune that the acting dean at the time, Bob Arrington, was the former philosophy department chair who had championed his hiring in the first place and happily rode to the rescue.

The philosophy department pounced again in 1995 when Prothero, Renick's number two, left for Boston University and the question arose whether to replace him or shut down the religious studies program altogether. Renick had already begun making the case for religious studies to Arrington's successor as dean, a brilliant but ruggedly secular microbiologist named Ahmed Abdelal. Now, though, his survival was on the line and he needed to do a lot more than explain why it wasn't Sunday school—an all too familiar jab. Renick chose to meet Abdelal on the scientific ground with which the dean was most familiar and present him with *data*—on course enrollments and majors, on the money these were making for the university, on the alumni who were going on to doctoral programs at Harvard, Princeton, Yale, Oxford, Cambridge, and so on. Data wasn't deeply ingrained in Renick's academic training, but he was not confrontational by nature and he liked the way the data could be made to speak for itself. Abdelal appreciated his pragmatism and the power of his presentation and let him live to fight another day.

Still, the tensions persisted. It was not until 9/11, when religious extremism suddenly became a subject of burning public interest, that the need for a religious studies program at Georgia State became too evident to refute. It helped, too, that one of Renick's hires, an Islamic scholar named John Iskander, was catapulted into a regular slot on cable news. "Suddenly," Renick later wrote, "the arguments we had been making for years about the importance of understanding world religious traditions were being made by others: not merely by former secretaries of state and magazine editors, not merely by the general public, but by college deans, provosts, and presidents—at times, even by our 'cynical, questioning, anti-authoritarian' colleagues." By then, Renick was working under a much more sympathetic philosophy department chair, George Rainbolt, who shunted some of the older, more scabrous analytical philosophers into retirement. Rainbolt also supported the idea that Renick should move out from under him and be given his own independent religious studies department, which came into being in 2005.

Two things stood out about Renick beyond his teaching: he worked as hard as anyone, and he was very difficult to dislike. In meetings he was unfailingly prepared, articulate, and on point. He was also personable, funny, and understated about his accomplishments, unusual qualities for an academic that served him well when he was most under pressure. "With Tim, what you see is what you get," Prothero observed. "There was never any bad blood there."

His preference for solving problems instead of arguing about them made him a natural fit for administration. He was elected early in his career to the Georgia State University Senate and ended up serving six years as chair of its flagship committee on academic programs. In the early 2000s, he also ran the university honors program, an obvious perch for a teacher with a celebrated ability to spot and nurture talent. Still, he didn't imagine he'd go into senior administration until the spring of 2008 when Lauren Adamson, Abdelal's successor as dean of arts and sciences, encouraged him to apply for the associate provost's position, with oversight over enrollment, registration, and financial aid.

Renick wasn't much interested at first. He was too attached to his own department, which was barely three years old, and he didn't relish a competition with the perceived frontrunner, George Rainbolt, who was still philosophy chair and occupied the office adjacent to his even though they now ran their own separate shows. It wasn't until Renick heard he had the backing of another powerful dean—Fenwick Huss of the business school, with whom he rarely saw eye to eye—that he threw his hat in the ring. Even then, he was determined not to become just another university bureaucrat shuffling student numbers around on a spreadsheet. He wanted to find meaningful ways to serve Georgia State undergraduates, as he had for the previous twenty-two years, or he would just as soon stay in the job he had.

He told Risa Palm's predecessor as provost, Ron Henry, that he didn't want the job if it just meant waving students in through the door. He wanted the authority to track their progress throughout their undergraduate careers, and he wanted to do so broadly, covering every area from classroom performance, course planning and scheduling, to the health of their finances. In short, Renick wanted the job to be about *nurturing* students, much as he had nurtured them in the classroom, only on a broader scale and with greater overall impact. He wanted to find the places where they were prone to give up and drop out, and come up with ways to support and redirect them.

It was a do-or-die pitch, but as it happened Henry had been thinking along similar lines. For several years, the provost had been piloting programs he hoped would offer the sort of supports Renick was talking about: "learning communities" of no more than twenty-five incoming freshmen to instill a sense of belonging; supplemental instruction that stronger students could offer to their struggling peers; and a computer lab that would give struggling math students the opportunity to move forward at their own pace instead of getting lost in a large, conventionally taught intro class. When Renick said he wanted to integrate these efforts and extend their reach across the whole student experience, it resonated immediately. It was the unifying idea that Henry had been reaching for but had never articulated for himself. "All my life I've been interested in integrating things, and to me, that was what was missing," Henry said. "We were dealing with a number of silos, and . . . we needed a person interested in pulling everything together. It was Tim who triggered those ideas."

Henry was a physicist by training, so the scientific method was in his bones, as it had been in Abdelal's. "His thinking was, we can find the truth by experimentation," Renick remembered. On that, they were of one mind.

There was a lot that needed fixing, because many of Henry's pilot programs, despite their initial promise, had sputtered or hit bureaucratic obstacles. And there was little time to make measurable progress, because Henry was months away from retirement and could not guarantee what would happen to Renick after he left. Still, Renick relished the challenge, and he took the job.

The first project Renick launched, like many that followed, was about money more than academics. And, like everything he would undertake from this point on, it was inspired by a close reading of the data.

The issue was a structural flaw in the state university funding system that Georgia had inaugurated in the early 1990s. The HOPE scholarship, as it was known, was available to any high school graduate with a 3.0 grade-point average or better, a merit-based system that nevertheless opened the door to many lower-income students who might not otherwise have found a way to college. Those who could hold on to it throughout their undergraduate careers could, at the time, expect about four years' coverage of the cost of tuition, books, and fees.

The problem was that not everybody could hold on to it, and the uncertainty was having a devastating effect on Georgia State's drop-out rates. Renick noticed case after case where students were doing just fine from an academic point of view, with more than respectable GPAs of 2.93 or 2.95, but found themselves unable to continue much past their freshman year because of the shock of losing HOPE. The blow was often psychological as much as financial. Indeed, the data showed that those who started out with HOPE stood only a 20 percent chance of graduating once they lost it, whereas those who never had HOPE in the first place—regardless of income level—stood a 40 percent chance.

"It was infuriating," Renick said. "If you finish freshman year with a 2.95 GPA, that should be cause for congratulations . . . And instead we say, sorry, this is not good enough, you're going to have to figure it out for yourself." It was a flaw in the system that struck Georgia State particularly hard, because students typically came in with high school GPAs in the 3.0–3.5 range, and those numbers tended to drop a half-point or so in college. What irked Renick the most was that the scholarship brooked no compromises or half measures: your GPA could go from 3.0 to 2.99 and still you lost the entire pot of money.

In response, he came up with an idea he called Keep HOPE Alive. What this entailed was a $1,000 scholarship, spread over two semesters, for any student whose GPA had slipped as low as 2.75. The money couldn't come close to replacing HOPE, but it could, perhaps, buy students some time to improve their grades and let them know the university still believed in them. Renick couldn't use university funds, because the state had strict rules prohibiting subsidies of tuition fees, but he persuaded Georgia State's private foundation to provide $40,000 to test his idea on an initial forty students.

This was a strategy that would come to define the entire trajectory of Renick's student success work: start small, show the benefit, then scale the program university-wide. As he would with many of his future initiatives, Renick bet that Keep HOPE Alive would more than pay for itself—that the outlay of a few thousand dollars would result in tens of thousands of dollars in additional revenue. The first time out, though, the experiment was a failure. Renick had hoped to see a significant improvement on the 9 percent of students who lost HOPE and managed to win it back on their own, but the figure refused to budge.

This was a blow, no question, and Renick and his team immediately set out to investigate what had gone wrong. What they discovered was that a lot of students who lost HOPE were putting their newly jacked-up tuition bill on a credit card and were ending up in default within a couple of months, if not also in collections. *That* was what was causing them to drop out. In response, Renick attached conditions to the scholarship money, including mandatory meetings with financial and academic advisors. And the difference was startling. In the second year of the program, the percentage of students who won their HOPE scholarships back leapt from 9 percent to more than 60 percent.

The program's benefits were about more than money. Brianna Cheek, a journalism major who started at Georgia State in 2012 and became a Keep HOPE Alive beneficiary the following year, remembered how the offer of help was both a morale booster and a wake-up call to take her life more seriously. She'd had one bad semester in her freshman year when she partied too hard and studied too little, but she hadn't been honest about it to her parents, her friends, or herself until she understood she might lose her prized independence and be forced to live back at home for a semester or more.

"I definitely felt like a failure," she said. Her attitude changed completely after she learned that she was being offered a stipend, along with a financial literacy class and guidance on organizing her study time better. She did not take the helping hand for granted and understood she had a responsibility to protect her parents' limited resources and her own future. "I needed something, and it was a boost to my confidence," she said. "It was a turning point in my life where I got to buckle down a bit. You figure out who you are, what you want to do, and who you want to be." Cheek had no trouble winning back HOPE in her junior year and ended up graduating, on time, with a 3.3 GPA.

Looking back, Renick would see Keep HOPE Alive as no more than a baby step, a program of limited scope applicable to only a fraction of Georgia State's students. But it was at least a concrete result he could take to the university's top administrators as proof that his approach was working. Those administrators were not all that focused on student outcomes and did not immediately appreciate the significance of the breakthrough. That, though, did not deter him in the slightest.

Keep HOPE Alive was not the only idea Renick was promoting. He also took a keen interest in the peer mentoring program and made sure that, when the most talented students looked for campus jobs, they got hired as instructors in their own classrooms. That was good for the students they were tasked with helping, but it was also good for them: Renick noticed that when students worked as peer mentors their own chances of graduating went up 15 percentage points.

Another important area was the use of computer learning in

introductory math classes, something that Lauren Adamson and
Bill Nelson, an associate dean in the College of Arts and Sciences,
were also pushing. Together, they understood that the faculty was
broadly skeptical of letting computers do their work for them,
but they also realized they didn't need the support of more than a
handful of intro class instructors to move forward with pilot testing. Once they could demonstrate the difference between students
who used computers to learn at their own pace and those exposed
solely to traditional classroom teaching, it became much easier to
persuade senior faculty to give the idea their blessing. Before long,
the program was extended to all students in introductory algebra
and pre-calculus, and the results were stunning. Pass rates jumped
from 57 percent in 2008 to around 80 percent four years later.
Better still, those who had been exposed to adaptive computer
learning started doing better in follow-on classes in natural sciences, accounting, and advanced math.

Renick's most profound insight, early on, was that, contrary to
conventional wisdom, academic performance was not the most
important predictor of student success or failure; the most important indicator was the level of unmet financial need. Every extra dollar a student had to earn or borrow to get through school
decreased the likelihood of making it to graduation, while every
dollar covered by the government or family funds increased it.
Grades, choice of major, degree of high school preparation, raw
intellectual talent—all of it was subordinate to the stark realities
of money, or the lack of it.

Renick did not reach these conclusions entirely alone. A few
months into the job, he recruited an essential partner in Allison
Calhoun-Brown, a political science professor who, like him, had
a reputation as a brilliant teacher and was now interested in ex-
tending her reach beyond the classroom. Calhoun-Brown had
limited administrative experience before becoming his deputy,
but she chose to turn that into a strength. Precisely because she
was unburdened by detailed knowledge of bureaucratic rules and

procedures, she felt able to look at things she found appalling and decide there and then that they had to change. "I'd ask pointed questions and I'd be quick to say, It can't be like this," she recalled. "People got used to hearing me say, *That is not a thing.*"

Calhoun-Brown was no charging bull. Even if she could be cutting she had a soft touch and a wicked sense of humor and a talent for making people, especially faculty, feel good about what she was asking them to do. She, like Renick, had a moral conviction about the mission that others found compelling. "I believed in individual students," she explained. "I've always believed in them. It's highly demeaning to think that they are limited because they are low-income, or from the country, or part of a minority. If you've been teaching for as long as I have, you see that's just not true. The students are more than capable. Often they're up against really tough odds, yet in many cases they are resilient and persevere. To believe that students are fundamentally unable to learn because of their circumstances—that's racist thinking, even if it's dressed up in 'reality' or some other level of sophistication. It belies all of history."

Renick knew Calhoun-Brown slightly before he hired her; they'd been on a doctoral committee together because one of her research interests, the black church, touched on one of his. But he would never have thought of her had it not been for Lauren Adamson. Adamson had seen potential in Calhoun-Brown for a while and encouraged her to apply for the chair of the political science department when it fell vacant a year or two earlier. Calhoun-Brown had demurred at the time because she had young children and wasn't sure she wanted the added burden. When the student success job came along, she was still unsure about becoming an administrator but figured if she didn't like it she could always go back to the faculty. She had no idea in that moment how passionate she would feel about the cause she'd undertaken. She and Renick were fighting for the soul of the university, and it wasn't long before she understood it was up to them to make the case for maintaining the broadest possible student access, because lives and livelihoods would be crushed if Georgia State opted for the greater exclusivity being pushed by Risa Palm and Fenwick Huss.

"Where are the kids, who are good students, going to go? Who's going to serve them?" she remembered asking herself. "We don't have weak students academically. They're B students on average . . . They should be able to succeed if we can serve them a little better, and there's no evidence we *can't* succeed. What choice do we have?"

The first time Mark Becker and Tim Renick met, at an introductory group session in the student center, the two men were sitting next to each other but Becker retained no memory of it. He didn't regard Renick—yet—as a member of the university's top leadership and his focus was elsewhere: on deans, vice presidents, and the senate executive committee. Still, Renick had a feeling it wouldn't be long before his data-driven approach would capture the imagination of a president who had started his career as a statistics professor. And he was right about that. Becker couldn't help but be impressed by the impeccably prepared student success coordinator who spoke the language of facts, figures, trends, and attainment goals. At one early meeting, Becker joked that Renick was "the person who found religion in data," a line that sounded flippant but was meant as a sincere compliment. "We were speaking the same language," Becker recalled. "As a statistician, I believe that data will set you free."

They started talking more regularly a few months later after Risa Palm became provost and she instituted daily team meetings in her office, next to Becker's. Renick would arrive well ahead of the 8:30 a.m. start time and wait in the common reception area on the third floor of Dahlberg Hall, then the main university administration building. Becker would show up around the same time, and they would chat. Becker described this as the "strategy of managing by walking around"; Renick didn't mind what it was called, he was just happy to develop a line of communication to the president and give him a different point of view from the one advanced by Palm and Fenwick Huss.

Renick also had a more formal opportunity to lobby Becker at monthly administrative council meetings where his role was to present the enrollment report, ostensibly a dry rundown of how many students were registered for class. Renick went much further than this, however. He would habitually talk about problems he'd pinpointed and results he was seeing from the programs already in place. Becker always looked forward to hearing it. "It was clear," Renick said, "that Mark loved engaging with the data, and he became increasingly impressed with the way we were moving the needle in some of these areas. It was not completely fair that I had that standing opportunity. But it was a way for me to reach Mark, and listen as he told others around the table that he wanted to see more of this—more data, more innovation. I had some kind of favored status early on."

Renick was favored enough, in fact, that he was asked to introduce Becker at his investiture speech in October 2009. And the honor was far from coincidental. Becker was starting to see Renick as the essential innovation partner he hadn't known he needed. "This wasn't just data," he said of the emerging student success programs, "but data wrapped around a story—the story that we were doing the right thing." Renick's approach appealed to every leadership instinct in Becker's body: it was fresh, it was against the grain and, best of all, it was self-validating because it was based not on opinion or assumption, like a lot of university decision-making, but on hard fact.

The budding relationship between the two men gave Renick the opening he and Calhoun-Brown had been looking for to speak frankly about Georgia State's admissions and Risa Palm's insistence that the university should aim to raise the average SAT and ACT scores of incoming freshmen. Renick had internal data to show that high school GPA was a far better predictor of student outcomes, and that aptitude tests were predominantly an indicator of how well-off or well-educated a student's parents were. He could also draw on a freshly published national study, spearheaded by a former president of Princeton, that echoed these findings almost exactly. "High school GPA is very positively and very consistently associated with six-year graduation rates, whatever the level of the high school that the student attended," the study found.

This was not a particularly new insight. Academic literature going back to the 1940s revealed school-administered aptitude tests to be "a fraud, a way of wrapping the fortunate children of the middle and upper-middle classes in a mantle of scientifically-demonstrated superiority," as Nicholas Lemann put it in his book *The Big Test*. But it was an insight that most of the academy, obsessed with status and *U.S. News* rankings, generally chose to ignore. "I hadn't known," Palm said. "I was very used to looking at SAT scores as a benchmark for defining high quality. That's the glasses I came in with."

Becker chose not to act on Renick's arguments right away. He was reluctant to undermine his provost when she had been in the job for such a short time. And Renick, at that time, still reported to her. The calculus changed, however, as Georgia State came out of the worst of the recession and Palm began clamoring for faster improvement in SAT scores. Renick ran the numbers and realized with some horror that to meet her benchmarks the freshman class numbers risked shrinking by 40 percent. Renick went to Jerry Rackliffe, the university's finance chief, to ask if Georgia State could afford such a drop, and Rackliffe was unequivocal: it couldn't.

When Rackliffe was summoned to the president's office, he said much the same. He told Becker he understood the theory that, by restricting the number of those admitted, Georgia State could foster a higher caliber of undergraduate and build a reputation that would pay off in the long term. "I'm not disagreeing with the theory," he said, "but is the time to do that when we're still dealing with a recession?"

Becker asked what would happen if the university shrank enrollment just for a year or two, and Rackliffe reminded him that Georgia State had recently been forced to cut its budget by $15 million in a single year. "Do you want to double that number?" he asked. He didn't see a way to take the hit and come out better for it.

Not everyone agreed. Fenwick Huss of the business school had already made his support of Palm's efforts plain, and he was not afraid of a little financial hardship along the way. He prided himself, in fact, on the cuts he'd been making to his own operation. They were painful, he said, but also "an opportunity to right-size," and the rest of the university would do well to emulate him. "I have the utmost respect for Jerry [Rackliffe]," Huss said, "but the heart of the matter is to ask, what choice do we want to make? If we opt for downsizing, can we be better on the other side?"

The issue came to a head in the third year of Palm's tenure, with a pool of a few hundred students that Renick wanted to admit and she wanted to turn away. Palm now understood the evidence that showed SAT scores to be poor predictors of student outcomes, but it didn't change her view that these were the weakest students in the admission pool and could only do harm to the university's reputation if they came and failed in large numbers, as she expected.

Becker had one baseline question, which he put to Renick at a meeting in Rackliffe's office, down the corridor from his own. Palm was not included in the discussion.

"If we admit them," Becker asked, "will they graduate?"

Renick argued that whatever else happened, they would succeed in greater numbers than those currently being admitted who did well on the SATs but did not have a GPA to match. Becker replied that he didn't care about SAT scores or how much money the students had or where their parents had been educated. He cared only whether the disputed students would leave Georgia State with a degree.

It was not an easy question to answer. Renick had no doubt they had the *potential* to succeed, but he also recognized that students with decent high-school GPAs and low SAT scores were more vulnerable than the rest and required extra support—because of their family background, or the low quality of their high school, or some other factor that suggested they needed easing into the challenges of higher education. Renick was working on providing that support but had not yet rolled it out, in part because he didn't know how many of the disputed cohort would be allowed into Georgia State at all.

Since the facts were inconclusive, Becker's decision had to be about where to put his faith: in the provost who wielded ultimate authority over admissions and academic standards, or in the student success guru who believed the university could overturn decades of received wisdom about the prospects of lower-income and minority students.

"All right," the president said. "Admit them."

It was, without question, the riskier choice. Average SAT scores immediately dipped back below 1100, and the university lost what modest gains it had made in the *U.S. News & World Report* rankings.

But it was also the choice with far greater potential rewards. When Palm asked what had swayed Becker's opinion, he told her: "If we do this, we're going to change the country."

3

WHO ARE WE?
WHERE ARE WE GOING?

In the fall of 2009, a Georgia State marketing professor named Ken Bernhardt was summoned to a lunch meeting in Risa Palm's office. He didn't know why. It turned out that a friend of his, a senior executive at Coca-Cola, had served a brief stint as New York's assistant secretary of education and overlapped with Palm when she was provost at SUNY, the state university system. A social affair, then. Only the lunch quickly developed into something else.

Palm mentioned that the president had asked her to put together a strategic plan to chart Georgia State's future and wondered if Bernhardt, as a marketing expert, had anything to suggest. Such plans are common currency in universities, and in many cases are taken as pro forma exercises, a state-mandated requirement to which administrators respond with many thousands of fine words that mean little and are soon forgotten. Becker, though, had a different idea. He wanted his strategic plan to announce to the world that Georgia State was doing things differently. He wanted to set the tone for everything the university aimed to accomplish over the next twenty years—or longer.

Bernhardt told Palm he had written strategic plans for corporations and public institutions for more than thirty years. He had strong opinions about what worked and what didn't, and he wasn't shy about expressing them. "If the plan summary doesn't fit on one page, it's worthless. It'll have no impact," he told her. "It can't be more than ten pages total, or nobody will know what's in there. You need a small committee of highly respected people who focus on a handful of attainable goals. Don't have representation from all units of the university, because the representatives will be interested only in looking out for the interests of their unit, not the university as a whole. You must have the big picture in mind. And you need to have a mechanism to track your progress, so once it's over you know if you're doing what you said you were going to do."

Palm said nothing at first. She just listened. Then she went to a filing cabinet and pulled out a planning memo of several pages that she'd drafted but not yet sent. Bernhardt leafed through and saw an elaborate scheme involving committees, subcommittees, white papers, discussion periods, feedback sessions, and more.

"I like your way better," Palm said, and put the memo back where she'd found it. She'd been thinking already that she needed an outside facilitator to keep the planning process professional and on track, and Bernhardt had just talked himself into the job.

Bernhardt was a natural networker, and he soon found an independent line of communication to Mark Becker through a mutual friend at the University of South Carolina. He and the president hit it off right away and talked about the strategic plan several times while it was still in its nascent stages. Bernhardt said that if the process was going to work, Becker and Palm would have to keep their distance. They could set the tone and sketch out their overarching ambitions—which is what Becker's "think different" presentation had been about—but they had to leave the heavy lifting to the committee so the university felt it was determining its own destiny. There was nothing to be gained by dragging people into the future against their will. If that happened, Bernhardt warned, the plan would simply collapse.

Becker did not need to be told twice, because he'd been thinking along similar lines himself. He wanted an actionable plan, which meant buy-in from the colleges and their departments but not a "Christmas tree"—an unwieldy, inert structure on which everybody got to hang an ornament but nobody was obliged to make meaningful changes. A Christmas tree, in his opinion, was what Georgia State had created with its previous strategic plan in 2005, when, among other things, it vowed to double research funding from $50 million to $100 million in five years but had failed to come close. "To me, this was Einstein's definition of insanity," he said. "You can't expect different results if you keep doing the same thing . . . Few people received gifts on Christmas Day, because most of the agenda items were never funded."

The key, he realized, was to identify campus leaders with the talent to put together a dynamic plan and the credibility to sell it to their colleagues across the university. He also needed to be very clear about what he wanted. For these reasons, he had sought and received approval from the Southern Association of Colleges and Schools, the university's regional accrediting body, to postpone the strategic-planning process by one year when he first arrived at Georgia State. By the end of 2009, though, he was ready to issue his directives, which did not stray all that far from Bernhardt's. He wanted no more than five goals that would be simple enough to summarize on a single sheet of paper but profound enough to have lasting impact. No Christmas trees or indigestible slabs of prose. The committee needed to be mindful that they were setting more than a broad-brush agenda. From the plan would flow budget priorities and performance metrics by which the university would judge its future progress.

That, though, was all he said. He left it to Palm to select the committee members and made a point of staying away as much as possible until the plan was close to completion. He wanted the process in and of itself to show people what kind of leader he was. If they were worried about him becoming an autocrat, this was his chance to prove them wrong. "Early in my career, I learned that if I gave everybody the opportunity to be heard and then articulated my decisions in a coherent way, people were comfortable with that style," Becker reflected years later. "What faculty do not like is when you do things without letting them be heard and without explaining why you did what you did."

Not everyone was persuaded this was a truly collaborative form of management, and as the planning process got underway there were concerns around the university that the committee's work would prove to be little more than window dressing for a vision that Becker had staked out in advance. Those actually picked to sit on the committee came to see things very differently, however. When Palm called on Jorge Martinez-Vazquez, an economics professor in the Andrew Young School of Policy Studies, he thought at first he was in for just another stultifying dose of bureaucratic paper-shuffling—"a pain in the ass," as he imagined it. Then he looked at the caliber of his colleagues and the mandate they had been given and understood this truly was a different kind of exercise. "It was a call to arms," he said. "Our committee had a lot of freedom and was willing to court controversy. The script did not come from the top."

Martinez-Vazquez was chosen, in part, for his expertise in international development. Michael Eriksen was there for his sharp mind and his expertise in public health, which Becker saw as vital in the home city of the Centers for Disease Control and the Task Force for Global Health. Paul Alberto, a rising star in the College of Education who chaired the university senate executive committee, was a co-chair, along with Pamela Barr, a managerial sciences specialist from the business school. Renick's student success shop was represented by Allison Calhoun-Brown. Of the other seven standing members, just one was a dean—Steve Kaminshine of the law school, who understood that his brief extended to all the professional schools including business and nursing.

Whatever else this group was, it was no rubber stamp. They had no clear idea, at the outset, what they were going to recommend, but they knew they had a mandate to bring fundamental change to Georgia State and it was up to them to deliver. If they worried about anything, it was that Becker was using them to further his own career ambitions at the university's expense. If he had his heart set on moving up to a Big Ten school, then their efforts could end up being for naught. It was a concern that would stay with them a while longer.

Nobody on the committee imagined at the outset that equity gaps and graduation rates would become a central focus of their work. The subject barely came up as they started, and Becker showed no signs—yet—of pushing for it. The committee members knew undergraduate education was on the to-do list, but when Palm first talked about it, at a senate planning committee meeting in November 2009, she sketched out a traditional agenda of classroom issues deemed important by *U.S. News*: lowering student-teacher ratios, hiring more graduate teaching assistants, expanding classroom and library space. That didn't excite the participants nearly as much as other things that were dearer to their hearts. As Pam Barr observed: "Get a bunch of academics around a table, and the first thing they are going to talk about is research. That became number one."

The mindset began to shift in January 2010 when two outside experts, a former president of the American Council on Education (ACE) and a higher-education planning specialist from the University of Wisconsin, were invited to address the committee and encouraged them to think about the university's natural strengths and core mission. One of the first PowerPoint slides displayed by Maury Cotter, the planning expert, posed some blunt questions. Not only: "Who are we? Where are we going?" But also: "Why do we exist? Who is affected by our work? What are their needs?"

David Ward, the former ACE president who had also spent eight years as chancellor at Wisconsin's flagship campus in Madison, was blunter still. Universities, he said, often make the mistake of aspiring to become something they are not, when they would be better advised to focus on what makes them distinct and work to excel at it. Georgia State, he reminded them, was not like Tech or the University of Georgia—and that was a good thing, because it had a different identity, a different niche, defined largely by the students it served. "Don't compare yourself to the wrong league," Ward recalled saying. "You do what you do, and become the top of *that* league." Allison Calhoun-Brown found this observation particularly heartening. And she noticed it making an impression on her colleagues, too.

The subject came up again ten days later when the planning committee, together with Becker and Palm, flew across the country to visit Arizona State University at the invitation of the country's most scabrous, most unconventional, most gleefully iconoclastic higher-education leader, Michael Crow. For eight years, Crow had been pulling ASU apart piece by piece and re-building it to conform to his vision of a new American univer-sity. That meant, among other things, bucking the national trend toward exclusivity and embracing the broadest possible access, particularly for lower-income students. It meant imagining a uni-versity that served a hundred thousand students both on campus and online—essentially, creating a vast urban hive of learning and research unbounded by class, race, or conventional wisdom. And it meant, most profoundly, letting the mission dictate the admin-istrative infrastructure, not the other way around.

Crow had been a javelin-thrower in college, and as president of ASU he remained unafraid to chuck spears at anyone he per-ceived to be blocking his path. He'd dismantled ASU's college of education and ditched forty-five of the people who worked there, because he didn't think it was minting great teachers as it was supposed to. He'd even fired tenured professors, an unheard-of trampling of academic norms. He believed in setting goals and sticking to them, and he believed in Joseph Schumpeter's theory of creative destruction to promote future innovation and growth. "If you don't break down the institutional structure, nothing will change," he said. He also liked to hand out copies of a short management self-help book, *High Velocity Culture Change*, knowing that the concept in and of itself was sure to send chills down the spines of university administrators reared on collaborative, incremental decision-making. The book sang the praises of tough love and issued the dire warning that a new culture cannot be born if people keep doing things the way they always have.

Becker was conscious that exposing the committee to Crow would be a shock, but he could think of no better way to broaden their ideas of what was possible. A lot of ASU's innovations were directly applicable to Georgia State and would soon be copied or improved upon, in particular the interdisciplinary approach to research and a proactive, data-driven form of student advising. Becker was also impressed that Crow had not allowed the devastating effects of the economic meltdown, even worse in Arizona than in Georgia, to crimp his strategic vision. Despite a state appropriations cut of almost $90 million in a single year, Crow had accelerated the expansion of ASU's branch campus in downtown Phoenix, his most ambitious project at the time, and had taken advantage of the budget strictures to further reorganize departments and colleges.

The committee members heard Becker's message about culture change loud and clear, and were open to Crow's ideas and approaches, at least in principle. But the visit also stirred some disquiet. "The way Crow talked, it was all me me me. *I* did it, *I* changed that, *I* fired them," Martinez-Vazquez recalled. "I thought he was a benevolent dictator. He knew the end, and the end was just . . . Of course there was a question at that time, whether Becker admired him for playing that role." Calhoun-Brown remembered similarly uneasy feelings. "People already had a concern that Becker was going to be this autocrat," she said, "and Michael Crow seemed to be his hero. They thought: if this is how our president is going to be, no thank-you."

The issue boiled up over a dinner in Arizona when Michael

Eriksen, never one to shy away from contentious issues, asked Becker directly what his plans were and how long he intended to stay at Georgia State. "His response was: it depends," Eriksen recalled. "It depended on whether the senate and the faculty supported his efforts to move things forward. If they did, he would stay. If they didn't, he wouldn't." Eriksen was struck by how unafraid Becker was to address the issue head-on and how willing he was to acknowledge people's concerns. That boded well for his sincerity.

The bottom line was, Becker had no intention of running Georgia State the way Crow ran ASU. "The point of the committee was to redesign the university from the inside out. That's the opposite of Arizona State," he reflected years later. "Our approach was not to disrupt the status quo by blowing things up, but by changing the basis of our operating procedures." He assumed that was obvious, or soon would be.

Still, the mistrust persisted. Over time, Martinez-Vazquez, Calhoun-Brown, and Eriksen all came to appreciate and admire Becker's leadership, not least because he was willing to delegate authority and trust people to do their jobs unhindered. But at this early stage he was still an unknown quantity and prone to being misunderstood. His friend Harris Pastides had warned him about this. "You won't do your best work at the beginning," he had counseled. Pastides was among those who worried Becker might have half an eye on the presidency of a more prestigious university, and offered him advice on that, too. "You need longevity," he stressed. "You need time in office to do transformational things."

Becker, though, was in no hurry, and he had a hard time recognizing the calculating careerist that others seemed to see in him. "I've never thought in terms of five-year plans for myself," he insisted. "I never saw one job as a stepping-stone to another. In places where they've most questioned my intentions, I've stayed the longest."

———

Seven weeks after the Arizona visit, just as the strategic planning committee was beginning to enjoy the autonomy it had been granted, Becker threw them off balance once more by firing the dean of the Andrew Young policy school.

It happened in the thick of the budget crisis triggered by the recession. Erroll Davis, at daggers drawn with the legislature as usual, was told abruptly at the end of February to find an extra $300 million to cut on top of $265 million he had already pulled out of the system. These new cuts met with howls of public protest and were never enacted—indeed, Bob Smith of the higher education subcommittee later acknowledged they were strictly for show, his way of saying "to hell with you" to the system office—but in the moment Georgia State had to take them seriously and scrambled to find an extra $34 million in savings. At a meeting of the deans and other senior administrators, Becker wondered aloud if cutting here and there was still enough or if they needed to do something more dramatic—merge Andrew Young and the business school, perhaps. It was an off-the-cuff remark that never crystallized into a formal proposal. But Bart Hildreth, the dean of the policy school who had been appointed by Becker a few months earlier, became so alarmed that he drafted a five-page memo laying out reasons why the merger would "destroy arguably the most successful quality academic enterprise on campus." It would have been one thing if Hildreth aired such thoughts in closed session, but he distributed the memo to faculty without copying in the president, and Becker took that as an unforgivable act of defiance, an attempt to circumvent or undermine his authority. A loose memo was almost bound to become public, and indeed it later emerged that a reporter for the *Atlanta Business Chronicle* was chasing the story.

Becker had only one question when, with a copy of the memo in front of him, he summoned Hildreth to his office. "Are you stupid or are you insubordinate?" he asked.

Hildreth, in Becker's telling, replied: "Neither."

"Well," Becker went on, "this document is either stupid or insubordinate, and we can't have either of those, so you are no longer dean." He gave Hildreth until noon the next day to submit his resignation.

Since most of the university was not yet privy to the details, the firing sparked all sorts of anxious rumors. Was Becker channeling Michael Crow after all? Were deans no longer in charge of their own budgets, or even privy to deliberations that could result in the erasure of their colleges? Jorge Martinez-Vazquez, who had competed against Hildreth for the deanship, called it "a disagreeable and confusing moment." Another strategic-planning committee member was heard saying: "This is a monarchy. Becker and Palm are the king and queen, we're the aristocracy, and at any time they could say, 'Off with their heads!'"

Many of these concerns turned out to be overblown, because there were no secret deliberations and the policy school was never seriously under threat. Becker came to understand he needed to be more careful about airing spontaneous thoughts in university meetings. But Hildreth's fellow deans were not wrong to think they were being sent a message. Soon after Becker arrived in Atlanta, he had asked Tom Lewis, his canny political advisor, for his thoughts on how to make a difference at Georgia State. And Lewis had answered: "You need to fire a dean." Becker was nonplussed, but Lewis went on: "Don't misunderstand me, it's not going to happen today. You're new. But they need to know you mean business. It might be a dean or someone else, but it will come, and it needs to be swift. It will help you line up everyone else, like a line of ducks."

Lewis was one of the first people Becker told about firing Hildreth. And Lewis, who was as surprised as anyone that it was this particular dean, told him: "You're going to get a phone call from Andy Young."

Andrew Young was a legend in Atlanta, a civil rights veteran, a popular former mayor who had brought home the Olympics, a former congressman and ambassador to the United Nations who was always looking for ways to lift the city and put it on the global map. Lewis was right to think Young would be upset about an unexpected change at the school that bore his name. Over lunch, Young asked Becker to reconsider the firing. But Becker stood firm. If someone had gone behind *your* back and undermined *your* authority in the mayor's office or at the UN, Becker said, wouldn't you have felt compelled to do something?

Young didn't answer. "I always felt it was Dr. Becker's call who runs that school," he said many years later. "I'm not part of the administration, but part of the insurrection." Still, Young was concerned it would so much as occur to Becker to close the school, because he saw it as vital connective tissue between Atlanta and the broader global community, something no true internationalist would think to disrupt. Young later formed a more positive opinion of Becker, but at the time he thought the new president was in way over his head.

The strategic planning committee met sixty-eight times over the course of 2010, and as the year went on they put their doubts and suspicions behind them. Ken Bernhardt limbered them up with questionnaires and analyses of the university's strengths, weaknesses, opportunities, and threats, and helped them through several rounds of faculty feedback. They came up with four priority areas at first—research, student performance, the university's profile as an urban studies center, and internationalization. They later added a fifth, on graduate studies, because Fenwick Huss, the business dean, worried that the emphasis on interdisciplinary academic research might leave the professional schools in the cold. Risa Palm attended most of the sessions, to signal the seriousness with which the work was being taken and to make sure the committee members stayed on target and on schedule, but she did not push them one way or the other. She enjoyed supervising a group she had handpicked and enjoyed the respect they had for each other. Jorge Martinez-Vazquez, remembered her playing a "fantastic role": "She was the catalyst to the whole process," he said. "It was very useful having her there all the time."

Becker, true to his word, did not come to meetings and did not review the committee's work until the plan had gone through multiple drafts and revisions. He intervened just once in the early running, to shut down a debate about breaking up the College of Arts and Sciences, by far the largest of Georgia State's academic units that some wanted to split into smaller pieces. The issue was raised by P.C. Tai, the chair of the biology department, but other members of the committee worried it would be a distraction, and Becker agreed. The president was more than willing to consider shaking up the university's leadership structure, but not if it meant bogging the committee down in turf battles and the stultifying detail of organizational charts and hierarchies. The strategic plan had to be about bigger things.

Student success slipped into the proceedings with remarkably little fanfare, and that only benefited the agenda that Calhoun-Brown and Renick, working behind the scenes, were hoping to promote. David Ward's talk had opened the committee's eyes to the importance of the topic and made it easier to shunt Risa Palm's more traditional vision quietly to the side. Another helpful push came from a report by the Education Trust, a Washington-based advocacy organization, which came out just a couple of weeks after Ward's visit and praised Georgia State as one of the few American universities taking concrete steps to close the achievement gap between white and minority students. The study was based almost entirely on progress made on Ron Henry's watch, but that, arguably, made its message all the more powerful: that meaningful progress on student success had to be possible, *because it was happening already*. "Georgia State's example," the study authors wrote, "demonstrates that public institutions can foster access and strive for excellence simultaneously. They do not face an either-or choice." Mark Becker was not only delighted by this endorsement;

it also opened his eyes to the idea that becoming a national model for student retention and graduation—something he'd been talking about for months—might in fact be within reach.

Still, student success was set only as goal number three out of the five. And in terms of the time and attention that most of the committee paid, it might as well have come in dead last. The committee didn't come up with any language of its own on the topic. Paul Alberto ended up requesting some, which Renick was happy to provide. The result was a document that promoted a remarkably radical agenda but couched it in matter-of-fact, undramatic, straightforward language that slipped past the committee almost unnoticed.

Among the items Renick included were the introduction of proactive, data-driven student advising and a reduction in the ratio of students per advisor from as many as 1,200:1 to 300:1; new scholarship funding streams for lower-income students along the lines of Keep HOPE Alive; and a new teaching and learning center where faculty could experiment with new pedagogies. Taken together, these ideas were to have profound budgetary and organizational implications, and would eventually transform Georgia State beyond recognition. But the committee was too disengaged from the issues to care all that much beyond the fact that they could tick the box and move on. Either they didn't read the text carefully enough, or they were just glad to have one section that read fluidly and did not have to go through multiple drafts. "We were flying under the radar," Calhoun-Brown remembered. "There was review, but not a lot of input on what those goals would look like."

One key person who failed to understand how profoundly the student success agenda would affect his future until well after the planning process was over was Dean Huss of the business school. By his own admission, Huss wasn't much interested in undergraduates, and he allowed himself to be distracted by the question of whether professional schools would get their due. Once graduate programs were included, and placed second in the order of priorities, he was more than happy to sign off on the plan as a whole. "It wasn't as clear to us then where we would come out in the end," he acknowledged years later. "How many students does Georgia State have now? Fifty-five thousand? I don't think anyone was thinking about anything like that."

The committee's own big preoccupation was with communicating their vision in a way that would excite and motivate the rest of the university and alert public opinion that Georgia State was embarking on something truly special. They were pleased with the substance, particularly the parts outlining new cutting-edge interdisciplinary programs and the need to tie academic projects more closely to research dollars. But they also knew that early drafts of the sections *not* written by Tim Renick were hopelessly overloaded with vague, jargon-filled formulations that obscured many of the exciting things they were proposing. Who outside the academy knew what "translational research" was? Who wanted to read sentences that began "Investments and strategies will be adopted . . ."? The insipid summary line said Georgia State's goal was "to rise among the nation's leading public research universities and successfully educate a diverse student population for the challenges of the twenty-first century." In other words: we're going to keep doing what we're doing, only a little bit better.

Some of these problems were fixed in committee, but the draft was still far from perfect when, at Ken Bernhardt's suggestion, it was sent out to a select group of alumni, donors, civil leaders, business luminaries, and elected officials for comment in the fall of 2010. And the feedback, gathered by a former graduate assistant of Ken Bernhardt's on behalf of an outside market research firm, was correspondingly underwhelming.

The most common reaction was that the plan was "fine." One respondent commented: "This is a camel—a horse designed by a committee." A legislator offered: "I am thinking ahead to when I am going to have to ask people for money to support this plan. I can't sell it as it is. There's nothing compelling to me in this plan."

Such comments prompted many on the committee to sink into a deep gloom. It was now November, and they had been at work on the project for ten months. Michael Eriksen asked: "Does this mean we start over?"

The news was not all bad, because one part of the plan enjoyed unanimous approval—the one that said Georgia State aimed to be "a national model in undergraduate education where students from all backgrounds succeed." Those had been Renick's words from the get-go, and they were a clear winner. "This is motherhood and apple pie," one respondent said. "How can you be against this?"

It was at this point that Becker stepped in and made some decisive changes. He was nowhere near as dismayed by the feedback as some of the committee members were. One of the comments had been: "Rewrite it so the common man knows what you're talking about." And the president did that. Alberto recalled: "Mark took out his pen, crossed out each aspiration and rewrote each one while I was standing there. He had already been thinking about it, and he went right at it."

The research goal was now to "become a leading public research university addressing the most challenging issues of the twenty-first century." The urban goal was to "be a leader in understanding the complex challenges of cities and developing effective solutions." Becker touched up the student success language, too, taking what was already an ambitious goal and making it loftier still, to "become a national model for undergraduate education by demonstrating that students from all backgrounds can achieve academic and career success at high rates."

The more Becker thought about it, the clearer it became that the student success goal was key. "I had a gut feeling this was the winner," he said, "that this was really going to make noise." So he

moved it from goal number three to number one. And he upped
the ante further by committing Georgia State to a graduation rate
of 52 percent within five years, and 60 percent within ten.

The subtext of this was arguably more powerful than the words
themselves: *We're going to do what everyone in higher education
says is impossible, and we're going to come up with results to show
just how wrong they are.* Becker understood this was brazen talk,
with as much risk as potential reward. "It was make or break. I set
the bar really high," he said. "But I felt we could attain graduation
rates more typical of a public research university. I knew Tim was
working on it. My mentality was the same as in competitive athletics. If you think of yourself as a six-minute-mile runner, you're not
going to run a five-minute mile. So I set the goal high. And Tim
never pushed back on the language. He rose to the challenge."

The radicalism of the plan was not just in the wording, or in the
targets it set for research dollars and graduation rates. It also laid
out the terms for a new leadership structure, because college deans
were no longer free to set their own agendas and haggle with the
central administration to get them funded, as they had in the
past. Now they were obliged to abide by the strictures of the plan,
which came with timelines and performance expectations that
Palm, as provost, set about enforcing with an iron rigor. Becker's
view was that he had been careful to seek a broad swath of faculty
and staff input, but now that the plan was in place he intended to
drive it as hard as he could.

Everything changed, more or less overnight. If a budget proposal was tied to the plan, it was given serious consideration. If
it wasn't, it was dead on arrival. With the university still in a recession, the leadership—Palm, mostly—insisted that if academic
departments wanted to spend money on new faculty or facilities they had to identify a revenue source to offset the extra cost.
"Risa was fierce and focused about it," one of the university's top

administrators at the time, Peter Lyons of the office of institutional effectiveness, remembered. "It was a big deal."

The old guard was far from happy, but their pushback was short-lived. Hugh Hudson, the AAUP representative who had already bristled against the Becker administration's more assertive leadership style, was so upset that faculty was no longer empowered to haggle line by line over the budget that he lodged a formal protest. The president, he argued in a meeting with Becker that both men remember vividly, was making the same mistake as the Romanovs in the dying days of Tsarist Russia by cutting himself off from his best sources of advice. Becker was entertained by Hudson's erudition and found him engaging and well-spoken. But he also had no doubt he was neither weakening the budget process nor disregarding the faculty in violation of AAUP rules. In fact, he pointed to a section in the AAUP's bible, known as the Redbook, to demonstrate that he was still consulting with faculty as the rules required. He was just doing it in a different way.

Hudson's shock was understandable, because this was about more than the workings of a single committee. Georgia State's management structure was now entirely at odds with its own past practices, and with the practice of most other universities. Pamela Barr put it succinctly: "In the past, individual colleges decided what they were going to do and how they were going to do it, and they worked with the university leadership to make it happen. That relationship was reversed." Maury Cotter, the systems expert from Wisconsin who had advised the strategic planning committee, thought this may even have been an understatement. "The former is how higher education works," she said. "The latter is not. The entire higher education culture got flipped."

It was about more than power dynamics. Without the flip, much of the student success agenda Georgia State was about to pursue would not have made it out of the gate, because the deans would have had the power to preclude any encroachment on their territory and squash Renick's key ideas like gnats in the Georgia summer heat. As it was, Renick and his team had a green light from the president to set the performance metrics they felt best served the students' interests, knowing that the deans would be obliged to meet them. "Hurricane Becker" was how Tom Lewis described these changes.

The beauty of the arrangement was that nobody suspected Renick himself of unleashing any part of the whirlwind. The broad assumption was that the strategic planning committee had put the student success plan together piece by piece over months of work, and all Renick had to do was enact what they had laid out for him. "It was very valuable to us that this was people's assumption," Renick said, "because they were much less inclined to question what we were doing."

Another administrator in his position might have been more eager to claim credit, but hogging the limelight was never Renick's way. When it came to internal politics, he believed in speaking softly, moving quietly, avoiding open confrontation, and building alliances based on results that everyone could feel good about. The ultimate beneficiaries of this approach were the most vulnerable of Georgia State's students, who after decades of neglect now had a champion they could call their own. And there was no lack of work to be done.

4

THE PATH TO DESTRUCTION

Gabriel Woods arrived at Georgia State as a transfer student in the fall of 2007 with three trombones, an oversized tuxedo from Goodwill, and only one goal: to earn a music degree and fulfill his dream of becoming a band director. He was poor, black, highly motivated and bursting with talent, just the sort of student who should have thrived in a large, diverse university with access to the many amenities of a cosmopolitan city. Instead, his experience turned into the stuff of nightmares, a vivid illustration of how fast—and how needlessly—things could go awry, and a compelling argument for the student success revolution that would come just too late for him.

Woods had auditioned to be accepted into the school of music, but right away he struggled to be taken seriously. Having spent his first two years of college at Armstrong State in Savannah, he was late to the party, and the relationships between professors and students seemed to be cemented already. He suspected that many of these relationships predated college: a number of his peers had played in the Atlanta Youth Orchestra while in high school and had taken private lessons with Georgia State faculty members. Woods hadn't had those opportunities because he wasn't from Atlanta. He'd grown up in Brunswick, almost three hundred miles away on the south Georgia coast. And he hadn't had private lessons, because he could not afford them. He didn't consider himself a lesser musician for it—he was a three-time all-state band member and played professionally throughout high school—but when he arrived in Atlanta he was placed in a lower ensemble, behind a number of musicians he felt he could easily outplay.

"I was told, 'Gabriel, you're not ready, you're not good enough,'" he recalled. At first, he thought his placement was an administrative problem. He asked what was wrong with his audition. He appealed to his trombone professor. But nobody gave him a straight answer, or even seemed to care that much. Then he learned that the credits he'd earned at Armstrong were not being recognized, either because they had not been transferred correctly or because his professors did not want to recognize them, and he had to retake the courses from scratch.

One battle for recognition followed another. Woods eventually made it to the top ensemble, but his new practice times clashed with a required theory course. When he asked if there was a workaround, he was told there was not, even though he knew the school had made just such an accommodation for another student. The advice he received, and took only with the greatest reluctance, was to drop back to the lower ensemble. At length, he was told not to come to practice at all, because the next performance on the schedule called for three trombones and he was the fourth. Woods asked if this meant he would receive a bad grade. Wasn't the ensemble what he'd registered and paid for? Could he expect to be reinstated for the next performance? "The response was, we will be back in touch," he said. "Then, nothing."

These weren't ordinary setbacks to Woods. They were devastating, because from the time he was in middle school he'd thrown himself into music heart and soul, and there was no plan B. He had taught himself the trombone, the euphonium, tuba, and bass clarinet. He also played percussion, and was good enough at the piano—which he didn't take up until he had access to college practice rooms—to get hired for Sunday services at churches around Atlanta. "My love for music was unreal," he said.

As a child, living in unremitting poverty in Brunswick, it had been the one pursuit to give him true joy. His father was a traumatized Vietnam war vet who had drifted in and out of construction jobs, and in and out of the family. His mother wasn't able to work because of an autoimmune disease, and she scrimped by on disability checks and food stamps. The lights were often out at their house because they couldn't afford the electricity bills. Sometimes, there was no money for food either.

As a poor African American in the Deep South, the odds were stacked against Woods, but from an early age he refused to settle or give up. When a fifth-grade teacher told him to his face he'd never amount to anything, the effect was to make him burn with desire to prove her wrong. And music showed him the way. His mother bought him his first trombone by saving up food stamps and exchanging them for cash, and an inspirational band director in middle school did much of the rest by giving him just enough technique to run with and letting him take home instruments other than the trombone that he was impatient to master. By high school, he was recognized by one and all as a star player, "the jewel of Brunswick High" as his childhood friend and bandmate Duane Carver put it, far outperforming kids from more affluent families who had been taking private lessons for years. Soon, he was a regular player for the Coastal Orchestra of Georgia, two of whose patrons, a retired colonel and his cello-playing wife, were impressed enough to pay for his first tuxedo.

Woods understood that music was more than a talent; it was his most likely ticket out of Brunswick and the poverty he'd grown up with. When he started a job at Sears, he spent every penny he could spare on musical instruments, on sheet music, and on a used tux once he outgrew his old one. Instead of buying himself a used car, he walked the three miles to and from Sears, even though the heat was often punishing and it was far from safe for a black teenager to be out on the streets at night.

His high school grades fell just short of the threshold for a HOPE scholarship, so he took out loans and trusted that determination and hard work would see him through before his money ran out. The financial pressure accounted for much of the dismay every time he was turned down for an ensemble or told to repeat a class. He thought that transferring from Armstrong to Georgia State would take him "to the next level," but instead he kept looking at more time in school with no good idea of how to pay for it.

Woods was far from the only student to hit such obstacles. The music school at the time had a solid reputation for instruction, but not for designing courses and curriculum with the students' interests in mind. The auditioning process was a mess, with way too few slots to meet the demand from incoming freshmen. Faculty members were often unsympathetic to the general education requirements of a Georgia State music degree, which meant that scheduling clashes went unresolved and students received bad advice on what classes to take when. If anything, faculty were happy if the time to graduation was dragged out to five or six years because, in their minds, it gave students more time to mature musically. According to Maria Gindhart, a professor of art and design who would later become an associate dean overseeing all of Georgia State's arts programs, the faculty at the time acted more like a performance conservatory than a school within a large public university. Music directors would, for example, hire professional players from the Atlanta Symphony Orchestra to play in ensembles, thinking it would give students a chance to learn from a seasoned pro but overlooking the student or two who was necessarily excluded as a result. "It was really crazy. Why *pay money* to take an experience away from a student?" Gindhart said. The financial consequences for the excluded students were hardly considered. "In 2007, the university was just beginning to be aware that food insecurity and homelessness were major problems," she added. "But the response of most faculty and staff was, 'What do you mean? We don't have homeless students. We don't have students who are starving.' They didn't see it. It was not even on anyone's radar."

The dysfunction was such that students would suffer deep

crises of self-esteem or face significant hardship because of the time they were being induced to waste—*and the faculty hardly noticed*. Teachers of specific instruments, according to Gindhart, were frequently the worst offenders, "completely divorced from the larger picture of the university," and they came and went with alarming speed. Woods, not atypically, had three trombone professors in his first two years.

Was race also a factor? Woods feared that it was. Invariably, in his experience, the students who were unjustly overlooked were poor, or black, or both. It was a pattern he recognized from his school days in Brunswick, the good ol' boy system at its worst that he hoped to have left behind when he came to the big city. To encounter something like it again filled him with a weary resignation. He was eager, good-natured, well-mannered, very hard to dislike—yet he had the feeling that people at Georgia State did not like him one bit. "Something triggered in me," he said, "as if I didn't belong. Perhaps there was a procedure I missed, but nobody told me." It may have had something to do with his overall appearance, because he was a big kid and was self-conscious about a gold top-front tooth, the result of a childhood accident in the bathtub. He knew it worked against him, especially when he met people for the first time.

Gindhart said it was possible some form of discrimination was in play, although she saw it primarily as a byproduct of certain professors being too wrapped in their own preoccupations and failing to understand the challenges facing lower-income students of all ethnicities. The ensembles were often highly diverse, suggesting the bedrock issue may not have been race itself but rather the class divide that many young black men, like Gabriel, found it difficult or impossible to breach. At the same time, it did not help that the faculty was nowhere close to reflecting the diversity of the student body and could not easily relate to their life experiences. "It's a real problem, and not just at Georgia State," Gindhart said. "Often, old white men don't understand that there's a problem."

Woods spiraled rapidly downward. By the end of his first year, he was running out of money and his grades were dropping. His instinct was to ask questions of his professors and advisors so they'd understand he wanted only to find a path to success and do everything it took to get there. "I was constantly emailing and going to the office," he said, "trying to find professors and waiting my turn for an appointment." But often professors would not show up, and when they did they gave answers he came to mistrust. "I never got the feeling that they were thinking, *I want you to learn*," he said. "There were times I would not see a professor for months." Over time, he stopped speaking up, because he was afraid of being marked as a troublemaker and penalized for it in class. "I was being led on a path of destruction," he said. "I had this fear that I'd have to go home and say I'd dropped out. I could hear my mother saying, *I told you not to go to Atlanta*."

Woods made one last appeal for help, telling the school's assistant director about his futile quest for reliable advice and complaining about one advisor he found particularly detrimental. "Her attitude," he wrote, "has emotionally taken a charge on me to the point where I can't sleep and I feel like I have been called out because of my race." In response, the assistant director said he took accusations of racial animus very seriously and invited Woods to substantiate them if he could. But he also pointed out that there were several levels of bureaucracy within the school, and Woods had made the mistake of going two levels above the problematic advisor when the proper procedure was to go up one level at a time. So he should redirect his query to a different administrator, the director of musical education—and best of luck.

The assistant director may have meant well, but Woods took the email as a colossal brush-off. He had deliberately appealed to a senior figure who did not teach classes, because he didn't want his complaints to alienate or enrage anyone directly responsible for his grades. He began to lose heart. Worse, he lost his passion. "I said, forget this," he recalled. "I didn't want to do music. I didn't want to do band." In his mind, he imagined becoming a teacher instead of a player, but he had no idea how he was going to manage that because he was no longer on track toward a degree. He'd hit a wall.

By the end of his second year, in the summer of 2009, Woods's grades had dropped below a 2.0 average and he was "excluded," which meant he was on academic probation and, effectively, out of the music program for good. This sickened Woods to his core. "How can a person go from one of the top players in the state to not doing music?" he asked. The loss was almost unbearable. "In a way," he said, "they took my soul. Music was my first love. They took something that meant more to me than anything I'd been doing for years."

This was not, fortunately, the end of Woods's story, but it certainly felt that way. He had nowhere to go, nothing but debt to his name, and little prospect of continuing his education in any capacity. This, he knew, was the way that tens of thousands of college careers came to a crashing halt across America each year—not for lack of talent or hard work, but because of unexpected obstacles that students found strewn across their path and did not have the resources or the support system to overcome.

Reluctantly, Woods pawned off his three trombones, at a shop around the corner from the Georgia State College of Education, which he might at one time have dreamed of attending. He didn't do it because he was giving up. To Woods, giving up and going home was not an option. But he knew he was in deep trouble. He knew, too, he needed somewhere to stay, and money for food. *That* was why he was saying goodbye to his instruments—to keep body and soul together while he explored his dwindling options. It was an agonizing price to pay, but if it could give him even a glimmer of hope of one day earning a degree he would force himself to pay it.

———

Tim Renick and his team would soon develop a name for students like Woods who seemed to drift ever further from graduation the longer they stayed enrolled. They were called "swirlers," because they would go around in endless circles in pursuit of a goal they were never going to reach. This was a particular problem in programs that imposed extra entrance requirements on students beyond the university's basic admissions criteria: auditions for music, say, or a portfolio for art and design. And it was a problem, too, in the professional schools, particularly business and nursing, that required students to meet a minimum grade-point average in their core and introductory courses before they could be admitted into the program proper.

Nobody begrudged these programs the right to impose such standards. The standards have, if anything, *risen* over the last decade, as Georgia State has rethought its approach to undergraduate education. The problem was, nobody offered students a realistic assessment of their chances, much less an alternative pathway if in fact they couldn't crack pre-calculus, say, or first-year chemistry. A swirler with her heart set on a business degree—a common choice for lower-income kids looking for a quick route to a high-paying job—would typically fail at intro math in her first couple of semesters, creating not one but two significant problems. Not only would she now have to retake and pass the math class; she also had to worry about the blow that the failing grade had dealt to her GPA, because it might have fallen too low to qualify her for a business major at all. To remedy the second problem, she might take an elective unconnected to business—introductory geology, say, or history of jazz—in the hope of doing well enough to bump the GPA back up again. Often, that plan would pan out. Then she would retake the intro math class and either fail it again, which would put her right back to square one, or pass it, only to stumble at the next hurdle where her wobbly math skills risked being exposed—introductory accounting, perhaps, or finance.

Nobody was on hand to tell her that maybe she might find greater joy and a better use of her talents in a cognate field like marketing or managerial science. Nobody was at her shoulder to warn her that her state and federal money was running low and pretty soon she'd have a whole lot of electives to her name and no prospect of finishing a degree.

Some proportion of the students in this situation would figure out the futility of endless tail-chasing and switch to a different field of study within a year or two. But unless they had someone reliable to guide them, and most did not, there was no guarantee they would choose a major more wisely the second time around. When Tim Renick took over the student success shop, he found that even those Georgia State students who made it to graduation were changing majors *2.6 times* on average. Such woeful inefficiency meant that crucial numbers of students were not finishing, not because they couldn't find their groove academically, but because they had run out of time or money or both.

Behind the swirling lay a mindset that was singularly inhospitable to the needs of low-income and first-generation students. Individual departments and schools had a tendency to load the first-year curriculum with courses that had little or no application to any other field of study. So when as many as *90 percent* of aspiring nursing freshmen were turned away because they hadn't made the 3.8 GPA cutoff, they found themselves burdened with unusable credits and facing extra semesters in school to acquire others they could apply to a new major. In many cases, this disregard for the students' needs was simply tone-deaf. And sometimes it was a matter of deliberate policy, arising from misguided notions of what constituted a quality education.

The Robinson College of Business was the worst offender in this regard. Fenwick Huss, the dean, was interested above all in polishing and enhancing his school's reputation, and he was forever fearful that low-performing undergraduates would drag the enterprise down. He saw nothing wrong with large numbers of students failing intro math and accounting; in fact he saw it as his job to weed out as many of them as possible. "It made no sense to let most of these students progress," he said. "I used to liken it to medical school. Do you want to go to a physician who got through medical school, *barely*? It matters to me that a physician has Stanford on his wall." Renick remembered a similar line of argument from a math department chair in the early 2000s who thought it was his job to eliminate students whose high school education had not adequately prepared them for college. "He saw it almost as a badge of honor," Renick said.

The problem with this weeding logic was that it easily became a self-fulfilling prophecy: *because* we believe in quality, we feel duty bound to deny an education to large numbers of admitted students even though they are crying out for the very thing we are refusing to give them. It's a short road from that sort of thinking to a teaching environment in which the courses are purposely designed to deter and dissuade. Before Renick took control of Georgia State's student success initiatives, the math department resisted the widespread use of adaptive learning computer labs, despite evidence showing that students able to learn at their own pace were likely to succeed in far higher numbers. Ron Henry had tried repeatedly to make the case for adaptive learning, but could never win. "Maybe it poked at their manhood or something, because they're no longer in charge," he said, "We were not the only university that had difficulty . . . It sputtered along, but never really took root."

Students came to fear intro math because they saw it as a mechanism for crushing college careers, not a tool for advancement. The same was true of the intro accounting classes in the business school. Huss, who taught some of those accounting classes himself, acknowledged that he had "an extraordinarily high failure rate," but took vigorous issue with the idea that students were being demoralized on purpose. "It was not a dog-eat-dog environment," he insisted. "The students knew the reputation of the classes . . . I'd tell them, it's you against the material, and it's my job to help you master it. But if you don't master it, I can't *give* you a grade. You have to earn it."

Many of the students who enrolled as business majors did not experience accounting classes this way, however—and not always because they weren't capable of doing well. Kyle Stapleton, a high-performing marketing major who graduated in 2009, got a D the first time. His friend Terrance Rogers, a star first-generation student who would go on to Harvard Business School and a career on Wall Street, got a C; he remembered being bored out of his mind in a large auditorium and wondering: "Why are they going so slow? Why are they making this all so complicated?" Jovan Paige, another first-generation student who dazzled just about everyone from the moment he arrived on campus, heard so many horror stories that he switched majors from business to public policy at the start of his sophomore year so he wouldn't have to take accounting at all.

Perhaps the most insidious part of the "quality" argument was that it took no account of the difference between students who had every advantage handed to them and those with no less potential who had attended mediocre high schools and had no viable family support. Too often, this latter group encountered a teaching mentality unwilling to look past—or work through—the disadvantages they came in with. The expectation in many classes, particularly the large intro sections, was that only half the students would follow along, and only 20 percent would truly absorb the material. It was an insidious mentality, not only because it was so defeatist but because teaching styles were tailored accordingly. Little wonder, then, that the failure rate in intro math reached 43 percent in 2008, or that the graduation rate of the university as a whole remained stuck well below the 50 percent mark. Too many people on campus saw this as the inevitable nature of things.

A big part of what Renick and his team set out to do was to give teachers reasons to believe in their students again. The trick, they believed, was to base classroom decisions on evidence, not suppositions fueled by ideological blindness. Instead of assuming that large numbers of students were doomed to fail, the student success team started from the opposite premise, that these were good students who deserved the education they'd come to Georgia State to receive. If that was so—and the admissions criteria indicated it was—then the university needed to take responsibility for students and *help* them carve a path through the thicket of majors and core courses and electives, not to mention the additional, complicating thicket of financial aid forms, registration requirements, scholarship opportunities, and work-study placements. "The university doesn't exist just to provide for people who can figure it out for themselves," said Allison Calhoun-Brown. "The mentality always was, it can't be our fault if they're not able to graduate. But it was costing them too much for us to remain cavalier about it."

One obvious way to ease the burden on students was to provide them with effective academic advising, particularly in the first few semesters when they were navigating their core requirements and settling on a major. The individual colleges had their own advising units but, as Gabriel Woods experienced, these tended to be subject specific. Often, the advisors were faculty members, not staff professionals, and did not necessarily understand the workings of the university at large. They were of little use, for example, to anyone contemplating a change of major. Routinely, students would navigate that transition alone and then start again with new advisors in a new department.

Ron Henry had made a first attempt to address this problem when he was provost. On his watch, a young researcher named Elisha Jarrett was sent on a fact-finding tour of universities with centralized advising offices and, after she reported back, Georgia State set up its own Student Advisement Center to cover the first forty-two credit hours, equivalent to a year and a half of full-time enrollment. The center was woefully understaffed, however, with fewer than a dozen advisors to serve more than ten thousand freshmen and sophomores, a ratio of 1:1,200. They had no capacity to reach out to students who did not come to them and could barely manage even those who did, particularly at peak times ahead of registration deadlines. Forty-two credit hours turned out to be the wrong cutoff, because many students needed longer to map out their path to a degree and were often most vulnerable at the point that the service dried up.

The service itself was also beset with problems. Advisors took notes spottily, if at all, which meant nothing was tracked properly, and kept such a strict schedule that students who arrived even a few minutes late risked being turned away. There was no attempt to match students to advisors familiar with their study areas. "I had students last name H through L," Jarrett recalled. Most of them she never saw.

By 2007, the center had lost its inaugural director and had burned through a number of interims. "The administration called and said, 'You're not moving the needle. Y'all have a year to figure it out,'" Jarrett recalled. A new, tougher-nosed director was installed, but she proved so unpopular the staff petitioned for her removal and she resigned after just eight months. Dysfunction abounded. The office administrator responsible for recording the credits of incoming transfer students developed a habit of calling in sick at the busiest times of the year, leaving an unknown number of credits unrecorded and forcing an unknown number of students—possibly including Woods—to repeat classes they had already taken. She was eventually pressured into leaving.

Jarrett came close to quitting several times herself. The reason she did not was, ultimately, the students. She knew what it was like to fight for an education. She had been one of just eight African Americans out of a class of 223 to graduate from her high school in Kalamazoo, Michigan (her twin sister was another). And she had been a first-generation college student at Jackson

State in Mississippi, learning, like so many Georgia State under-graduates, to balance the demands of studying, working two jobs, figuring out who she was, and what her path should be. It did not always go smoothly. In her junior year she was almost thrown out because her grades were not up to snuff. Then she got pregnant; she sat her finals with a baby on her knee. Only slowly did she dis-cover her passion for education and dedicate her lifeblood to it. "I am 80 percent of our students," she said. "I look at them and say, that was me. That's huge."

Where Jarrett and her fellow advisors found they could have the biggest impact was with students whose grades had dropped below the required minimum, because a hold was automatically placed on their registration and they were forced to come into the office if they wanted to have it lifted. Indeed, by the time Gabriel Woods found himself in trouble, the SAC had developed a reputa-tion as Georgia State's last chance saloon. Many of the "excluded" students never recovered. But, for a crucial handful, the interven-tion made all the difference in the world.

Help for Woods came in the form of Crystal Mitchell, a last-chance specialist with a college background as checkered as Jar-rett's and a similarly huge heart. It shouldn't have come down to one person, and a few years later it wouldn't have, but this was the one chance Woods was given and he embraced it. Like so many members of the emerging student-success team at Georgia State, Mitchell had been a first-generation student. She'd started at Spelman, the premier black women's college in Atlanta, where her mother worked in the arts department, but felt overwhelmed and underprepared and dropped out in her junior year. Slowly, she clawed her way back to a degree by way of Atlanta Metro—which Princeton Nelson later attended—and Clayton State in the southeast Atlanta suburbs, where she graduated in marketing while simultaneously working at Georgia State, first as a records coordinator in the registrar's office, then in admissions and ultimately in advising.

By the time Woods came to see her, Mitchell was one of the most valued members of the team, known for her ability to draw things out of students that others couldn't, and to fight with everything she had for those she believed in. Woods was one she believed in.

He told her: "I have the weight of the world on me. I don't know how to get through this." She told him he was too smart to fail and should ask for whatever he needed. "No, really, here's my direct number," she insisted.

Mitchell had a different style from many of her colleagues, more like a therapist than a motivational coach. She was calm and guarded, not effusive or exuberant; she listened intently and chose her words carefully. In that way, her sensibility was not unlike Woods's, and they bonded easily. Nobody at Georgia State had talked to him with such sympathy and authority, and it filled him with a renewed hope.

Under the terms of his academic probation, Woods was allowed to take six more credit hours. If he got his GPA back up to 2.0, he would be granted another twelve, and so on until he was fully reinstated. He told Mitchell he'd enjoyed taking journalism, so she sent him to community college for the summer to pick up communications credits more cheaply than he could have done at Georgia State. It worked. The next step was to convince him to forget music, because it would take more years than he could afford to pick up the credits to qualify for a music education degree, even assuming he could overcome his bruising personal struggles with the department. She urged him to stay on the communications track instead. Woods listened, taking a lot more journalism classes and other core requirements. He started to imagine a future as a speech pathologist.

The summer he was put on probation, he stayed with his childhood friend Duane Carver, a brilliant student who had won a full ride to study computer engineering at Georgia Tech and was on his way to graduating in just three years. Woods didn't say a word about dropping out of music. He mentioned only that he was having financial problems. Carver and his roommates agreed that Woods could sleep on the couch. He got up early, took the bus to class, worked at a Sears in the predominantly black suburb of Lithonia, picked up $50 or $100 a week playing Sunday services, and spent any extra time studying in the library.

Carver wasn't offended that Woods did not tell him everything—and would not, for many years. He'd had an equally challenging upbringing, including a period in his teenage years when he and his mother were homeless, and he understood. "When you're from a different environment, you go through these weighing patterns," he said. "You have to protect yourself and be on guard. You learn that you have to lean on other people to be successful." Their friendship was founded on something arguably more important than full disclosure. They both knew, given where they came from, that one mistake could be enough to undo everything they had worked toward. The best favor they could do each other was to keep their eye on the goals they had set for themselves regardless of the pressure. Duane may have been the one on the more promising trajectory in the summer of 2009, but it was Gabriel, Carver said, who maintained the unrelenting focus.

He needed every bit of it. Once the fall semester rolled around, Woods had to move out of Carver's dorm but could not afford student housing of his own. He could have found more working hours, but his priority at that point was on rescuing his academic career and he preferred to devote every spare hour to study. So he found a way to live in group homes with ex-felons and recovering addicts for $50 or $60 a week, for as long as he had student loan money to cover it. When the loan money ran out, he moved into his dilapidated nine-year-old Saturn. At night, he'd park at large apartment complexes where he felt moderately safe. One was near Turner Field, just a few blocks south of Georgia State, and another was next to the Stonecrest Mall in Lithonia, which he knew from working at the Sears there. When he had extra change, he used the washer-dryers in the apartment buildings to clean his clothes. For personal hygiene, he'd arrive for class early and use the bathrooms in the General Classroom Building in the center of campus. His go-to meal was a Church's 69¢ special, two pieces of chicken and a biscuit. In the evenings, he'd go to the library and stay until it closed at midnight.

Academically, he was soon back on track, but keeping body and soul together was another matter. In the spring of 2010, he had enough money to move back into a group home west of Downtown, not far from the historically black campuses—Spelman, Morehouse, and Clark—known collectively as the Atlanta University Center. When he was truly pinched, he'd turn to Carver for a loan, including one time in the summer of 2010 when Carver, who had just graduated, agreed to risk money he'd saved for an apartment down payment in North Carolina, where he was about to start a software engineering job. Woods, true to his word, repaid Carver in time.

There were things Woods flat-out could not afford. At some point he lost the plastic cover on a second top-front tooth damaged in the childhood bathtub accident, and he didn't have the means or the insurance coverage to replace it. Now his smile had a chip as well as an off-putting sliver of gold. Sometimes, Woods was so hungry he ate out of dumpsters behind the Landmark Diner, an all-night dive restaurant next to the building where he was taking Spanish classes, or behind a row of cheap student eateries a block further south along Broad Street. "It was embarrassing for me," he recalled. "But I could only think, I have to do this by any means necessary. I just have to do this. I can't fail."

Slowly, and despite these extraordinary hardships, the music bug returned. One of the most heartbreaking aspects of leaving the music program was that he had nowhere to play the instruments he loved. "I would have needed to swipe my Panther card to get into the practice room," he said, "and I wasn't welcome there." Still, he decided to pursue an alternative teachers' credentialing program that did not involve Georgia State. He passed the Georgia Assessments for the Certification of Educators at the end of his junior year, qualifying himself to be a public school teacher. And he aced a separate music test on the first try, despite having little or no opportunity to practice and nobody to coach him.

Just once, at the start of his final semester in January 2011, Woods doubted whether he had the fortitude to go on. He was homeless again, and a snowstorm of rare severity blew through Atlanta, closing the university for three days. It was too cold to sleep in his car, and with the library off-limits he had nowhere to spend his waking hours either. Not knowing what else to do, he rode the MARTA public train system for as long it ran and spent the first couple of nights in a MARTA station. Then it occurred to him that, with the bag he carried around, he could pass as a stranded traveler, and he spent the next few nights at the airport, which never closed even though hundreds of flights were being canceled. He slept in snatches and studied as much as he could, but mostly the goal was to survive. At one point, he found himself sitting at a TGI Fridays, sipping a glass of water and ignoring the ache in his belly because he could afford nothing off the menu, and he made up his mind he was going to be grateful, not desperate, about his plight. "Ordering water from TGI Fridays was an upgrade from drinking water at our home in Brunswick," he decided. "I was in Atlanta. For me, that was almost an upgrade in itself. I told myself, my luck will eventually turn."

Nobody knew the extent of the bind he was in: not his friends, nor his mother, nor even his girlfriend Brittny in Savannah, who didn't find out until much later that he was no longer a music major. After the snowstorm, though, Woods could no longer hold it in and broke down in front of Crystal Mitchell. She listened, and asked him questions, and told him she'd find financial aid to see him through to the end of his studies. Graduation was only another couple of months away.

He completed his coursework on time, only to hit another obstacle: he had no funds to register for graduation. His parents had no money either, and no car to come to Atlanta, so he assumed he would simply skip the ceremony. Mitchell, though, insisted that he deserved better. She found grants for the graduation fee, and money for a cap and gown. When she learned he had no shirt, she bought him one herself. When she learned he had no tie, she bought him a tie. She said: "You've earned your degree. I want you to look comfortable and confident. You belong here."

After the festivities they met up one last time, and Woods confided that he had no money for gas to get back to Brittny in Savannah. Mitchell pulled $200 out of her wallet and told him: "You made it. Now go find a job."

But Woods had one last surprise for her. He already *had* a job. Starting that August, he was going to be the band director for a middle school in Savannah. Brittny had told him about the opening a couple of months earlier, and he'd driven four hours each way to meet the principal on her lunch break. It was a short interview. The principal was thrilled to find someone with the background and passion to teach poor, predominantly black kids with no access to instruments or private lessons. And Woods made quick work of charming her. She'd later joke she wished he was old enough to marry her daughter.

After that, he did not look back. He earned another teaching credential during his first year at Myers Middle School and went on to pursue first a master's, then a doctorate in music education from the University of Georgia. Eight years out from graduation, he had passed his love of music on to hundreds of kids at Myers and risen to assistant professor of music at Savannah State University, with a growing national reputation as a music educator and lecturer. He was also married, to Brittny, had medical insurance he could use to fix his teeth once and for all, and owned his own home.

Despite his bruising undergraduate experience, Woods made a habit of wearing a Georgia State lapel pin. It wasn't that he didn't feel bitter. He did, about a lot of things. But he chose to look past it. "I've learned to say, as a man, that I graduated from a reputable institution," he said.

And he was in no doubt about who made that possible. "Crystal Mitchell was an angel," he said. "She was sent. There was nobody else."

5

MULTIDIMENSIONAL CHESS

When Tim Renick's team set about transforming student advising at Georgia State, their ambition, in essence, was to take what Crystal Mitchell had done for Gabriel Woods and systematize and scale it so every student was in a position to benefit. Renick and his colleagues did not know the particulars of Woods's case—they were just getting started when he hit rock bottom—but they were aware of the needless suffering of untold numbers of undergraduates and felt a pressing need to end it. Granted, it was unusual for a student to descend to quite the level of penury that Woods endured, but debt and poverty were ever-present realities in the lives of most Georgia State undergraduates and it was clear just how stark the price of failure could be. As Joshua Okinola-King, a highly successful student from a lower-middle-class family of Nigerian immigrants, put it shortly before he graduated in computer science in 2019: "It doesn't take much. That's the scariest thing. You're just one misstep, one false move away."

Renick's team certainly understood the power of steady guidance and timely intervention to turn students' lives around, but they also knew that individual advisors, no matter how extraordinary, were not going to solve the problem on their own. For decades, campuses across the country had leaned on the golden-hearted dedication of people like Crystal Mitchell and Elisha Jarrett to rescue students who fell through the cracks without acknowledging that they were merely pecking away at the edges of a vast and deeply embedded problem. What was needed was a thoroughgoing overhaul to address the *causes* of the crisis, so intervention of the sort that Gabriel Woods required became a rarity, not the only safety net on offer. It was no longer enough to expect students to figure out the complexities of obtaining an undergraduate degree on their own, because more than half were failing to do so. It had to be the university's responsibility to keep them on track, from the moment they stepped onto campus until the day they walked away with their diploma.

The big question was how to achieve this. When Renick started as associate provost, Ron Henry felt that enhancing academic advising was as much of a lost cause as convincing the math faculty to embrace adaptive computer learning. He had been ready, in fact, to give up on his idea of centralizing the advising service and to redistribute Jarrett, Mitchell, and their fellow advisors to the individual colleges instead. It wasn't just that Henry was unable to find the right leadership for the Student Advisement Center. He couldn't convince the college deans to support him and was disinclined to browbeat them into it. "I'm not for big government," he said. "In the end, I ran out of time and I ran out of patience." Renick, though, wasn't so sure that the SAC had reached the end of its usefulness, and he talked Henry into giving him six months to explore ways to resuscitate it.

Renick's fundamental idea was to take the scientific approach embraced by Henry and build a data set he could use to lobby for broader changes. He applied this idea not just to advising, but to every program within his purview—learning communities, near-peer mentoring, adaptive learning, centralized advising, and more. He wanted to run randomized controlled trials to test the efficacy of each of these innovations and use the results to press the case for their expansion. Renick knew he'd get faculty pushback, because it came with the territory, but he had also been toughened by his fights with the philosophy department in the 1980s and 1990s and remembered how data had helped him keep the skeptics and detractors at bay. He had faith now that if he could amass data to show that intro math students learned faster and obtained better grades when they spent several hours a week in a computer lab, then mathematicians, of all people, would have to accept what the numbers showed to be true.

Advising presented particular complications because, at the beginning, Renick and Allison Calhoun-Brown had no data to go on. One of the first things they asked the SAC office was how many students were using the advising service, and no one could say for sure. "I remember feeling a great frustration because the way we counted students was on pieces of paper," Calhoun-Brown recalled. "If someone didn't sign in, or if the advisor didn't put down a hash mark, it didn't happen. Our systematization of the data started with the most basic question: Who are we seeing? And we couldn't answer it."

Renick and Calhoun-Brown weren't working in a complete vacuum. They knew that the majority of students coming in for advising sessions were either at the high end of the performance curve and seeking guidance with the same diligence as they went about everything else, or they were at the low end and obliged to seek guidance because they were on academic probation. In other words, advisors were seeing students who were almost certain to succeed anyway, or almost certain to fail anyway. What they were missing, and what advising services around the country were generally missing, was the large contingent of students in the middle, "the murky middle" as the parlance would soon have it, a broad pool of medium-level performers who were most in need of guidance because they were the ones teetering most precariously between success and failure. Indeed, research would soon confirm that the largest concentration of college dropouts nationally had a GPA of between 2.0 and 3.0 after their freshman year, the very definition of the murky middle. If the university could stop these students from choosing the wrong major, or taking courses out of sequence, or missing vital credits that would cost extra time and

money to recoup, it might steer their lives in a dramatically different direction.

From these insights, Renick made a number of preliminary
determinations. First, advising had to be proactive, not reactive,
because that was the only way to reach the murky middle. Second,
the SAC had to extend its reach, because it was seeing students
only up to the end of their first forty-two credit hours and the risk
of dropping out was just as severe after that point as it was before.
And, third, Georgia State would have to find a way to hire a lot
more advisors. NACADA, the National Association of Academic
Advising, recommended a student–advisor ratio of no more than
300:1, but Jarrett, Mitchell, and their colleagues were responsible
for four times as many. How Georgia State was supposed to go on
a hiring spree in the middle of a recession Renick did not know.
But he convinced Becker that the university needed to work toward the 300:1 target anyway, and he had it inscribed as a goal in
the strategic plan.

That was one piece of the puzzle. Another piece was building
up an advising service capable of keeping track of its own activities
and generating the data Renick needed to make the case for continuing change. At first glance, this seemed a near-impossible task.
The SAC was still suffering from a revolving-door leadership and
other staffing dysfunctions. The deans and faculty were already
skeptical of deploying advisors who were not themselves academics, and the skepticism was all the greater when the advisors were
not under their direct control. Then there were questions about
the mission itself. Why would the university want to invest in
underperforming lower-income students, when the conventional
wisdom viewed them as lost causes? If these students were unable to take advantage of the opportunities that higher education
already offered them, wasn't this tantamount to throwing good
money after bad?

Renick, though, never wavered. "Tim had some sense of hope

or faith or belief that the plan would be realized," Becker recalled. And that was no small thing. "When you have decision makers playing in the same park as you," Elisha Jarrett observed, "that's what made this thing work."

Renick enjoyed one early piece of good fortune, because the associate director of the SAC, installed just a few months before he began his own job, turned out to be a perfect partner for the reforms he had in mind. In short order, he made her head of the office and, later, director of all advising services. Not only did she help him navigate a path through the many challenges; she was, in many ways, a kindred spirit.

Carol Cohen came from the world of athletics where she'd been used to keeping a close eye on her students' every move. Now she found herself running an office where the staff seemed to keep an eye on almost nobody.

It was an excruciating assignment for the first year or so, because Cohen didn't know if she was destined to be the center's savior or its undertaker, and as long as the uncertainty lasted she became a lightning rod for many of the office's insecurities and frustrations. Her staff whispered behind her back about her sports background, as though having been head of academic support for student athletes was somehow unqualifying. They resented being questioned about what they did and how they did it, and complained about being overworked even before Cohen asked them to do anything new or different. "I was in charge, sort of," she recalled.

Still, Cohen was energetic, outgoing, full of ideas, and noticed *everything*: how advisors chatted to some students way past their allotted time and kept others waiting; how they would send late-arriving students away instead of taking them for whatever time remained; how one advisor worked from home and, as a result, saw hardly any students at all. "I'd say, wait a minute, we're advisors, we're here to serve. We need to meet the students where they are, not where we think they should be," she remembered. "I was not the most loved person."

Cohen had a good eye for advisors who were going to be her allies (she made Elisha Jarrett her deputy) and didn't worry unduly if she couldn't make friends with the others. This was, after all, a fight for survival, not a popularity contest, and she understood that the office was going to have to generate evidence—*data*—to prove its worth. No longer could the advisors scribble notes in any manner they saw fit; Cohen insisted on uniform record-keeping on Excel spreadsheets. No longer would students without appointments be turned away at the door; she instituted a rotating advisor of the day to handle walk-ins. She also promoted meet-and-greet sessions, with free donuts and orange juice, to familiarize students with the center and to encourage more of them to use it. The lines for these events invariably snaked out the door and into the corridors. "That showed me people were hungry for advisement if you reached out to them," she said.

Cohen made these changes not only because they made sense to her, but also because she knew what Renick and Calhoun-Brown were looking for. Early on she wrote her bosses a six-page memo making the case for keeping SAC open, and it was an almost exact echo of Renick's philosophy that what mattered was not winning political battles but producing results. "We were joined at the hip to work that office into shape," Renick remembered.

Knowing that the student success leadership had her back emboldened Cohen to do things she knew would be unpopular with some of her staff—for example, pushing them to pay special attention to the 1,200 freshmen who arrived each year without a declared major. The extra work sat so badly with some of the advisors that they filed a complaint about Cohen with human resources. But she never swerved from the belief that she was doing the right thing.

Cohen developed a particularly close alliance with Calhoun-Brown, her direct supervisor. They had different backgrounds and skill sets, but took advantage of these to form a compelling double act. "It was powerful to have a faculty person and a staff person together," Calhoun-Brown recalled. Typically, Calhoun-Brown would be the one to pinpoint something the students needed, or the hassles they *didn't* need, and Cohen, with her long administrative experience and detailed knowledge of Banner, the university student database, would be adept at devising solutions. The relationship worked well in the opposite direction, too: if Cohen needed someone in authority to correct a problem above her pay grade, Calhoun-Brown would gladly intercede on her behalf.

One example of this came when Cohen turned to Calhoun-Brown to help students on academic probation overcome a maddening bureaucratic procedure that required them to have their reinstatement plans signed both by the SAC and by someone in their college advising office. Since a lot of the college offices had limited opening hours and appointment slots, it would often take several tries to get the second signature, and many students lost heart and walked away. Cohen and Elisha Jarrett called this the "Panther shuffle," or more straightforwardly, the "walk of shame," because it struck them as a needless humiliation for students whose self-esteem was already at a low ebb. Often, it involved an actual walk across campus with no certain outcome.

Calhoun-Brown put her head in her hands as this was described to her. "Students were being run around and nobody was taking responsibility for anything," she said, still mad about it years later. "It's not reasonable to have a student who's fought traffic and taken the time to talk to the right people, only to be told, no, you've got to go back and do something else, you've only solved one part of the problem." Calhoun-Brown told the colleges what Cohen did not feel empowered to say, that academic probation was under the SAC's sole jurisdiction, and the practice came to a rapid end. "It was supposed to be a one-stop shop," she fumed. "That was a lie. There was no one-stop shop."

From the beginning, technology was key to the changes that Cohen instituted. She did not just fire the manager who begged off sick when she should have been making sure that transfer students had their credits moved over correctly; she hired a new articulation manager capable of automating large parts of the process. Cohen was also an advocate of GradesFirst, a student tracking system she'd used in athletics, which collated everything from class assignments and attendance rates to advising and tutoring appointments. Once it became apparent that centralized advising was going to survive and could lobby for its share of budgetary resources, she asked Renick if she could bring the system over, and Renick agreed. In fact, he told her he would go further and look for a system that could synthesize and analyze student data more closely still, so advisors would see at a glance who was on track and who was heading for trouble.

There was, however, a more fundamental problem to address first. If Renick and Cohen were going to provide reliable advice and, especially, if they were going to develop predictive models based on students' past performance, they had to know that the data in the system was correct. And they didn't, because Georgia State's record-keeping was an unholy, undisciplined mess. The problem was so big that Renick alone did not have the clout to fix it. Mark Becker was going to have to step in. And that meant making another case the student success shop could not afford to lose.

Georgia State started digitizing its records in the late 1990s, which meant Renick and his team had more than a decade of data to draw on for their advising models. That was all to the good. The problem was that the record-keeping lacked rigor to the point where Renick and Calhoun-Brown couldn't even figure out how many students were enrolled in which majors. The Banner system did not impose rules or standards on data entry, so students enrolled in "biological sciences" were counted separately from those enrolled in "bio," and separately again from those in "biology." Everything depended on the quirks of the individuals entering the information. If someone transposed an *i* and an *e* and wrote "political sceince," that too created a new major. This had been going on so long that the colleges had all but given up and preferred to keep their own records, separate from Banner, thus defeating the whole purpose of a university-wide system. Many of them used Excel spreadsheets accessible only on their own servers. The College of Education kept paper records stored in manila folders in the dean's office, where even the college's own administrators couldn't easily access them.

It was not difficult to convince Mark Becker, a trained statistician, that this state of affairs was unacceptable. The question was how quickly the president was prepared to move. Since Becker knew he'd have to knock some heads, he wanted to be sure ahead of time that the effort was worth it. Renick's task was not merely to sell him on the importance of good data, but on the broader vision of a revamped advising service that could transform the lives and prospects of Georgia State's students. "This," Becker said, "was his recruitment of me." It took a few months, but Renick was persuasive enough that Becker ended up telling the deans at a senior staff retreat in January 2010, just as the strategic planning process was getting under way, that if they didn't fix the data problem he would ask someone else to fix it for them. "There are certain nonnegotiables," he remembered saying. "And this is one them."

The man Becker picked to be his enforcer was Peter Lyons, the associate provost for institutional effectiveness, an amiable and quick-witted professor of social work from Liverpool. Together, Becker and Lyons performed something of a good cop–bad cop routine as they insisted that the new data warehouse had to be the sole incontrovertible source of factual truth across the university. Becker would threaten as necessary, and Lyons would be the playful bearer of tough news. "I would play a joke with Mark," he recounted. "I'd say to him, 'Tell me the university needs a single authoritative data system.'" Lyons wouldn't let up until Becker parroted back: "The university needs a single authoritative data system." Lyons would then go into a meeting and say: "The president said: *There will be a single authoritative data system!*"

The double act, though, was only so successful. Lyons put together a team to integrate dozens of third-party servers and data systems—he never found out exactly how many. But he couldn't get the colleges to put their trust in the new system. For months, he reiterated the message that the colleges needed to fix Banner, not run away from it or fudge the numbers, and Risa Palm did much the same. But the message simply would not get through.

Lyons thought the best approach was to "smooth out the deans"; in other words, to reassure them that everything would be all right and to show sympathy for the many pressures they faced. Renick also favored a diplomatic route, because he was going to need a lot of cooperation once the data question was settled—to reorganize class schedules, for example—and he didn't want to alienate anyone. Becker, though, was furious. He thought the deans were dragging their feet, plain and simple, and a few months after his initial warning he issued what everyone understood to be an ultimatum. From now on, he said, he would base all budgetary decisions on data in the warehouse. If information important to a college wasn't in the warehouse, he wouldn't act on it. Becker told Renick: "I've got fire coming out of my ears and nostrils, and I'm not going to take another year of this." He told the deans: "If it doesn't get fixed in the next iteration, I will take a different approach."

It got fixed.

Becker didn't insist solely because he wanted the deans to respect his authority. He saw an opportunity to put Georgia State in the forefront of transformative change in the Atlanta region by providing a reliable new pipeline of skilled workers with bachelor's degrees and offering a dynamic vision of the post-recessionary future that he could sell to the board of regents, the governor's office, and the legislature. Becker thought of his job as a game of multidimensional chess, and he was forever seeking to move his pieces in the right sequence, whether that meant forging new relationships or leaning on existing bonds of trust to win permission for changes that, on their face, seemed impossibly ambitious. Once Renick convinced him that data-driven advising was the essential engine of the changes he had in mind, Becker was willing to go to the mat to make it happen.

The timing seemed right, and not just because of what was happening at Georgia State. The university system had pledged, in its own most recent strategic plan, to raise graduation rates and ensure "high-quality academic advisement" as part of an overall renewed emphasis on undergraduate education. If that wasn't an invitation to bold action, what was? It also helped that in 2011 Georgia had a new governor, Nathan Deal, and Deal appointed a reform-minded university chancellor, Hank Huckaby, to take over from Erroll Davis.

Huckaby was the consummate insider, a native Georgian with a long track record as a higher education administrator, including stints at both Georgia State and the University of Georgia. He had also served as budget director to Zell Miller, the governor who introduced the HOPE scholarship in 1993. Huckaby was a Republican who knew how to work with Democrats, and an educator who knew how to talk to politicians. He was gentle, avuncular, and impeccably mannered. In the wake of all the mistrust stirred up by Davis's standoffs with the legislature, he seemed an ideal peacemaker. But he wanted to be much more than that. When Governor Deal approached him, Huckaby said he needed to know right away if he'd have a mandate to make major changes. It was, he said, his "primary drop-dead question" because it was going to take major changes to deal with the legislature and leverage the university system to help break Georgia's recessionary fever.

On the face of it, Deal did not look like much of a champion for education. One of the first things he did on taking office was to broker a bipartisan deal to cut back the HOPE scholarship from full coverage of tuition and books to something closer to 60 percent for the average student. Like Becker, though, Deal understood the difference between the short-term pain of budget cutbacks, which were unavoidable given the depth of the recession, and longer-term strategic opportunities. "Chess, not checkers" was the mantra around his administration. He didn't hesitate in saying yes to the big changes Huckaby wanted. "And he was as good as his word," Huckaby recalled.

Huckaby's goals weren't wildly different from his predecessor's—he described Davis as "an honorable man committed to the right values"—but he had a striking ability to deliver on them. Within a couple of months, he had talked Governor Deal into committing Georgia to retention and graduation goals espoused by Complete College America, a nonprofit founded in 2009 with funding from the Bill & Melinda Gates Foundation. And Huckaby went one step further, not only subscribing to CCA's list of "game-changers" but also formulating some of his own. The resulting Complete College Georgia plan included "identifying and removing common barriers for minority, part-time, military, disabled, low-income, and first generation students" and "developing new paths for students to earn a high quality degree in a timely manner." In other words: exactly what Tim Renick was seeking to achieve at Georgia State.

Becker saw this as a golden opportunity and he wasn't going to squander it. He and Jerry Rackliffe had been talking for more than a year about bringing Georgia State's student–advisor ratio down to 300:1, and they knew they couldn't do it alone—not quickly, anyway. Rackliffe had managed to rustle up a little extra money for new advisors in the 2012 fiscal year, but that cut the ratio only to about 630:1. "It'll take us forever to get to 300:1," Rackliffe told Becker. When Becker asked what it would take to do it by the next academic year, Rackliffe told him: $2.1 million, or forty-two new advisors at a cost of $37,500 each. It seemed a little crazy to ask the regents for money at a time when the university was still making cutbacks and students were being asked to carry the burden of higher tuition and fees. But Becker told Rackliffe he should ask anyway. They had new budget instructions now: the system office decreed that everything they asked for should stem either from their own strategic plan or from the system's, and academic advising was an explicit part of both. At worst, the regents would say no, or give Georgia State less than it wanted.

Rackliffe submitted the request in January 2012 without a lot of hope. A month later, an equally doubtful Tim Renick delivered his best pitch at a budget meeting with Chancellor Huckaby, arguing that the investment would more than pay for itself as "murky middle" students stayed enrolled instead of dropping out. Becker, meanwhile, kept reminding the system office that Governor Deal, a Republican, and President Obama, a Democrat, had committed themselves to offering new educational opportunities to lower-income students, because they both understood that America needed to produce more university graduates to remain competitive in the global economy. Did the regents *want* students to keep swirling around in a major they were never going to complete, when Georgia State had identified the problem and found a way to fix it? "It was a big ask," Becker said, "but it was the right big ask . . . There's a time and place for some things, and it seemed to me that the stars had aligned."

Huckaby was certainly enthused. By the time he received Georgia State he had sat in on a lot of budget meetings with other institutions and had developed a habit of pressing them on their plans to boost graduation rates. This time, he hardly needed to ask. He remembered being particularly excited by the concept of *data for a purpose*, which sounded like something he could use as a model for the university system as a whole. It did no harm that he had a long personal history with Georgia State—he'd earned a business degree there before coming back to work as an administrator—and that he knew and trusted Jerry Rackliffe from his time as finance chief at the University of Georgia. Things could easily have been rocky between the two men, because one of Huckaby's first moves as chancellor was to fire Rackliffe's wife as the system's budget director. But Rackliffe chose not to utter a peep about it. He knew what was at stake. In fact, he turned right around and volunteered to help train his wife's successor.

Huckaby approved the full $2.1 million, and the regents soon followed suit. "It *was* a big ask, a bold ask," Huckaby said. "But the governor told me he supported bold asks and bold moves. We weren't going to get there incrementally. For me, it was a throwback to Zell Miller . . . Zell would tell me, 'I didn't run for governor to do nothin'.'"

Becker, of course, felt similarly. And having an asset like Renick to win over the waverers made a vast difference. "Usually you don't get accolades at budget meetings," Becker said. "Usually, when you ask for money, they don't thank you. But we had a very good working relationship with the system office. And Tim is a master communicator."

The last constituency to win over was in many ways the trickiest: the deans. The colleges were going to have to cede significant control over their in-house advising services, because there was no question in Renick's mind that all forty-two new advisors would be working centrally under Carol Cohen and handling students well past the middle of their sophomore year. Renick considered pushing to take over advising entirely, the "nuclear option," as he called it, but politically he knew he'd be better off leaving the colleges with some residual control at the upper end of the undergraduate experience. The math pointed to the same conclusion: Jerry Rackliffe showed him that the numbers lined up best if the colleges remained in charge of advising after the third year. Cohen's staff would be stretched too thin if they had to service all undergraduates from start to finish, and the central administration couldn't appropriate extra money from the college offices to cover the shortfall, because the budget didn't work that way.

The system that emerged from this split-the-baby approach created its own challenges, because it required a lot of streamlining and coordination, and college advising offices did not have a strong track record of either. They were entirely unused to communicating with the central administration or with each other, and followed different rules and standards on everything from training to record-keeping. Sometimes, faculty members acted as advisors, and sometimes staff members were shunted into the role more or less at random. Renick was horrified to stumble on an office assistant advising students even though she had no training on federal confidentiality rules and had not been told what to do if a student reported being in psychological or physical distress. This was, as he saw it, a lawsuit waiting to explode.

Renick asked Risa Palm to speak to the deans about these issues, but she wasn't sure she could make the case without Becker's help. Many departments were bitter to see new advisors being hired at a time when they were still lobbying to refill positions left vacant by the recession and to raise salaries left frozen for the past three years. Becker agreed that the deans were likely to resent anything that smacked of a loss of control and promised to broker a meeting. But he also had some advice for Renick: to let the deans know that the student success office would be doing the heavy lifting of training staff and providing a book of uniform rules—in other words, to take the hardest part of the problem off their plates. "I don't think any of them were of a mind to say, I'm going back to my college [to] get this right so the president and the provost and

Tim Renick don't centralize it," Becker said. "They didn't have the resources or means to fix it."

Renick knew he could count on the support of the university legal department, which had a reputation for being cautious and conservative and was as jumpy as he was about possible violations of FERPA, the Family Educational Rights and Privacy Act. He also forged an alliance with human resources to make the case that all advisors should receive the same training and be paid according to the same salary structure. As much as possible, he wanted the deans to hear a uniform message from all sides.

In the end, the deans and their senior staff did not put up much resistance. They understood that the changes Renick was proposing stemmed from the strategic plan, which meant the president was putting his full authority behind them and was not going to relent. Only Fenwick Huss of the business school raised any objections openly. He offered the usual reasons: he believed in the quality of his own college, including the quality of its advisory service, and he didn't see why he should fix something that was already working. "He was very much of a mind that anything the business school could do was better than what the university could do," Becker recalled.

Huss played down the extent of his opposition when asked about it seven years later but did not hide his philosophical disapproval of what Renick was seeking to do. To him, centralizing the advising service wasn't in itself the problem; rather, it was having students who weren't strong enough to stick to their first choice of major and thus created the need for a robust advising service in the first place. "If the university is going to admit them and they want to find somewhere they can fit," Huss said, "I suppose it makes sense to have the advising centralized."

Behind the scenes, disquiet among the deans was more widespread—not because of anything in particular that Tim Renick was doing, but because they felt power shifting away from them and did not like it. One who found the adjustment especially difficult was Lauren Adamson, who as dean of arts and sciences ran by far the largest college at Georgia State. She had come into the job in 2004 with assurances about maintaining the college's size and autonomy, but it became apparent over time that Becker and Palm had no interest in holding to those assurances. She was alarmed when she heard talk of arts and sciences being broken up—an idea that did not stem from Becker or Palm—and alarmed, too, at what she saw as an erosion of the administration's trust in the colleges to make good decisions unsupervised.

Adamson was widely respected, both as an administrator and as a scholar of child psychology, and she had an undoubted eye for talent, as she'd proven by recommending Renick and Calhoun-Brown for their jobs. But she struggled to stay quiet about her misgivings and had a particularly fraught relationship with Palm, another formidable woman used to being in charge who found it as difficult to conceal her frustrations as Adamson did hers. By 2011, Adamson understood she was in a battle she could never hope to win and decided to stop fighting. She had the promise of a National Institutes of Health grant for her research, and grandchildren in New England she wanted to see more often. "I didn't leave because of Risa," Adamson insisted, "although I can think of more pleasant people to work for." Palm's assessment: "I did not fire her, but we were all relieved when she left."

It wouldn't be long before more deans used to a different way of operating would follow Adamson out the door.

6

MONEYBALL ON CAMPUS

On the eve of the great recession, a higher education researcher named Ed Venit stumbled on a journal article that laid out what it called "a simple method that works" to boost graduation rates at large public universities. The idea was to track students' progress by computer and lay out a map of which courses they should take in what order to graduate on time. In too many universities, the article said, this basic support mechanism did not exist. Not only was course information not computerized; it tended to be presented department by department, making it difficult for students to construct a multidisciplinary course load without missing classes they needed or wasting time and money on classes they didn't. The tracking program reorganized the information sequentially so students could easily see what they'd already taken, what requirements still remained to fulfill their choice of major, and what electives they had time for on the side. If a student wanted to consider changing majors, the program would instantly adjust to show what that looked like. The lead author of the article, Betty Capaldi, had introduced such a system when she was provost of the University of Florida from 1996 to 1999, and had seen a significant boost in retention and graduation rates as a result. At the time of the article's publication in 2006, Capaldi was about to become provost at Arizona State University, under Michael Crow's leadership, and would soon introduce a new iteration of the same concept called eAdvisor.

Venit worked for the Advisory Board Company, a health-care

analytics firm just beginning to branch out to the education field, and he wanted to know how other institutions could acquire a nonproprietary version of Capaldi's tracking program. He was surprised to discover that they couldn't; nothing like it existed in the public marketplace. And so he lobbied his company to create one: to do everything eAdvisor did and incorporate all the other things he was learning about student success and the obstacles that typically stood in the way of undergraduates in public universities. Capaldi had identified some of the important ones, but he knew of many more.

Venit had two baseline ideas. The first was to make his system *interactive*. Capaldi had given him the seed of this, because her program created a marker every time it found evidence, based on grades or course sequencing, that a student was struggling. But Venit wanted to dig deeper, into all the available student data, and expand those markers into a system of alerts that faculty and academic advisors would receive every time a student missed a critical benchmark. The alerts wouldn't just monitor whether a student was taking the right classes in the right semester. They would track whether a student was late registering for those classes in the first place; whether there was a hold on the registration and, if so, why; whether a student was routinely late for class, or failing to hand assignments in on time; and so on. Venit even thought about flagging considerations beyond academic performance: signs of financial trouble, or a transcript request that might indicate the student was thinking about leaving.

The second idea was to make the system *predictive*. Venit's research had taught him that it was not enough for students to receive passing grades in the courses they took. An early C in organic chemistry might not matter all that much to an English major fulfilling a core science requirement, but it could be a giant red flag for someone interested in pursuing a degree in natural sciences. Too often, universities paid no attention to these red flags, or *hidden risks* as Venit thought of them, allowing students to proceed on their chosen path until, more likely than not, they started failing and were forced to reckon with a lot of time and money they could not recoup. What if Venit could create a program to bring such hidden risks to light much sooner? A computer fed a critical mass of data on past student performance—years of it, ideally—would be able to assess just how damaging that early C in organic chemistry was and assign a number to it. If a student could learn in the first year, or even in the first semester, that the chance of completing a degree in natural sciences was only 15 percent, but that other avenues based on other grades were more promising, it could be a life-changing insight.

In 2010, the Advisory Board Company (soon to branch out as the Education Advisory Board) asked Venit to develop this idea into a full-blown commercial venture. One of the first people he called was Tim Renick, to find out if Georgia State was interested in acquiring his product once he built it, and to see if there was a way to collaborate on its development. This initial inquiry came crucially too early, because there were still too many other pieces around advising that needed to fall into place before Renick could think seriously about acquiring a software system. They chatted amiably enough, but the conversation went no further.

By early 2011, that picture had changed substantially. Renick and Calhoun-Brown were now *very* interested in a software system and couldn't find what they were looking for. The closest they came was with a company called Starfish, whose product incorporated elements of predictive analytics but not ones that seemed especially usable. "Their system could tell you the retention of people based on whether they ate breakfast," Calhoun-Brown said. "But we're not in charge of breakfast. Our thinking was: what helps the students pass their classes? We weren't finding it, and we were frustrated." Then, serendipitously, she and Renick ran into Venit on an escalator at an education technology conference in Denver. They did not know each other by sight, but Renick noticed Venit's name tag and asked if he was still building the system he'd talked about months earlier. Not only was Venit building it; three schools in the Midwest had signed up already.

From that chance encounter, a partnership was formed. Renick and Calhoun-Brown didn't just want Venit's product, they wanted to be involved in every step of its development so they could be sure it was built to their specifications. It became clear that they all thought about student success in similar terms, never more so than when Venit talked about the "murky middle," the large swath of students missed by most university advising services, including Georgia State's, who had the potential to succeed but not necessarily the diagnostic powers to assess their own strengths and weaknesses. "We were the original murky middle," Renick said. "We weren't seeing those students either." By the end of 2011, Georgia State and the Education Advisory Board had a contract, even though there was no product yet, just the promise of database intelligence beyond any seen in higher education to that point. "Luckily," Calhoun-Brown said, "they had the capacity to deliver on what they talked about."

There was little question, at the start of 2012, that big data was an idea whose time had come. Entire industries had sprung up to take advantage of instant processing of vast volumes of information, whether that was in applied fields like health informatics or business analytics, or in the packaging and selling of data itself, as pioneered by Google, Facebook, and others. In the political sphere, microtargeting of voters had helped power Barack Obama to the White House in 2008 and, two years later, helped the Republican Party retake the House of Representatives and wrest control of several state legislatures. When, in 2011, those legislatures were empowered to draw new electoral maps, they leaned on new data technologies that could break down partisan allegiances street by street and house by house and adjust district boundaries to achieve almost any outcome.

All these things were happening in plain sight, and it would have made perfect sense for universities to leap on the technological advances to improve the lives of their students. A number of emerging technology companies were proposing to help them do exactly that. In too many cases, however, administrators were prepared to live with what Ken Mauriello, a former derivatives trader turned baseball analyst, describes in the pages of Michael Lewis's bestselling book *Moneyball*, as "the inefficiency of sloppy data." Much like the ball clubs who, in Lewis's telling, were slow to recognize the utility of new data models, universities tended to be stuck in old habits of mind and did not see the imperative to change. Academic leaders who had been trained in the scientific method and treated it as a given in their research somehow could not see their way to applying it to the management of their own institutions. Mark Becker called this phenomenon "the disease of the university." Betty Capaldi was one of a rare breed when, in the 1990s, she understood that universities arranged courses and degrees from the perspective of the departments designing them, not from the perspective of students taking them. A decade later, Venit stood out from the rest of the ed tech crowd because he was willing to investigate the causes of dismal graduation rates and float a wide-reaching data solution. Likewise, Renick and his team, by their very job descriptions, were pushing against a powerful tide of administrators, at Georgia State and elsewhere, who preferred excuses for dismal student performance over concrete action to address it.

Their exceptionalism gave them a tremendous edge, of course. Like Billy Beane and the Oakland A's in *Moneyball*, they had an opportunity to become pioneers and demonstrate by example just how wrongheaded the conventional thinking was—to bring science, as Lewis described it, to an unscientific culture.

Venit took a team to Atlanta and was immediately impressed by the commitment and preparation of his Georgia State counterparts. "The whole crew was very, very vocal and ready to share what they wanted out of the system," he recalled. "They said, we'll

tell you exactly what we want and then you'll build it . . . We
don't normally have that experience with our partners, but they
had a whole plan. The leadership was really engaged. It wasn't long
before we said, yeah, they're going to be our favorites."

The overall attitude was one of nothing much to lose and everything to gain. Some on Renick's team worried the Education
Advisory Board might not be around long enough to see the project through to launch, but it was a risk they were prepared to take.
As guinea pigs of a brand-new system, they got to enjoy EAB's
services at a steep discount, so the budgetary pressure was minimal. Venit's top technical consultant, Rich Staley, remembered
thinking how refreshing and different it was that Georgia State
was willing to take a chance on something not yet fully formed.
"That's where most institutions fall short," he said. "If you wait for
perfection, you wait a long time." As it happened, Staley fell a little
short of perfect himself on his first visit to Georgia State, because
the tie he chose was red, the color of the University of Georgia,
and he had to rush to the university bookstore to buy a new one in
Panther blue. Renick wisecracked: "I'll bet that's the most expen-
sive tie you ever bought."

Staley's approach was to identify milestones for every one of
Georgia State's ninety-plus majors so he could apply markers to
them, graded green for safe, yellow for less safe, and red for vulnerable, and build out the alerts from there. Originally, his plan was
to add a Capaldi-style course map and wait until the system was
up and running before building more capacity. But Renick's team
wanted more right away. Several advisors were struggling with the
fact that to extract data from the Banner system before a student
appointment they had to open multiple screens—for grades, for
overall GPA, for the courses in which the student was enrolled,
and so on. Was there a way to reconcile all these data points in a
single screen? Yes, Staley said, there was. Which is how the system
he created—named Campus—became a dashboard.

Campus launched in August 2012, a brisk nine months after

the contract was signed, and the directive right away was to use it for all advising sessions. That was a challenge for many advisors, who were already uncomfortable that their jobs were being upended by new technology. Now they had to do battle with a rudimentary system not yet able to do many of the things it was supposed to. Much of the historical data, arguably the most powerful piece of the system, drawing on 144,000 students records and 2.5 million grades going back ten years, did not come online until 2013. GradesFirst, the student tracking system Cohen had used in the athletics department, was not incorporated for several months either, and until it was advisors had to switch screens and programs to keep track of notes, appointment times, and course maps. Even the ones who figured it all out had a hard time reconciling the familiar, qualitative side of their jobs, rooted in human interaction, with a less familiar, quantitative side that called on them to love numbers and probabilities and statistics along with their students. "It was a cultural shift," Crystal Mitchell said. "The seasoned pros said, *This is so different from what I've done for twenty-five years* . . . They struggled to understand why data was so important."

This was a time of rapid transition all around, as new advisors flowed in and the office worked to institute training both for its own staff and for the staff of the college offices. The SAC was about to become the UAC—the University Advisement Center—with new offices on two floors of the old SunTrust bank building overlooking Woodruff Park, which offered plenty of space and enough abandoned furniture scattered around the building to make do. Carol Cohen was understanding but firm about everything her staff had to adapt to over a short period. "If you want to get on board, we want you," she remembered telling them. "Nobody is off the team, but the expectation is that you are open to the changes we are making."

Almost all of them were.

The most immediate adjustment was to the large numbers of

"murky middle" students, who had been near-invisible before the launch of Campus but now became ubiquitous more or less overnight. The adjustment wasn't just about numbers. It was also about the assumptions that advisors, like everyone else, had previously made about a class of students who did not generally stand out and might at any moment stop registering for class, never to return. It was easier to stereotype these students, of course, when they never came in for advising sessions. Now that the office had a chance to get to know them, they adjusted their assumptions accordingly. Each one had a story. Often, they faced challenges in their lives that they were reluctant to talk about. But their desire to attain a degree was no less ardent than anyone else's and they lapped up the advice on offer. It was easier, perhaps, for advisors to break the stereotypes than for anyone else on campus, because they tended to be empathetic by nature and many of them had personal experience of struggling as low-income or first-generation students.

Crystal Mitchell certainly knew what it was like to face down failure. So did Elisha Jarrett, who recognized right away that there was no mileage in stereotyping or dismissing the murky middle students because, by their sheer number, they were the ones keeping the university afloat. Then there was Cary Claiborne, a new member of the advising team blessed with an abundance of both soft-touch and data skills—the head and the heart of the new operation. And his personal story was perhaps the most extraordinary of all.

The first time Claiborne applied to Georgia State, it was as a prospective student and he didn't get in. He'd been attracted to the large urban campus from the moment he set eyes on the student housing buildings from the Atlanta Connector interstate. But his grades weren't all that good, and he had little family support. His mother was in New Jersey, where he'd spent most of his childhood, and his father had moved from Atlanta to Baltimore as soon as he graduated high school. Still, Claiborne was gregarious and bright and trusted that if he signed up for the Gwinnett campus of Georgia Perimeter College, in the eastern Atlanta suburbs, he'd do just fine by himself.

He did not. He threw himself at everything, taking as many classes as possible while also serving as a vice president on the student government association, joining several campus clubs, and working on the side at Victoria's Secret and Bed Bath & Beyond. It was way more than he could handle. He was popular with everyone, including his professors, but he was also failing most of his classes. As his grades tanked, he kept switching directions, from education to communications to business. "Nobody ever stopped me changing my major," he recalled. "I just filled in a form. It was failing in a different way." His GPA shrank almost to the vanishing point—it hit a low of 0.4—and he was told to take a year off before re-enrolling.

Most people might have given up, and Claiborne himself did not know how he was going to recover. When his father could no longer justify providing financial support for his education, Claiborne took an overnight inventory job at CarMax and began to imagine a future as a used car buyer—until he learned that to be a buyer he needed a college degree. So he waited out his probationary period and tried community college again, only to flunk out a second time.

Then he lost his job with CarMax. It was now December 2007, the economy was about to plummet, and Claiborne's future, at the age of twenty-four, seemed entirely spent. "I felt worse about being laid off than about being excluded," he said. "How was I supposed to explain this to my friends and family?" His friends were notably more successful than he was. Even his girlfriend, whom he later married, was a HOPE scholar at the University of Georgia and would soon embark on a successful career in advertising. Deep down, Claiborne knew he was better than this. He held on to a memory of two professors at Gwinnett, a political science professor and a faculty advisor, *telling* him he was better than this.

In the absence of any firmer plan, he became an apprentice

electrician. He needed to learn something, and the Pat Murphy Electric company was offering to train him for free. He spent half his time on the job earning $8.50 an hour and the other half in trade school. He learned quickly and told himself he must be smart after all, just not *school* smart. After a few months, he was sent on a rewiring job at the Georgia State basketball arena, in the heart of campus, and he reassessed himself again. As he watched students walking to and from class, he told one of his co-workers: "That should be me." To which the co-worker responded: "If you're so smart, what are you doing in this job?"

What indeed? Claiborne knew Georgia State was out of reach, for now, but he kept seeing a highway billboard for Atlanta Metro college with the slogan, "Your Success Starts Here." It was a corny line but he couldn't shake it from his mind, and one day he asked the driver of his Pat Murphy truck to pull off the interstate so he could fill out an application. He was driven by more than pure impulse: he'd seen too many friends in the electrical business hurt themselves by falling off ladders, and he knew, with the economy melting down, that layoffs were coming. So he signed up for an initial twelve credit hours in the fall of 2009 and scored a perfect 4.0. "I couldn't believe it," he said. "Right there, I turned into an academic success junkie. I said, this feels really great. Let's do it again."

He kept enrolling in classes, and the A's kept coming. Just once, when he loaded up his summer with too many courses, he received a solitary B, but he made sure it didn't happen again. He was still working as an electrician but began to feel for the first time that he might belong somewhere else. "I'd be talking political philosophy to the guys in my truck," he remembered, "and they'd say, 'You're an electrician, none of that matters.' I was the one-eyed king of Blindsville."

The electrical work dried up just a couple of months before Claiborne earned his associate's degree, but by then he was more than ready to move on. He graduated in business administration with a 3.98 GPA and set his sights on transferring to Georgia State. Only Georgia State had other ideas.

The university turned him down because his cumulative GPA, going back to his earlier misadventures, was barely over 2.0 and the admissions office didn't think to look past that baseline number. Such was the price of sabotaging his college career the first time around—and also, perhaps, the price of being young and black and underprepared to face a world that had little patience for his stumbles, no matter how graceful the recovery. A transfer advisor at Metro told him: "The world is not designed for people like you to do what you want to do. You're *supposed* to fail out of school."

Still Claiborne did not give up. As a member of Atlanta Metro's honors society he'd helped welcome Georgia State's admissions recruiter to campus. He'd also told his peers about the amenities he worked on as an electrician at Georgia State—the rec center, the pool, the steam room—and got them excited about all of it. With the encouragement of his advisor, Claiborne wrote an appeal letter to Georgia State, and it worked, because this time he was offered a place for the fall of 2010. Still he was not satisfied, and he contacted the recruiter, Lynette Forte-Reid, to see if she could squeeze him in for the summer session. Why wait three months to get started? "I graduated on a Friday," he said, "and on the Monday I started my classes at Georgia State."

He started out as a business major, only to struggle with many of the same issues that had tripped up other bright business students before him. It wasn't just about maintaining his grades in the intro courses. It was also the culture: "Kids with briefcases and little business cards, talking about shorting stocks." So he switched to economics and was immediately more comfortable dealing with broader questions of wealth and poverty and the interrelationship between mathematics and real people's lives.

Advising came into his life largely because he needed a job, and the SAC had a flier advertising for student assistants. He didn't give much thought to what he was getting into, and it occurred to him only later that he was himself a living example of the sort of vulnerable student whose success depends on constant guidance. He credited the job with giving him the support he needed, because there was barely a time when he wasn't in class, or in the advising office, or aware of his advisees seeing him walking around and forcing him to think about the example he was setting. "I had a solid network 24/7," he said. "Someone was always keeping me in the net."

Many years later, it would occur to Claiborne that many of the student success initiatives pioneered by Renick and his team performed exactly this function—of keeping students *in the net*, whether it was by placing them in learning communities, or hiring near-peers to offer supplemental instruction, or building a proactive advising service that could offer every one of them the sort of support and focus that working in the SAC had given him. He was, in many ways, a vivid illustration of what the student success project was about, offering both a cautionary tale about how badly a talented student could fly off the rails and a feel-good narrative of what could happen to a student with the right sort of net built around him. His job now was to define that net, and systematize and scale it across the university.

Claiborne graduated in 2011 as a double major in economics and philosophy, and immediately applied for a scholarship to pursue a project examining the ethics of companies deemed too big to fail. He won the scholarship, too—until he was told at the last minute he was ineligible because he'd been in school too long and did not satisfy a "satisfactory progress" requirement. As it happened, Elisha Jarrett, now a colleague, sat on Georgia State's Satisfactory Academic Progress committee, and she encouraged him to appeal. "She gave me a way around the back," he said. "The system was not designed for people like me, but I got my scholarship back."

Claiborne stayed on in the advising center while he worked

through his graduate studies and, later, Georgia State's MBA program, and was offered a full-time position six months ahead of the launch of EAB's Campus program.

He quickly established his ability to connect with students. Claiborne was as outgoing and effusive as Crystal Mitchell was reserved, and he didn't hesitate to tell students about his own struggles so they could relate to him more easily. The first time he looked himself up online, he told them, he, too, was color-coded red for high risk. "I could speak to students who were like me," he said. "I would tell them, I know you can do it, not just in theory, but in practice." He also showed an extraordinary adeptness with the technology. "I was a data guy," he said. "Data boot camps, Excel boot camps, you name it, I was there. I was getting a lot out of it. What takes you all day takes me thirty minutes."

This second skill set made Claiborne a singularly useful source of feedback to Rich Staley's technical team as they sought to work out kinks in the Campus system, because he understood it and used it more intensively than most other people. He also proved to be a valuable asset when advisors started reaching out to the murky middle and the office found itself overwhelmed. Students, Claiborne remembered, did not need to be coaxed to come to their appointments anymore: "They were beating down the door like this was Beyoncé tickets to figure out how to graduate." He'd siphon them off in groups of thirty-five and have a student assistant help them fill out intake forms, all the while keeping them buoyed with his infectious energy. He wanted them to be glad they came, and he was eager to explain what the data showed and how it could help them.

For all his bravura, Claiborne also understood the misgivings of his less tech-savvy colleagues. They all wanted to help as many students as possible, and data entry inevitably cut down the amount of time they could spend doing the actual advising, especially if they were unable to enter the data quickly. "If you spend five minutes reporting data on every student, you lose 450 student slots over the year," Claiborne explained. "Balancing it all out is an art."

With that art came a lot of pressure. The system generated a weekly report to Carol Cohen detailing how many students each advisor had seen, which some of the older advisors found uncomfortably Big Brother–ish. They understood the need for efficiency, but they wanted to be judged on their advising skills, not on how adept they were at the computer keyboard. "In the end, it's still a people business," Claiborne said. "You have to have the connection with the students. If you don't have the connection with the students, you can do all the analytics you want, it's like driving an elephant down a highway in a sports car and trying to make a U-turn."

What Claiborne was picking up, even though he didn't experience it personally, was an anxiety inherent in any change to a new way of doing things, particularly one that involves a rapidly evolving new technology. The underlying fear, particularly among the older staff members, was of being sidelined or replaced. Cohen spent a great deal of her time reassuring her staff that Campus was a tool to make them more effective, not a substitute for human interaction. "If you don't pay attention to the numbers," she said, "you're not seeing the students you may be missing." Inevitably, though, the transition took an emotional toll. With the increased traffic, Cohen noticed that the UAC was getting through two large cases of paper tissues a year. Quite a few of those were being consumed by members of her own staff.

Tim Renick was ideally positioned to understand the conflicting demands on the advising staff, because he was a left brain–right brain kind of person himself. He had boundless empathy for students one-on-one, and at the same time was utterly devoted to the data. Still, he never doubted which element of the work made the more profound difference. "The aspect of Georgia State that's driven our student success is the data," Renick said bluntly. "A lot of people have a crude take on advising—let's do the personal relationship thing, and that's great. But it's very selective."

It's not that Renick had any philosophical disagreement about the importance of the human touch. Certainly, he wasn't looking to fill the advising office with data nerds incapable of relating to students as human beings. Rather, it was about understanding the issue from a macro as well as micro perspective. One-on-one, a strong bond between advisor and advisee was of course a valuable, even a life-altering thing. Every student had his or her narrative, his or her fine line to walk. No computer program was ever going to develop an understanding of the survival mechanisms and psychological complexities involved in navigating that line. But personal bonds were not the only thing that mattered. Nor were they, in Renick's view, the most important.

The most important thing was scale. Renick's focus was not on what could be transformational for the individual, but for *thousands of students* at a time. Any university could hire good advisors; the real question was how to deploy them, and with what tools. In Renick's mind, computers were there not just to replicate and automate what human beings could do on their own—to hand out a degree map, explain which courses needed to be taken in which order, and make sure the students registered for them on time. That might have been how Rich Staley and the EAB team started laying out their milestones, but it was only the start.

Renick wanted the data to tell him *how* to design those courses, to tell him which first-semester classes were predictive of future success and which were not; to tell him, for example, whether first-year business and economics students were better served taking intro macro economics followed by intro micro economics, or the other way around; to tell him if a 2.5 GPA was the correct cutoff for aspiring business majors, or if it needed to be set higher or lower. In short, he wanted and fully expected the data to help the university see things that individual advisors, on their own, could not, and that academic departments responsible for designing degree courses and class schedules could not. Data collection, in this mindset, wasn't something for advisors and faculty chairs to resent as a bureaucratic distraction taking them away from more important activities. It was the heart and soul of everything they did and thought about.

One thing Renick was particularly interested in learning was whether the data could identify the reasons why students were dropping out and address them before it was too late. The students themselves couldn't provide that information, because in most cases they made no formal declaration of their intent to withdraw. They would just stop showing up for class one day, and the university would decide after a year or so that they probably were not coming back. A big part of designing the alert system was looking for pivotal points in students' lives where it made the most sense to intervene. Renick and Staley thought initially they might come up with a few dozen—a weak or failing grade in an important class, say, or a poor choice of class for a particular major, or a negative balance on a student account. Over time, though, they found more than *eight hundred*. Not every alert was a sign that a student was about to drop out. Often, the student would be dealing with a temporary setback—a sick relative, say, or a car breakdown— from which he or she could reasonably be expected to recover. The point, though, was to ensure that the advising service left nothing to chance. An alert allowed them to investigate whether the problem was indeed temporary or something more consequential.

The process was designed to be as interactive as possible. When students came in to the advisement center, they could see all the data displayed on the Campus dashboard for themselves: the courses they were taking, the ones flagged as high risk, the likelihood that they would make it to graduation in their chosen major, and the comparative statistics for other fields of study they might want to consider. Since the university uploaded fresh data into the Banner system every night, an alert was never more than a few hours behind the problem that triggered it. All this was, to use

Cary Claiborne's parlance, a way of keeping students *in the net*, to let them know they were more than just a cog in the machine. Even when they weren't seeing their advisor or looking at the data directly, they knew they were being monitored and in some important sense nurtured.

That was how Savannah Torrance experienced it when she started as a chemistry major in 2015 and realized almost immediately that the subject made her miserable. Things got so bad she was calling home to her mother in tears, not only because she was failing in her core subject but because she had no idea what to do instead. Just a few weeks into her first semester, though, she was called into an advising session and forced to confront the tough questions she didn't have the fortitude to tackle on her own.

"Are you quitting because it's hard?" the advisor wanted to know.

"No," Torrance responded, "I'm quitting because it doesn't make me happy."

When the advisor asked which classes *did* make her happy, Torrance could think only of an elective she was taking in rhetoric and public speaking. Soon, her mood lifted—as did the data picture on the computer screen. In less than an hour, she had switched from chemistry to speech communications and had a full course schedule ready to go for spring semester. She never looked back, graduating in 2018 in the same class as Princeton Nelson, with a glittering résumé as a student ambassador, a student government leader, an orientation leader, and a member of the honors college.

Not every student who went through proactive advising could recognize its power. Many, perhaps even most, took it for granted as just another part of the undergraduate experience since they had known nothing else. Indeed, they were as likely to complain about wait times for walk-ins, or turnover in advisors, as they were to recognize the vital role the service played in keeping them on track. "Like going to the doctor for a checkup," was how one high-achieving student dismissed it, an unintentionally apt turn of phrase since of course medical checkups play a critical role in prevention and early treatment of disease.

Torrance, though, understood exactly how important the early intervention had been, not because she formed a special bond with her advisor (she saw three different ones in her freshman year), but because the analytics proved revelatory and life-changing. When asked what she most appreciated about Georgia State, Torrance had no hesitation in replying: "It helped me figure out who I was."

Once historical data was incorporated into Campus, Renick was able to pinpoint a number of factors affecting student performance that had previously been invisible. Most revealing, perhaps, was what he found out about nursing and business, two areas where students had to jump over extra hurdles to qualify for the major in the first place. In the nursing program, first-year physiology turned out not to be predictive of future success, even though it had been a requirement for as long as anyone could remember. First-year chemistry, on the other hand, was *highly* predictive, and also a core component of most natural science degrees, so it was valuable both to those who went on to complete a nursing major and to the majority who did not. Over time, Renick made the case that the pre-nursing program should be cut from two years to one, and that it should focus as much as possible on courses applicable to other areas of study. The change, when it came, was profound. Those who had failed out of the nursing program had previously been graduating at a rate 20 percentage points lower than the university as a whole. Now that gap closed.

The data on business studies revealed the full horror of the swirler problem, which was affecting around a thousand students every year. Carol Cohen came to think of them as the very middle of the murky middle, a group that needed to be saved from themselves as much as from Dean Huss and his undergraduate teaching faculty. The first thing the student success shop wanted to do was to get the business school to *own* its students—in other words, to agree that once students were admitted into the bachelor's pro-gram they were there to stay and could not simply be bounced out again because of a slight dip in their overall GPA. Renick knew this would be a hard sell with Fenwick Huss, so he ran data on the scores business students needed in their intro classes in econom-ics and math to stand a strong chance of finishing with a GPA of 3.0 or higher. The upshot was that the university raised the GPA cutoff to qualify for the business program from 2.5 to 2.8; once students were in, however, they stayed in as long as their GPA re-mained above 2.0. Huss was satisfied that the standards he cared about were being protected, and Renick was satisfied that an im-portant part of the swirler problem was now solved.

This was not the only issue in the business school that de-manded attention, however. Renick noticed that students were failing introductory accounting at an alarmingly high rate—fully one-third of them were doing so *after the first quiz*—and felt that an attrition rate of that magnitude indicated a problem with the faculty more than the students. Professors needed to meet stu-dents where they were. That didn't mean passing them all, regard-less of their classroom performance. But it was important at least to give them a chance.

Renick took the problem to Risa Palm, and Palm resolved to talk to the accounting faculty herself. She agreed it was unaccept-able simply to assume that most of students weren't good enough and to weed them out. The faculty needed to make more of an effort to *teach* them.

It was a testy session. One professor hardly waited for the pro-vost to finish her opening remarks before saying: "I don't remem-ber you. Have you ever been a faculty member?" To Palm, the implication was clear: she was just some bureaucrat who had never given out grades or interacted with students. "*Where do you think I came from?*" she remembered thinking. "*I didn't just materialize from outer space.*"

Palm didn't recall her antagonist's name, only that it was a man.

"Of course it was," she said. "This was the business school. There are always too many men in the business school."

In *Moneyball*, Michael Lewis describes such interactions as the "silent shrieks . . . of people who had no clue that they were on the receiving end of an idea." And the accountancy teachers were far from the only ones to shriek, silently or otherwise. Renick and Calhoun-Brown endured multiple accusations that they weren't enhancing student performance at all, merely dumbing down the university by shunting the lower-performing students into easier majors. The charge wasn't remotely true, because Georgia State in fact experienced a surge of students completing degrees in biology and computer science, regarded as two of the tougher majors on offer. Sciences generally saw an increase in graduation rates, particularly among minority students: the number of African American men obtaining science degrees shot up 60 percent in the first two years of proactive advising.

This was a period, in fact, when all the indicators of student success started not just creeping but positively somersaulting in the right direction. The overall graduation rate broke the 50 percent barrier during the 2011–12 academic year and jumped another three percentage points in the year after Campus was introduced. At least one-third of that gain, in Renick's estimation, was due to the advising piece. African Americans and Latinos were now graduating at rates *higher* than white students—who were themselves graduating at a rate 19 percentage points better than a decade earlier.

Renick's office noticed that freshmen were changing their majors more often as a result of the new advising system, but everyone else was changing much less. The obvious inference was that people heading down the wrong track were now reorienting themselves better and faster. Indeed, the data showed that in the first year of Campus close to 2,500 students went from being designated "off path" for a degree to being "on path." And 900 of them were correcting their schedules during the registration period—before they'd had an opportunity to *start* taking the wrong classes. The UAC was deluged in alerts at the outset—130,000 in the first month—but the number dropped to around 75,000 by spring. In other words, a lot of problems were being resolved quickly and others that popped up at the start no longer arose.

Proactive advising worked at Georgia State not because it was a miracle cure—Renick, for all his grounding in religious studies, did not believe in miracles in university administration—but because everyone from the president down was primed to accept it, money was available to fund it, and clear lines of authority existed to act on the insights it delivered. All these achievements were hard won, as Ed Venit would constantly remind other universities who signed up with EAB and couldn't understand why they weren't seeing the same results as Georgia State's. "When you've got a leak in your sink," Venit would tell them, "you need to do more than put a wrench next to it. We can build you a really nice wrench, but you also need the skills and the people in place to use it."

Often, Venit would find himself referring people to Tim Renick. And they didn't just get on the phone to seek his advice. Before long, schools around the country were descending on Atlanta to ask Renick in person how he'd done it and, in many cases, to offer him a job. Renick resisted the offers of alternative employment; he was very far from done at Georgia State and, with Mark Becker's support, was enjoying an increasing degree of autonomy. But he was unfailingly gracious about telling the Georgia State story to anyone interested in hearing it. And advising wasn't the only thing people were curious about, because he had a number of other tricks up his sleeve.

7

THIS IS NOT A SCAM, DO NOT HANG UP

In mid-2011, Mark Becker wrote a check to his own university for $40,000 and asked Tim Renick to do something bold and experimental with it. The Georgia State foundation had just launched a fundraising campaign, whose goals included the establishment of scholarships for deserving undergraduates, and the president wanted to lead by example by making the first of what would end up being multiple personal gifts. Becker and his wife could have contented themselves with a contribution to the general fund, which is the custom among university presidents at the start of a capital campaign. But Becker wanted alumni and donors to be able to focus on something more closely linked to the precepts of the strategic plan, which already had them excited. He had a feeling that, given the right jump start, Renick could come up with something special, something to put Georgia State on the national map. And he was not wrong about that.

Renick's greatest despondency at the time was over the numbers of students in good academic standing who were dropping out because they couldn't come up with the money to cover their classes. The problem was made worse by the tuition increases and budget cuts forced on the university in the wake of the recession, and it was made worse, too, by the fact that Georgia State was now enrolling many more lower-income students—51 percent of incoming freshmen in 2011, up from 31 percent four years earlier—who were by definition the ones most at risk. Many of these students hit a wall as soon as the semester started, because the state of Georgia had strict rules obliging them to pay for their courses in full within the first week. They would scrabble furiously before "the drop," as the deadline was known, and not all would make it. By 2011, the number of students unable to pay for classes for which they'd registered reached more than one thousand a semester, an attrition of more than 3 percent of the entire student body. The numbers were, in one sense, compelling evidence that Renick's initiatives were working—that lower-income students were cutting it academically and eager to take more classes. But it was also turning into a bloodbath. "Things were getting worse because we were getting better," Renick said. "It was overwhelming, thinking of those thousand students and the millions they owed. You feel helpless."

An injection of need-based scholarship money was obviously going to help. But when Renick and his team drilled deeper into the data, they saw that giving students that money at the beginning of their college careers was not the most effective way to attack the problem, because the largest cohort of student dropping out for financial as opposed to academic reasons were not freshmen or sophomores, but *seniors* just a few months away from graduation. The reasons for this weren't too hard to discern: many lower-income students came in with federal grants or HOPE scholarship money or both, and these kept them going for a good while. HOPE, for example, was good for the first 128 credit hours, which was technically enough to earn most degrees, but only as long as the student's course load was primed for maximum efficiency without extra electives, or a change of major, or a disruptive personal crisis along the way. In practice, HOPE tended to run out at exactly the point where Renick and his colleagues were finding the densest drop-out rate, a semester or two short of the finish line.

When Renick's team investigated how much these students owed, they were stunned, not because the amounts were overwhelmingly large but quite the opposite: less than $1,500 in most cases. The equivalent of just a couple of weekly pay checks separated these students from a degree, and yet large numbers of them were walking away, crushed by a burden of debt they might spend a lifetime trying to lift. When Becker said he wanted to find an unconventional way to reach students in need, Renick knew these were the ones to help. He didn't want them to have to apply for a scholarship, because the application would be just another barrier to overcome and the rigors of the drop date did not give them the luxury of time. Rather, Renick's idea was to zero out the students' accounts, pure and simple. His staff already knew who was on track to graduate and who was in danger of missing the payment deadline for classes. What else did they need to know?

Such was the germ of the idea that would become Georgia State's most celebrated and arguably most brilliant innovation. In the fall of 2011, Renick's team used the $40,000 from President Becker to pay off the debt of thirty-four students so they could stay enrolled, and within two semesters 70 percent of them had graduated. Not all of them were inclined to believe their luck when, days before the drop, Renick's office called to say their debts were cleared and they should plan to be in class the following Monday. "We had multiple students hanging up," Renick said. "They thought it was a scam. Their thinking was, there's no way someone from Georgia State just put money in my account. We'd call back and tell them to check so they could see it was true."

Renick's staff called these payments Panther Retention Grants, an anodyne name that scarcely did justice to the power of the underlying concept. When Jerry Rackliffe first heard about them, he was bowled over, not only because of the help they provided to students in need, but because they paid for themselves several times over: recipients who stayed in school continued to receive grant money and paid tuition and fees the university would have otherwise lost. Rackliffe explained: "You handed them $500, and now they're handing me $5,000. If you hadn't done that, I would have gotten zero." This was Milo Minderbinder math right out of *Catch-22*: buying eggs at seven cents apiece, selling them at five and still turning a profit.

With Hank Huckaby now in the chancellor's office and Complete College Georgia their new roadmap, the regents were delighted to embrace such an innovative program. And they could hardly argue with the return on investment. Once the program was running at full strength, the average amount paid out to grantees was $900, while the average amount paid back to the university in tuition and fees ran from $3,600 to $6,100, a return of anywhere from 500 percent to 800 percent.

Already by the 2012–13 academic year, the number of grant recipients had leapt to 2,600, a cohort more than half the size of that year's graduating class. The program was no longer a secret, and it was no longer restricted to students within view of the finish line. Anyone with a compelling case for emergency support was now considered—including Princeton Nelson, who didn't have a HOPE scholarship (he was too old to qualify) and needed extra support for summer school so he could graduate before his finances blew up entirely. He ended up with two grants of $1,500 each.

Renick's team added a stipulation that recipients had to sit down with both a financial advisor and an academic advisor, another way of keeping them *in the net*. And the graduation rate of recipients inched up to around 85 percent, a staggering result. It was a major factor, along with proactive advising, behind a six percentage-point jump in Georgia State's six-year graduation rate between 2011 and 2014.

One of the beauties of the grants was that they required minimal justification or auditing, because there was no question of where the money went. The students' need was a matter of record, as was their academic standing, and the money was used exclusively to pay down their university accounts. Huckaby thought the grants helped build a case for more widespread need-based support throughout the university system. In serving as a relief valve for individuals, they built a documentary record of a much broader problem.

It wasn't long before the country at large started to notice. Georgia's senior senator, Johnny Isakson, a Republican, bragged about the retention grants in a committee hearing on Capitol Hill, and Barack Obama, the Democratic president, singled them out at a White House College Opportunity Day of Action. In a country riven by partisan division, the grants were a rare point of consensus across the aisle. "They're good for social justice *and* they provide good return on investment for the taxpayer," Renick said.

Becker didn't just agree with that sentiment. He preached it. "In a world of red states and blue states, everyone can agree on the need for better education and a more skilled workforce," he said. "It was a priority for our Republican governor and for our Democratic president . . . Whether they emphasized social progress or the economic imperative, the case was the same. All we needed to do was a good job of delivering."

In the spring of 2015, Sharon Sample was in exactly the financial mess the grants were designed to fix, only she wasn't at all sure Georgia State *would* deliver. Sample was a mature student who had endured a roller-coaster early life before signing up for college at the age of forty to pursue her dream of becoming a teacher. She'd grown up with an abusive father who called her "stupid idiot" to her face. From him, she'd jumped into the military for four years, then into a bad marriage and a cult-like religious sect in Washington State, where she was forbidden to work or cut her hair. She stayed in the marriage just long enough to convince her husband to move to Georgia—she was afraid of losing her two children if she left the sect on her own—then drifted from one retail job to another until, one day, a man she was dating asked why she wasn't in school.

The question took her aback at first. She said she didn't have time. And, besides, she couldn't do math. The boyfriend replied: "I don't ever want to hear, you *can't*."

Sample signed up for community college shortly after. When she scored a perfect 4.0 in her first semester, her reaction was to stick her middle finger in the air and mouth joyful expletives at her faraway father. "Right there, 'stupid idiot' got thrown out the window," she said. That was in 2011. By 2014, having barely squeaked by her math requirements, she was ready to enroll at Georgia State and complete her bachelor's.

Her academic performance was never in question, but her finances almost always were. She was too old for the HOPE scholarship, which meant she had to scrape by on veterans' disability checks, odd jobs, and an unrelenting diet of boxed mac and cheese. By the spring of 2015, just six months away from graduation, she wasn't sure she could come up with the money for her remaining classes. At the same time, a professor specializing in historical preservation was encouraging her to join a trip he was leading to Cuba. Sample was torn. She started a GoFundMe site to take care of the Cuba expenses, but wondered if she should put the money toward her tuition instead. Then it occurred to her she could deal with the tuition problem by asking for a Panther retention grant.

The scholarship office did not take her request kindly. "You're going to Cuba?" they asked. "You have money for Cuba but not to pay your tuition?" She had no answer for that, only a conviction that she should seize her opportunities where she could. If the retention grant was out of reach, so be it. She'd figure something out when she got home.

She did not regret Cuba for an instant. It was, she said, like getting her brain factory-reset. She thought she knew what it meant to be poor, but next to what ordinary Cubans endured every day, her struggle to pay for her summer classes seemed suddenly trivial, a bump along a road far smoother than she'd credited.

Once back in Atlanta, Sample checked her student account to take in the news of how much she owed and how many days she had to pay, only to find that her debt had been erased. She couldn't understand how at first. Then she noticed a code under the rubric "payments supplied" and discovered through a phone call that she'd received a Panther retention grant after all. The scholarship office hadn't wanted to process her application, but it didn't matter. The data showed she was a deserving recipient, and the power of data trumped all. "I was blown away," she said. "I was humbled."

She also graduated on time that December and vowed on the spot that she would repay Georgia State for its immense faith as soon as she was able. Sure enough, in the fall of 2018, once she had completed her training and she was a freshly minted high school history teacher in the eastern Atlanta suburbs, she wrote the first of what she pledged to be monthly $100 checks to her alma mater. It was yet another way in which the system demonstrated it could pay for itself.

The next group of students Renick wanted to help were those who, unlike the retention grant recipients, were vulnerable academically. This was, essentially, the group with acceptable high school GPAs and low SAT scores that Risa Palm and Fenwick Huss hadn't wanted to admit and that Renick now had a responsibility to turn into successes in the face of considerable skepticism. Historically, these students had tended to drop out at a 50 percent clip before the end of their freshman year, the higher education equivalent of trench warfare. Under such conditions Renick was disinclined to admit them too. But the problem wasn't lack of potential. Rather, they came from a background that made it likely they would be overwhelmed by a large urban campus if they did not have some guide rails in the first couple of semesters.

What to do? A number of universities offered bridge programs, remedial classes in all but name that weaker students were either invited or required to take ahead of freshman year. Many of those universities, though, also had to offer financial support, because non-credit-bearing remedial classes did not qualify students for federal grants and loans. And financial support at Georgia State was a nonstarter because the student numbers were simply overwhelming.

Another option that offered actuarial temptations was to defer the weaker students to January. That way, they wouldn't be counted in the same cohort, and the drop-out rate wouldn't look as bad on paper. This, too, was a nonstarter, because students felt *more* lost when they came in a semester late. Renick and his team had tried it as a way of bringing some of the lower SAT students in through the back door while Palm was still insisting on raising freshman standards, and the results had been ugly. "January," Allison Calhoun-Brown said, "is the worst possible time of the year to admit them."

That left only one option: to admit the students in summer, not to enroll in remedial courses but to engage in college-level work and take advantage of the quieter time on campus to bond with each other and get a head start on their peers. Often, Renick and Calhoun-Brown realized, the biggest obstacle these students faced was not academic but psychological. "There was a mindset—a belief that they cannot succeed," Renick said. And so they structured the Summer Success Academy, as it became known, as a learning community, not a boot camp. The students were split into groups of twenty-five according to their common academic interests and given an opportunity to navigate the intricacies of student life together. Ron Henry had first introduced learning communities to Georgia State more than a decade earlier, but in his hands the idea never progressed beyond the experimental stage. Now, Renick's team saw it as an ideal way of easing students into university life without stigma. "We don't tell them, you're pitiful, poor, and at risk. That's not the tone," Calhoun-Brown explained several years into the program. "We say, we're going to provide you with the same attention as we provide to athletes."

Stephanie Tran, who was part of the very first Summer Success Academy, remembered being given exactly that message. She was aware of being a guinea pig in an experimental new program, but that did not bother her for long and she welcomed the chance to get a leg up on how the university worked. She knew why she was there: she suffered from "major testing anxiety," as she put it, and had not done well on her SATs. The extra guidance was welcome.

Summer students like her didn't just do coursework. They also got a jump on the rest of the university in peer instruction—the notion that those who were strong in a particular area could give extra help to those who were struggling. And they were the first to be exposed to a revamped version of Georgia State's basic orientation class, GSU 1010, which taught them how to access university services and introduced them to advisors who showed them, in person, how the interactive Campus system worked and what it could do for them.

Over time, it became clear that the Summer Success Academy was an ideal environment in which to pilot new ideas of many kinds. The concept of learning communities was extended to the entire freshman class. And it was given an extra twist, as students were no longer grouped by personal interest but by general area of study—business, liberal arts, computer science, and so on. These "meta majors," as they were known, would eventually become an organizing principle for all Georgia State students, applied to everything from admissions to the allocation of academic advisors.

For Tran, the array of services, even in its rudimentary first-year form, was transformative. She enrolled as a nursing major and not only knew by the start of fall that the odds were stacked against her making the cut, but developed the confidence and the familiarity with predictive analytics to switch to psychology and feel good about it. When she found herself struggling with medical issues at the end of freshman year and lost her HOPE scholarship, she barely blinked and won HOPE back a year later—without any additional support. "What students need," she said, "is a group of people to help them throughout their college career, and that's what I got."

The overall results were extraordinary. Close to 90 percent of that first summer cohort were still enrolled at Georgia State at the start of their sophomore year, a quantum improvement on the 50 percent retention rate that low-SAT students had recorded previously. Their average GPA clocked in above 3.0 and stayed there through their time at Georgia State—and in some years went above 3.2. After a few years, the data showed that they were graduating at a rate 7 percentage points higher than the university average. So much for Risa Palm's contention that these were students doomed to fail in large numbers because of their SAT scores. Pretty soon, students *not* admitted to the summer program were clamoring to be allowed in.

"What we were giving them," Renick observed, "was the mindset that they can do college work . . . They know where everything is, what the syllabus is. And it's a no-cost program. It absorbs no central resources. The more we retained, the more revenue we were generating." There could be no greater testament to a fundamental idea at the root of Georgia State's grand experiment: that the measure of a university lies not in the test scores of the students it admits, but in what it chooses to do with them once they arrive.

As more students started finding their confidence and their stride at Georgia State, a sense of indomitability began to spread across campus, a visceral feeling that no problem, no frustration or failure, was too big to surmount. Renick and his staff were forever on the lookout for the next data-driven solution, the next obstacle to identify and remove. That energy also extended to the students, who now had the self-belief to push back against adversity and *expect* to come out stronger on the other side.

One such student was Tyler Mulvenna, who arrived at Georgia

State in the fall of 2013 with all imaginable momentum working against him. He was the first in his family to go to college, and one of only a few from his high school in Newnan, forty miles southwest of Atlanta, to make it to the big city. Mulvenna knew he didn't want to end up like his mother, who had lost her job at a pharmaceutical company during the recession and now struggled to make ends meet as a checker at Kroger. He knew, too, that he didn't want to end up like his two older sisters, who both had babies when they were teenagers and led lives far short of what either had dreamed. Mulvenna was bright, athletic, and popular, and his mother had given him all the support and guidance she could to help him excel academically. But he also had no money—he'd worked from the age of fifteen so he and his mother could scrape by—and knew that if he couldn't figure out a way to pay for college a degree was going to be out of reach.

Mulvenna graduated high school with a 2.97 GPA, tantalizingly short of the 3.0 cutoff for a HOPE scholarship, so he made a plan to work for the summer before school and vowed he'd buckle down after that to make sure his grades improved and he qualified for HOPE the following year. That plan went up in smoke, though, when he crashed his car toward the end of the summer and was left with no transport to get to and from a job. Instead of arriving at Georgia State with cash in hand, he was flat broke and accumulating extra debt from a string of last-minute high-interest loans. Because he couldn't afford to live on campus, he was forced to take a 7:30 a.m. bus from Newnan and another back no later than 6:00 p.m. He had a weekend job as a stocker and cashier at a sporting goods store in Newnan, but he couldn't work during the week because he was enrolled in the Panther Excellence Program, a less intense, regular-session cousin of the summer academy that required him to be on campus full-time Monday through Thursday.

The program was very good for Mulvenna in that it provided him with a structure to excel and helped fill the gaps from his high school education. But it also created other problems, because the number of credit hours he could take was capped at twelve for the first semester and fifteen for the second. That left him three credit-hours short of the thirty required for the HOPE scholarship. Mulvenna applied for a summer study program in France, good for another six credit hours, and won a scholarship to cover some of the travel expenses. But he was still around $2,000 short. The HOPE money wouldn't come through until fall, and the bill for summer tuition was due up front.

This was where Mulvenna's refusal to be daunted kicked in. He happened to meet Crystal Mitchell through his GSU 1010 course, recognized her as someone with an unusual ability to make extraordinary things happen, and peppered her with questions to see if she could somehow get him to France, short of upending the laws of the universe entirely. Mitchell came up with the idea of applying for a Panther Retention Grant. In theory, students weren't supposed to apply for them at all, on top of which they were designed for seniors, not freshmen. But in Mitchell's mind Mulvenna was a good fit all the same—a promising student, with a 3.2 freshman GPA, facing a financial emergency that threatened his chances of earning a degree. So he applied and the grant came through, the France trip was back on, and with it his HOPE scholarship. Most importantly, he learned never to take no for an answer. "Every time I needed something, I went to Crystal to figure out a way to circumnavigate the system," he said. "What I learned from her was how to get around certain obstacles. I do a lot of that still."

Sophomore year was no less of a white-knuckle ride. Even with HOPE money, Mulvenna was drowning in debt, so much so that he received a second retention grant within weeks of his return from France. He needed to work at least twenty hours a week, and that was only going to happen if he could lay his hands on a car. He still had the 2000 Ford Fusion he had smashed up in the accident and, while it wasn't remotely roadworthy by any normal definition, he got a family member who was an auto mechanic to stretch out the crumpled bodywork to the point where it could do a plausible imitation of holding the road. Soon, Mulvenna wasn't just driving around in the car. For most of the fall semester, he was also sleeping in it to save himself the gas needed to drive back and forth to Newnan. That meant a singularly high-stress existence, because almost everything about the vehicle was illegal. "It couldn't pass an emissions test, so I couldn't get tags," Mulvenna said. "And I couldn't have it on the street for fear of getting tickets. I got four of them and couldn't pay them."

For a while, Mulvenna parked the car overnight at friends' apartment complexes so he wouldn't get cited or towed. Soon after Thanksgiving, though, he decided to ditch the car and take a job that he could walk to, selling memberships at a YMCA across the street from Georgia State's main administrative buildings. Not only was this more convenient and better paid than working in Newnan; it also offered networking opportunities with YMCA patrons that led him to a valuable internship with the IHG hotel group and, in time, his first full-time job. He moved in with his sister, who lived on the MARTA rail line in the north Atlanta suburbs, and slept either there or on his fraternity brothers' couches.

In short, he survived. By junior year, he was living on campus, racking up class credits and internships, and earning himself an invitation to join the prestigious student ambassador program known as the 1913 Society. None of this came easy: the stress of working thirty hours a week on top of his multiple campus commitments caused him to come down with one infectious disease after another—first shingles, then strep throat, tonsillitis, and mononucleosis. In his senior year, he was so close to penury again that he needed a third and final retention grant.

Mulvenna came through his trial by fire, graduating with distinction in international business, French, and marketing and going on to a high-powered career, first with IHG and then with IBM. At no stage did he lack in inventiveness or grit. But he also typified the sort of student who routinely drops out of most colleges; one who, through no fault of his own, is perpetually walking a tightrope and has nobody to catch him when he falls. Without Georgia State's array of student success programs and the can-do attitude they fostered, there would have been no France trip, no HOPE scholarship, next to no likelihood Mulvenna would have made it much past the beginning of his sophomore year. He would have been remembered, if anyone remembered him at all, as just another poor, biracial kid who didn't make it. And yet he was a model student.

The ascendancy of Renick's student success initiatives was mirrored by the ascendancy of the university as a whole, just as the strategic plan had envisaged. Along with retention grants and freshman learning communities, Georgia State launched new, interdisciplinary fields of study and research—everything from bioinformatics to new media—to meet the challenges of the digital age in a rapidly recovering Atlanta economy. Research funding hit $100 million, the elusive target Carl Patton and Ron Henry could never reach. And many of the key strategic planning committee members moved into leadership positions. Michael Eriksen became dean of a newly formed school of public health and Paul Alberto was appointed dean of the College of Education.

The prime mover behind these innovations in faculty organization and research was Risa Palm, who settled into her role as Georgia State's manager supreme and pursued the goals of the strategic plan, including the student success parts, with vigor and unerring focus. She might not have been the one coming up with the creative ideas, and she certainly hadn't agreed with all of them at the outset, but now that Becker and the university as a whole were committed, she was relentless about making them a reality.

She did this despite being sandwiched uncomfortably between the leadership team closest to Becker, which had a boys' club feel at times and kept her out of the loop on key decisions, and Renick, who still reported to her but carried ever more authority in his own right. She remained no less formidable than the reputation that had preceded her, but she also saw it as her job to enact the president's wishes, and she stuck to that through thick and thin. It helped that a lot of the bad blood from her first couple of years was gone, along with the senior figures she had found it hardest to warm to. It helped, too, that she liked and respected Renick, even though she understood she was expected to follow his lead now as much as he followed hers.

Every day, Palm would convene her top administrators for an 8:30 morning meeting and expected them to be at the very top of their game. The get-togethers were brief, no more than fifteen or twenty minutes, much like stand-up meetings typical of the military, only with coffee. "If you meet weekly or biweekly," she explained, "the meetings get too long and people end up checking their email or getting bored and expecting that nothing will get done." Attendees took stock of what was expected, offered their thoughts, and left. Peter Lyons of the Office of Institutional Effectiveness described the meetings as "a whiz-bang group of super-smart people—and me."

In some ways, the terms of the strategic plan were liberating, because they gave Palm clear metrics on enrollment, graduation rates, research, and fundraising by which to assess the performance of deans and other top administrators. Either the deans met the metrics, or they didn't; there was no need to become vituperative about it. She did not need to say much when Fenwick Huss continued to rail against the student success project and complain that it was forcing Georgia State to lower its standards. She merely pointed out where he was falling short—which was more or less everywhere.

Huss, for his part, sought ways to dress up this failure primarily as an intellectual disagreement between esteemed colleagues. "I was unwilling to tell my faculty and staff to lower admission standards to make numbers," he said with some pride years later.

At an administrative council meeting in 2013, he argued that the university's responsibility stretched not from matriculation to graduation but from matriculation to career. It was, he said, a very different approach to education. He wasn't wrong to argue that Georgia State lagged in the career support it offered undergraduates—particularly those from more modest backgrounds who could not lean on their families or peer groups to develop a professional network. But it also struck a number of Huss's colleagues as an argument of convenience; since his critique implied that some graduates were more equal than others, for reasons that went beyond the courses they took or the academic standards they satisfied. That attitude, to many ears, smacked of insufferable elitism.

Huss was well aware of the frosty reception. He remembered Becker responding tartly: "Our job is to graduate students." Becker himself thought Huss was simply resistant to change. And Palm was no more tender. "He didn't hit any targets," she said, "not in philanthropy, not in graduation rates, not in admission rates. At first, I gave him a warning. Then, the second year, I offered him a choice—either to resign or be fired."

Huss moved on at the end of the 2013–14 academic year, leaving a dust cloud of ill feeling and frustration in his wake. Nobody doubted his intelligence, and nobody begrudged the pride he took in the business school's reputation. But he also made it sound as if undergraduates were an obstacle to be worked around, not Georgia State's core responsibility. "You can't be a modern university and operate that way," Palm said.

Jorge Martinez-Vazquez, the economist from the Andrew Young school, offered a slightly different analysis, seeing the friction as a consequence of Georgia State's unusual twin ambition to be both a top-tier research university and a high-quality access institution for low-income undergraduates. The two goals weren't incompatible, but people of a more traditional academic mindset found the pairing difficult. "As a university we were being forced in some ways to take on a split personality," Martinez-Vazquez said. "We needed to be reaching out to students who would not otherwise get a college education. And, at the same time, our peers were judging us by standards that make Harvard and Princeton so selective and wanted. How do you do both?"

The answer, apparent to most of the leadership but not to Dean Huss, was to separate graduate and undergraduate programs and approach them differently, just as the strategic plan spelled out. "In graduate programs," Martinez-Vazquez said, "you can be more selective and competitive. It's okay to want to be like Princeton. There will not be a conflict. But, at the undergraduate level, you can't do that. And Fenwick got that wrong."

Then and now: Princeton Nelson, who was born in prison and grew up without parents, was working as a computer programmer in Seattle one year after graduating from Georgia State. "If people like me fail," he says, "we're going to fail *our life*." Photo by Yosef Kalinko for Georgia State

Savannah Torrance almost dropped out in her freshman year, but timely guidance helped her switch majors. Georgia State, she says, "helped me figure out who I was." Photo by Steve Thackston/Georgia State

A casually dressed Mark Becker addresses students at Homecoming. "Change is what I do," he says. "Maintaining the status quo would kill me." Photo by Meg Buscema/Georgia State

Tim Renick in his element, chairing a meeting of his senior staff. A former student remembered: "He exuded tremendous kindness . . . and had this capacity to bring the very best work out of people." Photo by Meg Buscema/Georgia State

Risa Palm in graduation regalia. As provost, Palm was skeptical about the student success revolution but ended up "fierce and focused about it." Photo by Meg Buscema/Georgia State

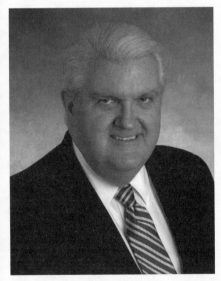

Fenwick Huss, as dean of Georgia State's Robinson College of Business in 2005. He opposed the student success reforms and resented having to admit large numbers of undergraduates he believed to be unqualified. Photographer unknown/Georgia State

Andrew Young, the civil rights icon and former mayor of Atlanta, came to see Georgia State as a vital engine of the American future. "I'm not part of the administration, but part of the insurrection." Photo by Meg Buscema/Georgia State

Hank Huckaby, Erroll Davis's successor, loved Tim Renick's idea of "data with a purpose" and approved extraordinary funding for student advising at Georgia State at a time when other budget items were being frozen or cut. Photo by Carolyn Richardson/Georgia State

Gabriel Woods (left) reunited with Crystal Mitchell in 2019 outside the University Advisement Center, which, crucially, did not exist when he was an undergraduate. Georgia State's advising reforms have systematized what Mitchell did for Woods and scaled it so tens of thousands of students, not just rare individuals, can benefit. Photo by Carolyn Richardson/Georgia State

Carol Cohen took over a troubled student advisement office and build it into the centerpiece of Georgia State's student success efforts. "We need to meet the students where they are," she said, "not where we think they should be." Photo by Meg Buscema/Georgia State

Cary Claiborne, assistant director of student success "at a school I got kicked out of," offers advice to a student at Georgia State's Decatur community college campus. Photo by Bill Roa/Georgia State

Allison Calhoun-Brown, Tim Renick's deputy, is known for her soft touch and wicked sense of humor and her talent for making people feel good about the changes she asks them to enact. Photo by Meg Buscema/Georgia State

Scott Burke, director of admissions, was a first-generation student himself and was quick to embrace technological solutions to problems facing incoming students. Photo by Meg Buscema/Georgia State

Sharon Sample was "blown away" when she received a Panther retention grant and graduated on time. She pledged to give $100 back to Georgia State each month as soon as she earned her first paycheck as a public school history teacher. Photo by Steve Thackston/Georgia State

Tyler Mulvenna was a model student who made it through Georgia State thanks to retention grants and other vital support mechanisms in the face of extraordinary hardships. "What I learned," he said, "was how to get around certain obstacles. I do a lot of that still." Photo by Carolyn Richardson/Georgia State

Noah Langdale, left, was the last university president of the segregation era and ran Georgia State "like a well-managed plantation" for thirty years. Bill Suttles, right, was his right-hand man, a part-time preacher with a fondness for fire-and-brimstone prayers. Photo by Charles R. Pugh Jr./*Atlanta Journal-Constitution* Photographic Archives. Special Collections and Archives, Georgia State University Library

Carl Patton (center), seen early in his tenure as Georgia State president with U.S. Housing Secretary Henry Cisneros (left) and Atlanta mayor Maynard Jackson (right). Patton broke with the good ol' boy culture he inherited from Langdale and Suttles and laid the groundwork for Georgia State to emerge as a national model of diversity and social mobility. Photographer unknown/Georgia State

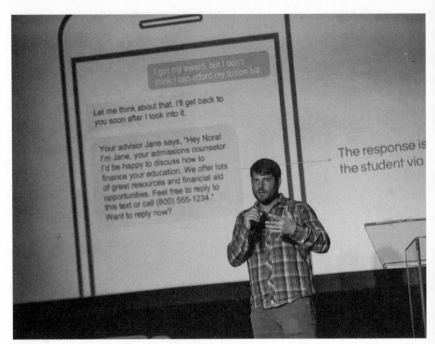

Drew Magliozzi of AdmitHub demonstrates the chatbot he developed for Georgia State at a Talkabot conference in 2016. Video screen shot courtesy of Howdy

Austin Birchell, left, shows Bill Gates how the chatbot works and why it rescued his college career. Photo by Steve Thackston/Georgia State

Tim Renick has given hundreds of presentations around the country to explain Georgia State's successes and to encourage others to follow suit. Photo by Carolyn Richardson/Georgia State

Terrance Rogers, left, and Kyle Stapleton, right, met as business majors at Georgia State and now raise money to help others find a similar path to success. Photo by Basil Iskandrian/Georgia State

Heather Housley, center, waits with two students leaders on the "blue carpet" for new student orientation. Housley transformed a "soul-crushing" experience into another compelling element of Georgia State's student success work. Photo by Meg Buscema/Georgia State

Mark Becker, left, congratulates a graduating student at the fall 2018 commencement, where he invoked "the magical power of thinking big." Photo by Meg Buscema/Georgia State

8

A WELL-MANAGED PLANTATION

When Mark Becker's predecessor, Carl Patton, came to Atlanta to interview for the presidency in 1992, it took only a few minutes with alumni and members of the university foundation board for him to understand how different their world was from his native Midwest. It was a world with no notion of how urgently it needed to change.

The meeting was in Wachovia Bank's executive board room, on the thirtieth floor of Downtown Atlanta's most distinctive skyscraper, at 191 Peachtree. Patton's hosts knew that the university was in need of fresh vision, because alumni donations were down to a trickle, state appropriations were being squeezed, and the adult evening learners who made up the majority of Georgia State's student body were rapidly moving out of Downtown along with the banks, law firms, and public relations agencies that employed them. Still, they had only two questions for the prospective new president.

The first was: *Who's the only American president without an accent?* Patton, who had not previously lived in the South, was nimble enough to come up with the answer. Georgia's own Jimmy Carter.

And the second was: *What's a nice boy like you doing getting a degree from Berkeley?* The last word flew out like an obscenity. It was all Patton could do to explain that he'd grown up without a lot of money and had gone for the biggest scholarship on offer. He didn't think it wise to point out that Berkeley was also one of the top public universities in the country, because these good ol' boys weren't going to accept it.

Patton knew already that Georgia State had a history of parochialism and reactionary thinking, but it wasn't until that moment that he could feel it in his bones. The board of regents had told him they wanted a president who could inject some much-needed dynamism and help revive a declining Downtown, assignments for which Patton, as an urban planner, was particularly well suited. They were excited about his vision of building Georgia State into a premier research university and excited, too, about the opportunities that the 1996 Summer Olympics coming to Atlanta would present.

Now, though, Patton understood he'd also have to deal with a moribund university culture. For thirty years, starting in the segregation era, Georgia State had been run by a gruff bulldog named Noah Langdale, a former University of Alabama lineman with a fondness for bear hugs but little patience for bold new ideas and an outright aversion to campus rebels and subversives. His deputy and ultimate successor, Bill Suttles, was a no-nonsense administrator and part-time preacher who liked to recite hellfire prayers at university meetings and public occasions. Both men kept offices on campus for years after their tenures were over. Patton was flabbergasted, at his first commencement ceremony, to hear one of Suttles's incantations admonishing anyone who strayed from the righteous path through Jesus. "I thought, what is this fire-and-brimstone prayer?" Patton recalled. "What is going on here?" At the next commencement, he had an assistant dean write a nondenominational, non-offensive reflection instead.

A significant part of the backwardness on campus was bound up with race, and in the spring of 1992, right around the time Patton went through his job interviews, the subject was coming to a rapid boil because of the Rodney King trial and the riots that erupted in Los Angeles when the four white police officers who had been caught on camera beating King to a pulp were acquitted.

The unrest soon spread to other cities, including Atlanta. Groups of young black men smashed shop windows, attacked a Korean-owned grocery, and set fire to cars in neighborhoods close to the Georgia State campus. The police tear-gassed protesters at Clark Atlanta University, a historically black college two miles to the west of Georgia State, and eventually the governor called in the National Guard. Patton remembered his friends at the University of Toledo, where he was still vice president for academic affairs, asking if he was sure he still wanted the job. Maynard Jackson, then halfway through his second stint as Atlanta's mayor, asked the same question. "My attitude was, it doesn't scare me," Patton said.

Once Patton started his presidency, it was a matter of days before the racial unrest reached his office door. A photograph appeared in the Georgia State Student Center showing members of the Pi Kappa Alpha fraternity in blackface and curly wigs performing a revue they called "Harlem Nights." In response, a restive Black Student Alliance demanded an apology and suspension of the fraternity. As the controversy rumbled on into the fall semester, a white student daubed a racial slur on a university garbage can and rolled it in front of the doorway to Phi Beta Sigma, a leading black fraternity. Instantly, the campus was in ferment. Outraged Phi Beta Sigma members wheeled the garbage can around to drum up support for a protest, and soon about 150 students were staging sit-ins at several university buildings, bringing the registrar's office and other services to a halt. A handful of the protesters burst into Patton's office and refused to leave until he had addressed a list of their grievances.

Contrary to the advice of his provost and a number of other top administrators, Patton opted to talk to the protest leaders instead of having campus police clear them out. He told them he was inclined to grant most if not all of the items on their list. Why not approve a department of African American studies, one of their top demands, particularly since Georgia State's black student population now made up a quarter of the total and was continuing to grow fast? Ahmed Abdelal, the newly installed dean of arts and sciences, had already been working on developing an African American studies major, a glaring omission at an urban university of Georgia State's size and diversity, and the extra step was mostly a matter of figuring out budgetary arrangements. Likewise, Patton was in favor of punishing student groups involved in racist pranks and in favor, too, of setting up an anti-discrimination hotline.

When he learned that the dean of students and two other senior administrators had misrepresented the gravity of what Pi Kappa Alpha and a number of other white students had done, he got rid of them. When the provost—already an unpopular figure on campus for other reasons—maneuvered behind the scenes not to go through with an African American studies department after all, it firmed up the determination of a key faculty committee to push him out, too, and Patton acquiesced.

Patton made these moves only with the greatest reluctance. It wasn't in his nature to manage with sharp elbows, and indeed some members of the faculty and staff worried he wasn't decisive enough. Many others, though, loved him for his principled stances, as well as his warmth and accessibility. A couple of years into his tenure, Patton gave up the official residence in Buckhead to which he was entitled and moved to an apartment on the top floor of a renovated building overlooking the Georgia State campus. It made a striking statement: that the president loved Downtown, believed in Downtown, and was intent on being at the center of a university that would at last embrace its identity and its geography instead of running away from them.

Forty-two years before the Georgia State sit-ins, a young black student named Horace Ward applied to the University of Georgia law school to test the resolve of one of the South's most die-hard segregationist governments. The end of World War II had created a rush of demand for higher education across the country, and the

GI Bill, passed in 1947, had given returning soldiers, black and white, the means to pay for it. Much of the South responded by integrating its universities, but Georgia was one of four states— Alabama, Mississippi, and South Carolina were the others—that dug in their heels. Ward, a graduate of Morehouse who also had a master's from Clark Atlanta, was refused admission to UGA, as expected, and he promptly sued.

The case dragged on for years and was eventually dismissed when the court discovered that Ward had lost patience and enrolled as a law student at Northwestern instead. Still, its implications terrified Georgia's political elite. In 1954, the same year as the Supreme Court's landmark *Brown v. Board of Education* ruling, the state passed a constitutional amendment empowering the governor to close any public school or college that crossed the color line. And that put the schools in a near-impossible situation. If they refused admission to black students, they risked being hauled into federal court for violating *Brown*. If they didn't refuse admission, the state could close them down overnight. And by the time they sued over *that,* their buildings would be impounded and their students paid by the state to obtain an education elsewhere.

Their solution was to do what state officials all over the South had done to keep blacks out of the voting booth since the Civil War: they erected barriers to maintain de facto segregation but gave themselves room to claim, however disingenuously, that the strictures were not motivated by race but by something else entirely. Thus, they insisted that any applicant to a state university needed a judge's certification and two alumni letters of recommendation. Most black high schoolers struggled to pry even an application form out of recalcitrant university admissions offices. They had little prospect of finding a sympathetic judge on an all-white Georgia bench, much less finding sympathetic alumni of an all-white institution.

A group called the Atlanta Committee for Cooperative Action sprang up to challenge the new strictures and find a way to enroll a black student at an all-white institution. Under the leadership of Jesse Hill, a black insurance executive who would come to be recognized as a major powerbroker in Atlanta, the ACCA decided this was no time to acquiesce to Georgia's governor, Marvin Griffin, and his vow to forestall school integration "come hell or high water."

The first place they targeted was Georgia State—or, as it was known then, the Georgia State College of Business Administration. This was hardly the large and bustling Georgia State of today. It was a sleepy, forty-year-old commuter school that had, at different times, been part of Georgia Tech and the University of Georgia but had never attracted more than a few thousand students to its limited curriculum of business-oriented programs. Georgia State's attraction to Jesse Hill was not that it was high profile, but that it had a large number of adult learners, which meant he could use established young professionals, not high school graduates, as his test cases. "People hesitated to send a seventeen-year-old kid into that hostility," he later explained.

The six applicants he lined up included three of his own employees. He worked every connection he had to find alumni and a judge willing to attest to their bona fides. Then, in March 1956, two of them walked into the Georgia State registrar's office to ask to be admitted. The registrar, J.D. Blair, took one look at them and, sensing trouble, nervously professed his "love for the Negro people." All the love in the world wasn't going to help these students, however, because Blair sent them to the Georgia State president, George Sparks, and Sparks told them the alumni who had written their references were no good. They had gone to the University of Georgia and UGA, as of a few months back, was no longer affiliated with Georgia State.

All six applicants sued, and the trial that followed was as nasty and personal as it was fraught with social and political tension. Two of the female plaintiffs were pilloried for their histories of divorce and childbirth out of wedlock and quickly disqualified on moral grounds. A third woman, who found work as a secretary to Martin Luther King as the trial dragged on, was accused of having "loaned herself to a scheme" cooked up by the NAACP and of having no interest in furthering her education. (It was not true: the woman, Barbara Hunt, later moved to Texas, where she obtained a bachelor's and a master's and pursued a career in urban planning.) The Georgia State campus newspaper, *The Signal*, penned one vituperative commentary after another, vowing to "fight until doomsday" to keep the student body white and telling the four remaining plaintiffs: "You will find no haven at Georgia State."

The trial outcome was mixed. The judge did not order the plaintiffs to be admitted and he did not issue a blanket condemnation of the excuses that universities and colleges were using to turn away students they found undesirable. Rather, he made a number of narrower rulings—that the requirement to seek alumni recommendations was unconstitutional and that Georgia State was wrong to deny admission to "qualified Negroes solely because of their race or color."

That was enough to push Georgia's apoplectic political leadership to new extremes. The state's freshly elected governor, Ernest Vandiver, saw the ruling as an act of judicial tyranny and ordered a temporary halt to new student registrations throughout the public higher-education system. To forestall future lawsuits by well-prepared black professionals, Vandiver also set statewide age restrictions on admissions—a maximum of twenty-one for undergraduates and twenty-five for graduate students. The board of regents introduced a new admissions policy tantamount to a "good character" test of the sort that had been central to Jim Crow across the South for decades. Students were to be judged not solely on merit but on "sturdiness of character and general fitness for admission to the institution."

Georgia State pushed this good character idea even further, proposing psychological testing and "moral-worth analyses of each matriculant" to be determined by an in-person interview. It was an absurd bar to set at an institution that demanded only a C average of its incoming freshmen. This, though, was the personal touch that Noah Langdale brought to the job after he took over as president in 1957. And the student body, for the most part, cheered him on. A startling editorial in *The Signal* remarked none too subtly that "in education today, many fleas come with the dog." The piece went on to decry "the fires of indignation and wrath" that it said the civil rights movement had kindled after "a hundred years of peaceful living, white and colored, side by side."

Langdale had been recruited to Georgia State as a safe pair of hands, someone who knew the system and could be trusted to look out for its interests. He was born into a well-heeled family in one of the most politically connected parts of the state. The Langdales of Valdosta, south of the "gnat line," were landowners heavily invested in Georgia's thriving turpentine business, and that more than compensated for the fact that "little Noah" had previously been just an ordinary professor at Valdosta State College with no administrative experience. It helped, too, that he was gregarious and charismatic and had a stentorian speaking style that marked him out as leadership material. Indeed, Langdale was told that if he could avert the closure of Georgia State and keep it white, he would be well positioned for a run at the governor's office.

That was far from how things turned out. The age restrictions proved calamitous to an institution so dependent on adult learners, and Langdale had his work cut out just holding on to his day job. Georgia State saw enrollment drop by 25 percent in a single year and by more than 50 percent over four years—from 5,668 students in 1958 to just 2,393 in 1962. The registrar was compelled to carve out ever more exceptions to keep the college's doors open, while finding ever more elaborate excuses to turn away the black students clamoring to be let in.

Georgia State was not where the color barrier was finally breached, but it could have been. Jesse Hill's gambit in response to Governor Vandiver was to find two unimpeachable Atlanta high school graduates with a year or two of college experience—he was still leery of using anyone too callow—and dare the system to turn them down. He found who he was looking for in Charlayne Hunter and Hamilton Holmes, both of whom were brilliant, good-looking, well-dressed, well-spoken, and light-skinned enough not to appear *too* black to a wary Georgia public. Hill's first idea was that they should try Georgia State. He knew the college was desperate for applicants, and he thought Hunter and Holmes might do better in an urban environment close to home than on a more isolated—and isolating—campus. Once his young charges visited, though, they changed their minds: the enrollment crisis had thinned out Georgia State's course offerings to the point where neither of them could find anything they wanted to study.

They applied instead to the University of Georgia, which had strategic advantages of its own since Governor Vandiver and a large number of state legislators were alumni and Hill calculated, correctly, that they might not have the heart to shutter their own alma mater. Hunter and Holmes were admitted in January 1961 and had to weather cross burnings and a riot in their first week. It continued to be an alienating and occasionally alarming experience. But nobody's world came to an end, and plenty of supporters came forward to counterbalance those who saw them, in the words of one of Governor Vandiver's aides, as harbingers of "dictatorship and tyranny."

By the time Hunter and Holmes graduated two years later, Georgia's entire higher education system had undergone a profound transformation. Georgia Tech admitted its first black students in the fall of 1961. The statewide age restrictions were lifted. And in the summer of 1962, Georgia State broke its own color barrier with a fifty-three-year-old black schoolteacher named Annette Lucille Hall, who was admitted to a summer course entitled Americanism and Communism.

Further change followed rapidly. Georgia State's first full-time black enrollee, Mary Belle Reynolds Warner, arrived in the fall of 1962. The first black graduate student came a year later, and the first black staff member three years after that. By the end of the decade, Georgia State had developed a program tailor-made for minority business students and established a black students' union.

Much of the work of building back up as an integrated institution was done by Bill Suttles, who became Langdale's deputy and took over the management of academic programming. But Langdale also pivoted from allegiance to the segregationist playbook to a more pragmatic understanding of the academic and financial opportunities available to a multiracial institution. By 1969, Georgia State had grown so fast it was no longer just a business college but a full-fledged university. While other institutions around the country were beginning to put the brakes on expansion because they'd already grown as much as they could, Georgia State was able to capitalize on pent-up demand in a rapidly developing Atlanta region and, because of a tightening academic job market, attract a wide array of high-caliber applicants for faculty positions.

The academic environment was dynamic and forward-looking and filled with exciting young talent. An interdisciplinary College of Urban Life, a precursor of sorts to the Andrew Young policy school, became a major engine for growing graduate programs, starting in the early 1970s, and helped give Georgia State an identity distinct from—not merely inferior to—UGA and Tech. A decade later came a law school, whose first graduating class included a future speaker of the Georgia House. Langdale and Suttles certainly understood the opportunities for growth and prestige in these and other initiatives. But, at the same time, they remained stuck in a quirky, old-fashioned, reactionary past, keeping a tight rein on the faculty and insisting on maintaining Georgia State as a quiet, apolitical night and commuter school. "A well-run Southern plantation," was how Jorge Martinez-Vazquez, the economics professor, thought of it after his arrival in 1977.

Suttles had a habit of standing outside his office, a benevolent patriarch shaking hands with passing staff and students and handing out candy from a tray. Nobody doubted his work ethic or organizational skills, but he had blind spots arising from his religious faith—a reluctance to endorse the study of genetics, for example—that may also have helped harden the philosophy department's hostility to religious studies after Tim Renick's arrival in the mid-1980s. The scuttlebutt on Langdale, meanwhile, was that he didn't seem to do a lot except eat. He was almost as broad as he was tall, a "yard wide, bull-necked, granite block," as the *Atlanta Journal-Constitution* described him, who would ask the cafeteria to bring him a second breakfast as soon as he came in and snacks for the rest of the day. Harvey Newman, a public policy professor who helped inaugurate the College of Urban Life, lived on Langdale's street in Buckhead and would see him after work in fast-food joints and grocery stores, hauling large bags filled with yet more food to tide him over until bed.

One thing Langdale took in deadly earnest was his belief that he needed to police the university for the slightest sign of agitation or rebellion. What started out as fear of the civil rights movement soon morphed into a generalized fear of the 1960s counterculture—the sex, drugs and rock 'n' roll, the long hair and campus sit-ins, the Black Power movement and the widespread opposition to the Vietnam War. Langdale insisted on interviewing every prospective new faculty member in person and was an enthusiastic advocate of a state-mandated loyalty oath, a relic of the McCarthy era requiring new hires to attest that they were not communists or, bizarrely, members of the Abraham Lincoln Brigade who had fought on the Republican side in the Spanish Civil War in the 1930s. Jorge Martinez-Vazquez found the oath particularly ludicrous since he'd endured the Franco dictatorship in Spain before coming to the United States. He also remembered Langdale shoveling chocolate cookies into his mouth from a table behind his desk and showering him with a spray of half-chewed pieces as they first shook hands.

Others hired in the same era retain similarly surreal memories. Tim Crimmins, who arrived as a history professor in 1972, remembered being asked if he had a "messiah complex" and what he would do if anti-war radicals were to start a campus organization. Ken Bernhardt, the marketing professor, remembered Langdale looking him over from top to toe and walking all around him as if inspecting a piece of meat. The president then launched into an unstoppable monologue, praising Bernhardt as a "fine-looking man" and firing off a volley of questions without once waiting for an answer. "Are you one of those Yankees coming down here to save the South?" Langdale asked. "If the students are out there marching on Courtland Street, are you going to be out there marching with them?" After about forty minutes of this, with Bernhardt unable to squeeze in a word, Langdale stopped, said thank-you, and sent him on his way.

Langdale was also unabashedly physical. He'd take pleasure in picking up an elderly department chair and swinging him around three times before putting him back down again. Once, when interviewing a candidate for a deanship, he recalled his college football career and hauled his three-hundred-pound bulk into a three-point stance to do blocking drills. His hapless interlocutor walked out of the room shaking his head and saying: "The man's crazy." On another occasion, Langdale threw an arm around Henry Ashmore, the visiting president of Armstrong State, and started rubbing Ashmore's stomach with his free hand. "How ya doin', Henry?" he asked. Quietly outraged, Ashmore responded: "Noah, I would feel a lot better if you moved your hand a little lower and a little slower."

Langdale pulled back and never laid a finger on him again.

The anachronistic culture wasn't confined to Georgia State. Two years after Patton arrived in Atlanta, torrential rains flooded two-thirds of Albany State University, a historically black campus in southwest Georgia, leading a number of community stalwarts to question whether the place should even stay open. One of them told Stephen Portch, then the chancellor of the Georgia university system: "This is God's message that we shouldn't be educating *those people*." To which Portch responded: "I'd say God's message is that we shouldn't be putting university buildings in a flood plain."

Georgia, at the time, had the highest incarceration rate in the United States and was spending five times as much per prisoner as the cost of college tuition. It also had one of the worst K–12 public education systems. It was *those people*—African Americans and other minorities—who bore the brunt of the imbalance, along with lower-income rural whites who often ended up as their prison guards instead of acquiring an education of their own. The failure to move with the times was baked into the system.

One person determined to address these structural injustices was the governor at the time, Zell Miller, who won the job by calling for a state lottery to boost education spending. Miller believed firmly in government intervention as an instrument of social mobility, and credited FDR's New Deal for lifting his own family out of destitution following the death of his father when he was barely two weeks old. "We can't all be born rich and handsome and lucky," he told the 1992 Democratic National Convention, in a keynote speech that did much to turn the tide of that year's presidential election to Bill Clinton, another child of the South who had started out with nothing.

Miller faced down Georgia's powerful evangelical Christians, who believed a lottery was inherently sinful, and instructed his staff to come up with a scholarship scheme that would open the doors of higher education to a broader swath of qualified high schoolers. His staff, who included Hank Huckaby, Miller's budget director, offered a variety of options for assessing families based on need. But Miller said that wasn't what he was looking for. One Friday, he retreated to the governor's mansion with a yellow legal pad, and by Monday he'd come up with the basic idea for a scholarship he was already calling HOPE—Helping Outstanding Pupils Educationally. Miller decided that a need-based system was too costly and might prove politically untenable in so conservative a state. Separately, he was interested in providing a financial incentive for the brightest and best of Georgia's high school graduates to stay in-state instead of heading to Yale or Princeton. So he made HOPE about merit, first and foremost, open to anyone with a 3.0 high school GPA or higher. When his office first rolled out the scholarship, it came with a family income cap—first $66,000, then $100,000—but the cap fell by the wayside because the system was simpler and cheaper to run without it.

The HOPE scholarship came in for a good deal of criticism, not least because of the large number of 3-Series BMWs, popularly known as HOPE-mobiles, that popped up in and around the University of Georgia once the money started flowing. At least one study has suggested that the scholarships *widened* the achievement gap between whites and nonwhites instead of narrowing it. Still, HOPE achieved its goal of broadening overall access to higher education by 7 to 8 percentage points over its first few years. And it utterly transformed Georgia State, which could now cater to a more diverse undergraduate body, reflective of the Atlanta population as a whole, and devise a greater range of academic programs to serve them. Carl Patton had been a skeptic about the scholarship at first, and not just because it wasn't directed at students who needed the money. He worried that high school teachers would systematically inflate their grades so more students met the 3.0 threshold. He soon recognized the benefits, though. "It did bring a lot of students who wouldn't have come otherwise," he acknowledged.

Another game changer was the 1996 Summer Olympics, an opportunity that fell more or less into Patton's lap and offered him a shortcut to establishing Georgia State as a residential campus. Andrew Young, Atlanta's mayor in the 1980s, had begged Noah Langdale to consider housing so lower-income Atlantans would

have an easier time affording an education. But Langdale was ada-
mantly opposed to anything that altered Georgia State's identity
as a commuter school. "As long as I'm on this campus, there'll be
no housing," Young recalled him saying.

The Olympics changed that calculus more or less overnight.
Young knew he needed to plan for a ten-thousand-bed Olympic
village, and he offered to build it either at the Atlanta University
Center, home to the city's prestigious historically black campuses,
or at Georgia Tech. He thought it was an unbeatable offer: give
us part of your campus for eight years and we'll give you $1 bil-
lion of improvements, no strings attached. AUC turned Young
down, though, because it didn't believe Atlanta could win the bid.
Tech said yes to building the units, but wasn't willing to commit
to keeping all ten thousand beds for its own students once the
Games were over. And that provided an opportunity for Georgia
State that Patton, once he arrived, embraced gladly.

Georgia State negotiated to take over an initial two thousand
units on the Tech campus. The number soon doubled, because
AUC backed out of a commitment to two thousand units of its
own and Patton was more than happy to pick up the slack. "We
took the whole village," he said. "First, we gave students MARTA
[transport] passes as part of their living fee, then we laid on shuttle
buses. It got us in the housing game. We could recruit students off
of it." Patton recruited so many students, in fact, that by the turn
of the millennium, a majority of Georgia State's undergraduates
were at last enrolled full-time. When Patton retired at the end of
2008, more than 70 percent were.

Part of Patton's leadership style was to organize regular listening sessions with students, and he knew that what they wanted
above all was a "real" university, with a full range of student facilities and a buzz of activity on campus, not just a collection of
teaching buildings and administrative offices. It was the Olympics that made that real university possible. Before he retired,
Patton built a new residential facility, the Commons, on the site

of a disused downtown car dealership, and another, the University Lofts, in the heart of the campus, which meant Georgia State didn't need the Tech housing anymore and its students no longer had to commute.

The effect was transformative, providing students with a connection to their university that they had never previously felt. "Housing brought student life to campus," Tom Lewis remembered. "The city loved it. It gave Downtown Atlanta life." Already, before the Olympics, Patton had organized a capital campaign to take over a disused Downtown theater, the Rialto, and convert it into a university arts center, with plate-glass windows that emphasized Georgia State's desire to embrace the surrounding cityscape. Now, more buildings followed: a rebuilt university library; a classroom facility, the Aderhold Learning Center, erected on a vacant lot near Woodruff Park; and the Petit Science Center, which boasted state-of-the-art labs instead of the cubbyholes endured by previous generations of students inside a converted parking garage, and elevators large enough that cadavers brought in for anatomy lessons no longer had to be propped up like extras in a zombie movie.

The ethos behind all these projects was to break with the idea of a campus at arm's length from the rest of Downtown Atlanta. No more would teaching or administrative buildings be erected on platforms above street level, as they had been during the expansions of the Langdale era. "We decided that we were going to be a part of the city," Patton said, "not apart from it."

There were many other changes, both symbolic and substantive. Georgia State reached tier-one research status in 1995. The basketball team hired a legendary coach, Lefty Driesell, the following year. In 1999, the Andrew Young policy school opened, making an immediate statement about the university's connection to the wider world. Patton ditched the old university colors, which he described as "confederate gray and maroon," in favor of the now-familiar Panther blue and white. And he helped design the modern logo depicting a flame of knowledge—a nod, in part, to the Olympics—inside a circle combining an uppercase *G* with an uppercase *S*.

The students didn't just notice. Many of them found inspiration in the new life that Patton was breathing into the university. "The place felt more serious. You could feel the shift," recalled Kyle Stapleton, who attended from 2005 to 2009 and saw both the Commons and the Petit Science Center open in his junior year. What Patton built was in many ways the essential foundation of everything Mark Becker and Tim Renick achieved after, as both of them have taken care to acknowledge. "There was," Stapleton said, "a groundswell of feeling that anything is possible."

9

BIRTH OF AN IDEA

When Ron Henry was provost at Miami University in Ohio, the job he held before coming to Georgia State, he couldn't help noticing that members of fraternities and sororities graduated at a rate 10 percentage points higher than the rest of the students. How so? He could only conclude it was because they were tight knit, talked to each other about their classes, and spent much of their study time together. So when he first heard about freshman learning communities and the positive effects education researchers thought they could have on academic performance and graduation rates, he knew right away he had to bring them to Georgia State. "I don't remember where I first heard about them," he said, "but I thought, that's a great idea."

The timing seemed propitious, because Georgia State in the late 1990s was going through a rough transition from a quarter to a semester system and students were struggling to schedule enough classes to graduate in four years. The idea was that the semester system would offer greater flexibility to the growing numbers of full-time students at Georgia State, but for those who did not live on campus it created all sorts of headaches, as the old block schedule was broken up and they were expected to come to class as often as five days a week instead of three. Henry saw learning communities as a vehicle to help freshmen support each other—by organizing car pools, covering for each other's absences by sharing class notes, and collaborating on homework assignments. Henry never developed the program much beyond a pilot, but it worked, leading to vastly improved first-year retention rates among those who participated.

Henry was unusually well attuned to cutting-edge ideas in undergraduate education. He made a point of following the work of think tanks like the American Association of Higher Education, which worked to improve outcomes for lower-income and minority students, and the National Center for Academic Transformation, which harnessed technology to develop new classroom techniques. One idea of AAHE's that Henry particularly liked was assessing faculty members on whatever they were good at; if someone was a gifted classroom teacher that would be valued in itself and they didn't need to face the usual pressure to crank out peer-reviewed books and journal articles on the side. From this idea came an initiative Henry launched with Ahmed Abdelal, the dean of arts and sciences, to create a career path for nontenure-track teachers. Georgia State found it could provide greater classroom consistency at lower cost if it identified the best of its adjuncts and offered them a fixed salary, plus benefits, to do all their teaching in one place instead of driving around Atlanta picking up classes here and there.

NCAT, meanwhile, had a study suggesting that if a university focused its efforts on improving the twenty-five or thirty most popular intro classes, it could have a huge knock-on effect on retention and graduation. NCAT's executive director, Carol Twigg, was one of the first people to advocate computer-based adaptive learning and what came to be known as a "flipped model"—that is, getting students to spend the majority of their time working at their own pace at a computer and only a small amount with a professor in a traditional classroom. "Students learn math by doing math," Twigg liked to say, "not by listening to someone talk about doing math." Her work was a direct inspiration for the lab-based teaching experiments that Henry started at Georgia State and that Tim Renick would scale up and standardize across the university.

It is difficult to overemphasize how unusual it was in the 1990s and early 2000s to engage in this sort of critical inquiry. Henry would take the best of the ideas to national provosts' meetings and find that they garnered very little interest. Incredible as it might sound, many colleges weren't all that interested in undergraduates, while others thought it was enough to expand access. If students subsequently dropped out, that was on them. Georgia State, though, had a financial as much as a pedagogical imperative to think differently. "We were going to be bankrupt if we didn't do something better," Carl Patton said. "We couldn't recruit more and more students and fail them out. That's not a good business model."

Henry hit the conference circuit, and in due time managed to make common cause with a small number of like-minded campus leaders willing to discuss and pool their ideas. If he found something he liked, he'd bring it back to Atlanta and try it right away. Learning communities were one such idea. Adaptive learning in math was another. Henry and his colleagues even came up with a rudimentary first stab at what would later become the Panther retention grants: short-term loans (as opposed to grants) of a few hundred dollars, taken from Georgia State foundation funds and offered to students who needed a little bit extra to meet the class registration deadline.

There was a heady, experimental quality to this operation, of ideas grabbed here and there and tested on the fly. "We never saw an idea we wouldn't steal," Patton said. Often, he and Henry would do something and tell the board of regents about it only later, relying on the strength of their relationship with Stephen Portch and others to stay out of trouble. They were, Henry said, forever asking "not for permission, but for forgiveness."

Nobody had a greater influence or offered more ideas to Henry than Larry Abele, the provost of Florida State University, who started out in administration assuming that students who dropped out couldn't cut it academically, only to change his mind in a hurry when he looked at the data. "Seventy percent were leaving in good academic standing, and of those one-third were A students," Abele recalled. "They were leaving because we were screwing them over on a regular basis."

Abele was a marine biologist, a scientist like Ron Henry, and he was not in the habit of ignoring evidence, even when it contradicted the received wisdom of his peers and predecessors. Soon after he took over as provost, in 1994, he realized that the faculty advisory group he'd formed wasn't going to help him improve students' lives because they were too wrapped in theory and not nearly familiar enough with what it was actually like to study at FSU as an undergraduate. He took refuge in the numbers instead.

The data wasn't nearly as sophisticated as it would become, but it was enough to tell him that students were routinely blocked from registering for classes they needed because they owed trivial sums for a late library book or an unpaid parking fine. "We did an Excel run on all the negative account balances, and the first four or five pages were under five dollars. It was insane," Abele recalled. "It wasn't always clear to these students why they had a hold, and by the time they'd sorted it out they'd missed their window and half the classes they needed were already filled." Abele quickly found other ways to deal with student debt that didn't impede academic progress and abolished library fines altogether.

He took a similarly pragmatic approach when he learned that FSU was not offering enough core classes, and that students who needed to get through calculus, physics, and chemistry were unable to register for more than one per semester because all three were scheduled in the same time slot. The reasons for such arrangements had everything to do with faculty convenience and nothing to do with the students, many of whom lost heart when they couldn't register for classes they needed, or ran out of money waiting. When Abele told deans and department heads this was unacceptable, they responded that scheduling was a matter of academic freedom and he had no right to infringe on it. "I'd have to say, it has nothing to do with academic freedom . . . and if you can justify screwing over 150 students, then we both have a problem," Abele remembered. "I'd tell them, I'm taking $50,000 out of your expense budget today and will keep doing that until you devise a system that works. I couldn't believe I had to be so unreasonable to get them to do the right thing. But if I'd blinked I would still be in the same damn situation."

In this and in many other respects, Abele blazed a trail for Georgia State. He, too, ran a large, urban institution—albeit in a city far smaller than Atlanta—with a hybrid mission to do cutting-edge research and also educate a diverse undergraduate population. When Abele realized that FSU's first-come, first-served approach to enrollment was penalizing lower-income and first-generation students, he gave them more time to complete their paperwork. He introduced a summer bridge program for the highest-risk students to familiarize them with the key people and places on campus and inculcate a sense of belonging. When Abele learned that Latina students from the Miami area were dropping out because their conservative parents didn't like them being in Tallahassee, at the other end of the state, he organized a bus service so they could more easily return home for weekends and holidays. He, like Ron Henry, paid attention to what others in the field were doing—the Betty Capaldis and Carol Twiggs—and was interested in establishing pathways for students to graduate as quickly as possible.

At the time, this was vital but lonely work. "People would say horrible things," Abele remembered. "They'd say, what do you expect, this is Florida State—look at the students." Like Henry, he'd find little interest among his fellow provosts who, in his experience, tended to fall into one of two groups. Either they were biding their time to apply for a university presidency, or else they couldn't wait to return to their old faculty positions because the job required them to enforce a lot of rules their colleagues did not like. Either way, they tended not to last more than a few years, lacking the stamina and longevity required for long-term institutional reform.

It didn't take long for Abele to see a kindred spirit in Henry—they met at a meeting of the Association of Public and Land Grant Universities—and soon they were working on projects together to introduce freshman learning communities and centralize advising. Abele went significantly further than Henry, by instituting a uniform training program for all FSU advisors, and in starting something he called "intrusive" advising to reach out to students on the wrong trajectory instead of waiting for them to come forward by themselves. Tim Renick later got to know Abele, and the influence on Georgia State continued to be profound.

These pioneering ideas remained outliers until the economic meltdown of 2008, when public universities across the country faced significant duress and started to see higher retention and graduation rates as essential to their financial well-being. After three decades of steady decreases in state funding—now accounting for less than 50 percent of overall revenues—the crash delivered a death-blow to any notion that the trend might one day swing back in the other direction. Institutions began to understand that letting more students in was not enough; sooner or later they would have to start working harder to hold on to them, because they were a valuable source of revenue that was very far from being maximized.

At the same time, state governments began to worry about the cost-effectiveness of their investment in higher education given the shockingly high drop-out rates, particularly of lower-income students. One organization that started from this vantage point was Complete College America, whose founders came from the world of politics. Stan Jones, who had been Indiana's commissioner on higher education, and Tom Sugar, a former chief of staff to Indiana senator Evan Bayh, started touring the country in 2009 to press the argument about squandered resources. They compiled drop-out data from thirty states and urged colleges and universities to do something about it.

The approach did not earn them a tender reception at first—either because universities were not yet ready to hear the message or because they did not want to hear it from *them*. "People were pissed," Sugar remembered. "We'd go out on the road to give speeches about it, and folks would sit with their arms folded and argue about the data. There was an unwillingness to accept what we were saying. Mostly, they hoped that these CCA people would just go away."

A turning point came when CCA teamed up with Abele and Renick and was able to hold up real-life examples of what was possible. FSU and Georgia State were distinctly unfashionable universities that rarely earned coverage in the Ivy League–obsessed higher education press. But Abele, by this point, had pushed FSU's graduation rate close to 80 percent, with a drop-off of only a percentage point or two for Latino and black students, and it wasn't long before Renick had some remarkable results of his own. It was still lonely work—Renick described them as "voices crying in the wilderness"—but CCA managed to build momentum with policymakers and persuade governors in more than thirty states to sign on to a list of student success and resource management goals, starting with the collection of more complete data.

Over time, CCA found that a number of other institutions were doing compelling work, too—either because they'd stumbled on their own innovative ideas or because they were starting to pay attention to the broader conversation. The City University of New York network, for example, was using block scheduling and a version of meta majors to accelerate the progress of community college students toward an associate's degree. Technical colleges in Tennessee were reporting graduation rates of 75 percent or more, in part because students had their classes sequenced and scheduled in advance. Austin Peay State University, also in Tennessee, was another early pioneer of meta majors, known there as "academic focus areas," and was helping to transform the national conversation on remedial classes by organizing them *alongside* college-level courses, as so-called co-requisites, instead of obliging weaker students to eat up time and money on prerequisites that did not earn them college credit or qualify them for federal grants.

Austin Peay's provost, Tristan Denley, soon became another regular on the CCA national touring circuit. He, too, was a scientist, a mathematician who not only grasped the concept of predictive analytics but wrote his own data analytics program to help students decide which courses they should take. If EAB's program was a little like Waze in providing students a route to a degree, Denley's program was more like Netflix—offering students courses they were likely to enjoy based on their preferences and performance to date.

One of the reasons Denley was able to push through such innovative ideas was that, in 2010, Tennessee became one of a number of states to tie funding for higher education to student success, as measured by speed to graduation, number of degrees conferred, and community college transfers. Denley still had to endure his share of pushback from deans and faculty chairs. But he also had an advantage over colleagues in many other states: a mandate from the legislature to show evidence of his effectiveness and, once he'd demonstrated it, to keep going. "Change is rarely something that people relish," Denley said, "but change that produces something positive—that's easier to deal with." That did not mean that the whole of Tennessee underwent a student success revolution, because the state funding formula could not, on its own, guarantee a better outcome for lower-income and minority students. That was still up to individual institutions, and many of them focused on improving student performance at the upper end of the income scale, where they viewed progress as more predictable.

Still, there were limits to the old model of improvement through greater exclusivity, and an increasing number of institutions were finding that they couldn't hit their budget targets if they didn't also work harder to hold on to the students they had. One such institution was the University of South Carolina, where Mark Becker served as provost before coming to Georgia State, and it got burned several years earlier than most. USC had pushed hard for exclusivity in the late 1990s, only to realize when the economy went into decline in 2001 that it needed to make up its numbers in a hurry and grow the undergraduate student body again. It worked hard on recruiting out of state, but that proved insufficient and the university was forced to admit students that many senior administrators regarded as undesirable. It then fell to Dennis Pruitt, USC's head of student affairs and de facto student success leader, to find ways to help these undesirables succeed anyway. Pruitt introduced a number of support measures—everything from peer-led supplemental instruction to writing labs to financial literacy courses—that proved successful, so much so that when the 2008 recession hit, he did much the same all over again. "It became a matter of survival," he said. "The lowest-hanging fruit for any institution is going to be retention. You gain in morale, in tuition revenue, all of it."

As more institutions struggled in the post-recessionary gloom, they started to come to very similar conclusions. "Student success went from something nobody talked about to something everyone talked about," said Hilary Pennington, the point person at the Gates Foundation responsible for setting up Complete College America. The shift hardly portended a national outbreak of moral courage, however, much less a narrowing of the yawning divide between America's richest and poorest students. Pennington noticed a sharp distinction between elite universities, which chose to become even more exclusive in the wake of the crash, and access institutions at the other end of the spectrum, which concluded, reluctantly, that they had to find a way to do more with less. She became so disillusioned with this disparity ("the capture of higher education by the elites," as she called it) that in 2011 she quit Gates to look for other ways to push universities toward a higher sense of mission. She found not one, but two, interrelated projects to help her toward that goal.

The first project was a report, co-authored by Pennington and issued through the New America foundation, that highlighted the work that institutions like Georgia State and Arizona State were doing to buck the national trend. More restrictive enrollment at public universities, the report argued, only exacerbated income inequality and risked making the next generation "the first in history to be less educated than their parents." By contrast, Georgia State, Arizona State, and a handful of other universities showed the benefits of taking a different approach and undermined the longstanding belief that large campuses could not improve student outcomes without a significant infusion of state money. Georgia State was a prime example of a university able to innovate fast, and at scale, to provide an education to large numbers of promising students regardless of their background or the quality of their high school preparation. "Public universities often insist that the only way for them to grow is with additional state subsidies to build classrooms, dorms, and hire an army of support staff to serve the new students," the report said. "But the six public universities studied [here] show that growth is possible in the face of shrinking state resources without sacrificing their core mission."

Pennington's second initiative was to bring those universities doing the most interesting, cutting-edge work into a single organization to pool and promote their ideas. The Gates Foundation, she knew, was not interested in funding individual institutions but was open to putting money behind an alliance combining several of them. And so, at an Aspen Institute meeting in 2012, Pennington brokered a meeting between Mark Becker, Michael Crow, and a cluster of other presidents. Within two years, they had launched the eleven-member University Innovation Alliance, with Crow as its chair and Becker its vice chair. Two other institutions featured in the New America report, the University of

California, Riverside, and the University of Central Florida, were founding members, along with several big midwestern schools. In time the UIA would become an effective platform for many of the ideas pioneered by Renick's student success team, including proactive advising, data analytics, and completion grants.

The alliance's inaugural executive director, Bridget Burns, was an indefatigable education researcher who had spent a year trailing Michael Crow as a fellow with the American Council on Education. She was ideally suited to the job of advising and recruiting college presidents because she'd spent time as a researcher inquiring what it took to make collaboration and reform happen. "My experience," she said, "is that people need to be dragged into it kicking and screaming most of the time."

Burns's perennial struggle was less to impress outside institutions with the work that Georgia State and others were doing than to convince them how difficult and all-consuming it was. There was no silver bullet, she'd tell them, just the long, steady grind of pushing against entrenched habits and opinions. She hesitated to tell institutions that they needed to find their own Tim Renick or Michael Crow, because she understood how exceptional each was. "Tim and Mike work harder than anyone I've ever seen," she said. "You're not going to find someone with Tim's humility, his incredible discipline, his ability to instill team loyalty ... Mike enjoys a similar level of loyalty—people pledge their lives and move across the country because they want to be around him and his crazy, exciting ideas."

What Burns *could* do was provide a platform for her superstars and introduce them to a broader public. The exposure was particularly valuable to Renick, because he was soon in demand to speak at conferences all over the country and attracted grant money from a dozen foundations that had either not heard about his work before or had admired it without necessarily taking the extra step to fund it.

Renick routinely blew audiences away with the power of his

presentations, which gathered all the techniques he'd picked up in the classroom and overlaid them with an unshakeable enthusiasm and sense of purpose. The rapturous receptions he received were about more than public speaking skills, though. According to Burns, they reinforced a powerful underlying message: that if you work harder than everyone else and are not obsessed with getting credit for it, you can achieve just about anything.

Smart communication has always been a vital part of the student success movement; it's rarely enough to show professors and administrators a bunch of data readouts and expect them to support changes that go against their cultural grain. Likewise, it's rarely enough to tell students struggling to scrape by that the data gives them a better-than-even chance of graduating. Much better if they *feel* part of something special, something infectious and irresistible, something they can sense in the air as soon they step onto campus. "I would wildly celebrate every little success," Larry Abele said of his time as provost of Florida State. The celebrations not only validated what he was doing; they shifted the mood from one where struggling students felt foolish for thinking they could possibly succeed to one where they felt foolish for ever thinking they couldn't.

Georgia State absorbed these lessons early on and used them not only to celebrate students but to let the world know the university existed in the first place. When the Atlanta Braves made the baseball playoffs in 1996 and ended up in a series against the St. Louis Cardinals, Carl Patton learned that a member of the Cardinals' ownership group had earned a business degree from Georgia State years earlier but never attended a graduation ceremony. So Patton dressed up in full university regalia, descended on the old Fulton County stadium, and had Elgar's "Pomp and Circumstance" march blasted over the sound system as he conferred an MBA on Drew Baur, live, on national television. He couldn't have bought himself better publicity.

Renick continued in much the same spirit, helping to craft news releases to celebrate every milestone, giving interviews to national news outlets and, above all, lecturing and talking to other universities from one end of the country to the other. He developed the ability to tailor his stump speech and accompanying slides to fit any time slot he was allocated, and he brought unceasing energy and enthusiasm to the task, coming across as both unassuming and utterly compelling. Tom Sugar credited him with putting Complete College America on the map—not quite single-handedly, perhaps, but not far off. "People around the country were doing good work, but they were not effective presenters. Tim was one of the most effective we could deploy," he said. "His moral commitment to the work just comes through."

Renick still met resistance, sometimes in the oddest and most surprising forms. "Academics like to think of themselves as the smartest people in the room," he explained, "and they think they know this field because they are in the classroom every day . . . It's very difficult to sway people." The pushback started at home, with members of the Georgia State faculty who accused him of grandstanding. They believed he was claiming altogether too much credit for an achievement that belonged to the university as a whole. An anonymous comment submitted to one of Renick's performance reviews made just this argument, asserting that his team was merely following instructions laid out for them in the strategic plan. The fact that Renick himself wrote the instructions in the plan was an irony lost not only on his detractor, but on much of the university, which had no idea of the extent of his involvement in the groundwork behind the student success breakthroughs.

Similar objections and skepticism abounded when Renick and other members of the Georgia State leadership went out on the road. Risa Palm remembered being taken aback when, at a meeting of TIAA Fellows in 2015 or 2016, the provost of Hofstra University questioned her results. "He gets up and says, you must have

restricted the number of students and raised your SAT requirement. It wouldn't happen otherwise," Palm recalled. (The provost,
Herman Berliner, had a different memory of the tone of the exchange, but acknowledged: "It is possible that I may have raised
some questions about the data or the results, which is expected of
an academic.")

When Renick gave his standard presentation at a symposium
in San Diego in 2018, a philosophy professor with strikingly long
hair pulled into a ponytail jumped up to say he had questions and
wanted to see more material, hundreds of pages of it ideally, to understand what the numbers meant. How could Renick be sure the
programs he'd enacted were responsible for the positive outcomes
he was claiming? Were the graphs he'd displayed drawn accurately, or did they exaggerate the jumps in student performance?
"I don't mean to take away from the presentation in any way," the
professor said, even though he appeared to be doing exactly that,
"but some of the facts and figures need more context. Since I teach
critical thinking for a living, that's something I notice quite a lot."

Renick didn't skip a beat. He gave the professor, Chris Nagel of
Stanislaus State in California's Central Valley, a website address
where he could lose himself in reports and charts to his heart's
content, and moved swiftly on to the next question.

10

THE FEELING IS MUTUAL

Like many tech entrepreneurs, Andrew Magliozzi has a vivid memory of the eureka moment when he stumbled on his big idea. It was 2014, he was recovering from surgery in a La-Z-Boy at his house in Boston, and he was talking to his friend Kirk Daulerio about their common passion: helping more kids go to college.

Magliozzi was, by his own description, a self-hating Harvard grad who couldn't decide if he wanted to be a business guru or a nonprofit do-gooder. Like his father and uncle, for many years the infectiously entertaining hosts of NPR's *Car Talk*, he had a notion that he could bring joy to aspects of life that most people consider mundane, but he wasn't yet sure how to apply that to his own life and career. He'd spent several years running a successful tutoring company out of Harvard Square and also had a nonprofit website to help kids pool their knowledge and collaborate on study projects. Daulerio, meanwhile, was a first-generation college student who had spent most of his career in admissions only to grow jaded by it. Inspiring high schoolers to see a future full of possibility and excitement remained thrilling to him, but after several years working for elite institutions, including the University of Pennsylvania and Bowdoin College, he was tired of saying no far more than he ever got to say yes. Lately, he'd come to joke that his business card should read: "College admissions officer: crushing dreams since 1863."

Together, Magliozzi and Daulerio knew they wanted to use technology to make college more accessible. Daulerio remembered how clueless he had been as a teenager applying for an athletic scholarship at a whole jumble of schools, and he wanted to help younger first-generation students avoid the mistakes he'd made. "Beyond that," Magliozzi said, "we had no idea what the 'it' would be." The conversation drifted to Magliozzi's tutoring company, and the difficulty he had in reaching students because they wouldn't respond to emails or phone calls and often texted at ungodly hours of the night. Idly, Magliozzi said he wished he could build a robot to handle the communications for him. Better still, what if there was some crazy way students could *text* their way into college? "Before I could say, that's the stupidest idea that ever came out of my mouth," Magliozzi remembered, "Kirk said, 'Yes! Let's do that.'"

Such was the spark that would eventually push the boundaries of student success into the unexplored terrain of artificial intelligence and establish Georgia State, once again, as the pioneering institution in the field. But it took a while to get there.

At first, Magliozzi and Daulerio imagined they were building a virtual college counseling service. They would gather information from prospective students and use it to build a list of colleges that looked like a good fit. They wouldn't ask the students to fill in forms or answer email questionnaires, because they knew that wouldn't work. Rather, they created a mascot, Oli the Owl, to ask fifteen basic questions by text message and give at least the appearance of being a purely technological beast that could think and interact with the students by itself. In reality, in those early days, Daulerio was "the bot behind the curtain," feeding Oli answers to students' questions and marshaling all the information about colleges and their requirements.

Where Magliozzi and Daulerio struggled was in finding a meaningful connection between their student clients and the target colleges. They weren't interested in selling information about students, because that crossed ethical lines. But they did need someone at each institution who would be willing to reach out to the ones they had identified as promising candidates and engage them in conversation. And they weren't finding any takers. "Universities absolutely did not want to talk to the students," Magliozzi recalled. "They said, if it's a small number, maybe. If it's a large number of people, no."

Just one piece of feedback offered a glimmer of hope. If Magliozzi and Daulerio could *automate* the conversation, some of their interlocutors might be interested to see where that led. And the interlocutor that showed by far the most interest in that avenue was Scott Burke, the director of admissions at Georgia State.

For almost as long as he had been in the job, Burke had seized on Georgia State's growing reputation to recruit students as widely and as creatively as possible. He wasn't content to let individual admissions counselors reach out to high school students in their target areas at random, as they always had. He hired an external marketing and communications team to study the data and find out with some degree of scientific certainty where the most promising recruiting grounds were. The Atlanta area was of course a major focus, along with the rest of Georgia and neighboring states—Florida, Alabama, the Carolinas, and Tennessee. But Burke also discovered vivid interest among high schoolers in Texas, New York, Chicago, and Washington, DC. "These were people either with a family connection to Atlanta, or looking for an urban school of a type they didn't have at home," he said.

Since he was open to new ideas, Burke was happy to respond when a Boston-area startup invited him to join a free forum for university admissions officers and interact with an artificial intelligence chatbot named Oli the Owl to learn about students who might be a good fit. By this point, Magliozzi and Daulerio had a name for their company, AdmitHub, and were assiduously courting members of the University Innovation Alliance whose pioneering spirit seemed to align with their own.

Burke was interested but skeptical at first. He, like so many other members of the student success team, had been a first-generation college student, and he had no problem with the idea of offering applicants extra support. He had vivid memories of the peer group that had helped him through the college application process when he was in high school in Amesbury, Massachusetts. Neither of his working-class parents could take on that role because they did not know the right questions to ask. It made sense to him to involve adult professionals in matching students with suitable colleges. But an artificial intelligence device that could generate conversation without human intervention? That wasn't something he'd ever considered.

Then it occurred to him that the chatbot might play a role in attacking a *different* problem affecting Georgia State's freshman classes: the fact that a startling number of students who confirmed they were accepting a place at Georgia State were failing to show up on their first day—or at all. Burke and Tim Renick had been discussing the issue at length, because the number of no-shows had doubled over the previous five years and now accounted for a staggering 18 percent of each incoming class. Burke and Renick used National Student Clearinghouse data to track the no-shows of 2015, about 600 students in all, of whom 278 failed to attend classes at *any* college over the following year. Academics were not at issue, because the students had an average high-school GPA of 3.34. But money and lack of family support almost certainly were. More than 70 percent of them were lower-income, and more than 75 percent nonwhite. It seemed likely that the complications of filling financial aid forms, signing up for university services, meeting payment deadlines, and providing proof of immunization records had in some way defeated these otherwise promising students. Could the chatbot be harnessed to a solution that had otherwise eluded them?

The phenomenon was hardly unique to Georgia State. Two nationally renowned researchers, Lindsay Page and Benjamin Castleman, had given it a name, "summer melt." And Georgia

State's melt rate was pretty typical. Page and Castleman found that as many as one in five high school students who enrolled in college backed out before the start of freshman year "as a result of unforeseen challenges." Often, these students would receive inadequate guidance from high school counselors, then lose access to that guidance altogether once the school year was over. They couldn't easily seek alternative help from their prospective colleges, because they weren't physically there yet, and any offices they might try to reach were either overwhelmed or short-staffed over the summer, or both. In some cases, students would not realize they had paperwork to fill out at all. In other cases, they would find the paperwork overwhelming, particularly the financial aid forms, which Page and Castleman described in a 2014 book as "daunting for college-educated parents, let alone students who are the first in their family to go to college." Sometimes, the process itself would act as a deterrent to kids already harboring doubts that they belonged in college at all.

Clearly, summer melt was a class issue. Page and Castleman cited a 2002 study of Fulton County, Georgia, the heart of metro Atlanta, which showed a melt rate of 37 percent for low-income students and just 7 percent for everyone else. One obstinate structural problem was that the very people who needed financial aid the most, those with an annual family income of $50,000 or less, were the ones pressed by the federal government to provide the most detailed information. They had to fill out a four-page form detailing income, assets, expenses, and tax status, an onerous and complex process, while everyone else could simply sign a one-page statement confirming they were above the $50,000 cutoff. The costs of this socioeconomic disparity were stark. Summer melt kids who might otherwise have powered their way to a degree and a middle-class life typically drifted into minimum-wage jobs in retail or fast food, if they found work at all.

Page and Castleman's book became required reading in the Georgia State student success office, and it triggered considerable soul-searching about the way the university was reaching out to prospective students. Renick calculated that those admitted would typically receive about three hundred emails from dozens of different campus offices, with little or no differentiation between the ones they could safely ignore and those alerting them to hard deadlines for financial aid, housing, and other vital components of their future campus life. Most of these emails were never opened, and even the ones that were did not necessarily offer the help students needed. FAFSA, the Free Application for Federal Student Aid, became known in the student success office as "the five-letter F-word," not only because students struggled to complete it, but because in more than one-third of cases the government would follow up with requests for verification and a few more students would melt away as a result.

Georgia State did not close its offices over the summer, but as its student population swelled it found itself unable handle the traffic or coordinate efforts between different departments. "Our admissions officers were overmatched. Their inboxes were stuffed," Burke remembered. Students would get bounced between offices for tuition, billing, financial aid, and registration. Sometimes offices acting independently of the admissions staff would send out bad information, or deliver instructions for a step in the process that many of the email recipients had already completed. "We'd have to urge people not to send out a 'have you sent your FAFSA' message to students who had already finished theirs," Burke said, "because we'd get deluged with calls from students worried that something had gone wrong when nothing had."

Magliozzi and Daulerio not only devoured the summer melt book; they called Lindsay Page at the University of Pittsburgh and proposed working on a solution together. The book confirmed what Magliozzi had experienced firsthand in his tutoring service—that phone and email were not nearly as effective in reaching students as texting or social media platforms. Texting was best of all, since it did not require a student to have access to a computer or even a smart phone, and did not require the counselor to "friend" a student or jump through other social media hoops before initiating contact. The question they asked Page was this: what if, instead of using Oli to determine what colleges a student should apply to, they deployed him later in the process to text deadline reminders and other vital information to students who had already chosen where they wanted to go? Page loved the idea, and together she and AdmitHub started scouting for a university willing to let them conduct a trial.

Scott Burke was one of the first people they approached, and he didn't hesitate. "I immediately said, we need to be your beta partner," he recalled. He'd already been thinking about a texting solution to summer melt and had looked at a service called Signal-Vine. But SignalVine wasn't a chatbot. It required a human being to manage the messages, and Burke worried that he didn't have anywhere close to the manpower he'd need to interact with an applicant pool of more than sixteen thousand. The opportunity to help develop a cutting-edge new technology and shape it to the university's needs, as Georgia State had already done with predictive analytics, was far more appealing. If it worked, it wouldn't just ease a logistical nightmare. It would further burnish Georgia State's reputation as a national leader in higher education.

Magliozzi and Daulerio felt similarly excited. "We got off the phone and said, *My God, they are the perfect partner.* More than anything, because of the demographic makeup of that school," Magliozzi said. "There was some desperation there as well. They had a significant challenge, a problem that was running away from them. As an entrepreneur, that's the kind of partner you want, someone who is willing to be innovative and let us be in the driver's seat with them. It was a match made in heaven."

AdmitHub, at this stage, was still a shoestring operation, funded only by friends and family, so Magliozzi and Daulerio had a lot riding on success at Georgia State. Together with the university, they identified fourteen different steps that students needed to take between February, when Georgia State sent out its admission letters, and the start of the fall semester. They pulled together an initial list of two hundred and fifty questions and answers, which they fine-tuned with Page and with Hunter Gehlbach, an educational psychologist and linguistic consultant from the University of California, Santa Barbara. Together they constructed a flowchart of exchanges with the chatbot, which they thought of as a matrix of possibilities akin to a choose-your-own-adventure, not a straightforward briefing book or website FAQ.

The chatbot wouldn't be Oli the Owl anymore. He was now Pounce the Panther, in deference to the Georgia State mascot. And he had a personality—playful, friendly, engaging, and big on emojis—so he wouldn't be all business. "One of our core principles," Magliozzi said, "was to infuse joy into the process. A lot of messages colleges traditionally send are very transactional: Do this by this date or else . . . Almost none of the enrollment process is optimized for happiness."

By February 2016, they were ready to launch, but Georgia State wasn't. The university's legal department was still sorting out the details of the contract and double-checking that there would be no infringement of student privacy. A week went by, then two, then four, and Magliozzi's anxiety started to flare. "Already, we had no idea if the chatbot was going to work," he said. "It was a recipe for sleepless nights and gray hair."

When April rolled around and the procurement process was still incomplete, Magliozzi thought it might be too late. Students were already enrolling for the fall semester, and the May 1 deadline for committing to a place in the freshman class was looming. Page was more relaxed than he was—in her previous summer melt intervention work she'd typically been most active in June and July—but she didn't exclude the possibility that they'd be missing people and diminishing their impact because of the delay. Magliozzi did not find this analysis remotely uplifting.

In mid-April the AdmitHub team had the green light at last, only to run into an entirely new set of problems. The questions they had anticipated were not at all the ones the students ended up asking. What threw them more than anything was the *form* of the questions, if they were even expressed as questions at all. "Nobody asked, *How do I apply for financial aid?*" Magliozzi said. "They said, *I have no money.* Or: *What the heck is FAFSA?*" Until the AdmitHub team adjusted for these variations, the chatbot stalled, and in the rush to improvise it did not always provide accurate information.

About a week into the trial, Magliozzi flew to San Diego for an ed tech conference and sat down with Tim Renick, who was also attending. "I was honest about the errors we were making. We were screwing up," Magliozzi said. "We were getting most of it right, but we were screwing up. We're not perfect."

Renick, as it turned out, was not nearly as anxious as Magliozzi, because Georgia State had invested only seed money in the trial and had nothing much to lose if it didn't work out. Renick also happened to think highly of Magliozzi and had faith that his team would iron out the problems as they arose. The one point on which Renick (and Georgia State's legal department) insisted was that since the chatbot was an official university platform, it could not be allowed to disseminate information that was not 100 percent correct. "We have to have more control and better vetting of the writing of the responses," he recalled saying. Magliozzi took this criticism as a gut-punch and half-expected Renick to tell him there and then that Georgia State was pulling the plug. But Renick remembered walking away from the meeting feeling that things were going well.

It was Renick's instincts that proved more reliable. The chatbot could learn as fast as its programmers, and the mistakes that arose did not stay mistakes for long. It took some time for students to understand the prompts and realize they could engage in actual dialogue. Once they figured that out, though, many became enthusiastic users, not least because they knew they would have answers to their questions in a matter of seconds. Participants interacted with Pounce fourteen times on average over the course of the trial, and the more active among them had closer to a hundred interactions. Very few opted to unsubscribe. Students would treat Pounce almost like a friend, sharing their personal fears and aspirations, laughing and joking and apologizing when they took their time to respond to a prompt. Pounce, on the other hand, was always on hand—unlike the university offices, which were wide open when chatbot traffic was lowest (10 o'clock in the morning), but emphatically not when traffic was highest (1 o'clock at night).

The bot would ask nonintrusive personal questions—*What is your spirit animal? What's your favorite emoji?*—and offer a lot of positive feedback. When students completed their FAFSA form, for example, Pounce would send an animated GIF of Tiny Fey making it rain money. "The seemingly useless stuff is what builds the trust," Magliozzi said. "If you were talking to a person, you might think, *Oh, he took the time to ask me this thing, it must matter. I'm cared for.* But of course it took no time to come up with these things because it wasn't a person, it was a robot."

The mistakes, when they happened, were often technological glitches, not something to do with actual content. AdmitHub was supposed to make sure, for example, that if students did not respond to an initial query about financial aid forms they would receive a reminder after twenty-four hours and a second reminder after forty-eight. But the AdmitHub team inadvertently set the interval at twenty-four *seconds* instead of twenty-four hours "That," Magliozzi said, "had interesting ramifications."

Sometimes, it was the chatbot's imperfect efforts to think for itself that proved its undoing. One exasperated student texted: *I hate you.* Since Pounce didn't know what hate was, it jumped to what it thought was the nearest match, *I love you*, and responded: *The feeling is mutual.* Pounce suffered a similar confusion when a student texted: *I'm dropping out.* Nobody on the team had anticipated that students would be using that term before they had so much as set foot on campus, and Pounce was once again left floundering. *That's great*, it answered. *Keep it up.*

The concern these mistakes caused was not that students would take offense. They rarely had time to, because a human minder would invariably follow up with a *Sorry, what I meant to say was . . .* Rather, the worry was that Pounce would promise something Georgia State couldn't deliver, like a nonexistent scholarship, and thus land the university in financial or legal trouble. "We had to be very cautious and slow at the beginning so we wouldn't make those kinds of mistakes," Burke said. Magliozzi was painfully aware of the dangers and couldn't help but take every slipup personally. "After a while you don't observe what's working anymore," he said. "All you think about is, boy, we're bound for failure."

Things *were* working, though, and slowly the AdmitHub team stopped feeling quite so sick about the quirks in the system and found ways to laugh at them. The specificity of the questions was always fascinating. *Can I keep a salamander in my dorm? Is there a Chipotle on campus? Is Kanye coming to spring fest?* If the AdmitHub team could find a reliable answer on the Georgia State website, they would provide it. Otherwise, they'd have to wing it with something vague (*there are definitely burritos to be found!*) or refer the query to a university office and wait for an answer. Pretty soon, team members became founts of trivia for after-work conversation. (Yes, salamanders are permitted, as long their tanks are less than ten gallons. And, sorry, no Kanye, but enjoy the Bengali new year celebration.)

By the time the trial was over, the need for human intervention had dwindled and Pounce could handle almost every question by itself. The overall results, meanwhile, were remarkable. The trial indicated that if the chatbot were extended to the full student population, Georgia State's summer melt rate would go down 21 percent. The cost of running the chatbot was negligible, no more than $15 per student. The revenue the university could ex-pect to receive from students who would now show up for class far outstripped the system's cost.

Magliozzi has a vivid memory—as vivid as the eureka moment in the La-Z-Boy—of opening an email from Lindsay Page with the good news about the trial results. At the time, he was desper-ate for some proof of concept to satisfy the venture capitalists he'd been courting to fund his company, and when the email landed AdmitHub was just eight days away from going bankrupt. He'd never felt so relieved in his life. "I've been practicing meditation for a decade," Magliozzi said, "but one thing that bothers me is when I ask others to put their reputations and livelihoods on the line."

One thing that worked to AdmitHub's advantage was tim-ing, because 2016 was the year when venture capital companies fell in love with chatbots in the commercial sphere, too. A year or two earlier, Magliozzi and Daulerio might have struggled for funding, and a year or two later the venture capitalists might have steered them away from the education space because it came with too many strings attached. "Higher education is a very conserva-tive industry when it comes to implementing new technology," Daulerio said. "And they are right to be conservative . . . If a tech-nology goes wrong or turns students off, it's a reflection on them."

As it was, Georgia State took the chatbot technology and ran with it, increasing its automated texting traffic close to tenfold over the next eighteen months and reducing its summer melt rate not just by 21 percent, as it had in the trial, but by 37 percent over the full student population. The technology also provided the university with new insights into problems it had been seeing for years, but had not fully understood because students hadn't previ-ously volunteered their thoughts the way they were doing now.

The reason some of them weren't turning in their FAFSA forms on time was not procrastination, as Renick's team had of-ten assumed. Rather, they were hitting genuine obstacles, like an estranged parent they couldn't reach for a required signature or for immunization records. These insights, in turn, led to policy changes to ease the students' burden. In 2019, for example, the university rolled out a bio-bus at freshman orientation to offer shots to students who still needed them. "It made no sense," Renick said, "to let first-generation, low-income students leave orientation without immunizations in the expectation that—what? They will just go to their rolodex to find a qualified physician?"

The advent of artificial intelligence technology was not universally welcomed. Some faculty administrators began to worry what was next: humanoid tutors, maybe, or a university run top to bottom by robots. Such sentiments generally reflected the anxiety that had greeted every one of Georgia State's technology-driven innovations: a fear of *replacement*. Professors shuddered as they read articles put out by Google's Singularity University telling them they would no longer be a "sage on the stage" in their classrooms but rather a "guide on the side"—a powerless observer watching the takeover of virtual reality–based immersive environments, cognitive enhancement drugs, and computer-generated learning "playlists."

The students actually using the chatbot did not think in nearly such dystopian terms. To them, the technology was a practical tool, a deft way of sidestepping many of the frustrations of dealing with university bureaucracy, exactly as it was intended. "I think it's amazing," said Jasmine Twine, a navy veteran who went back to school in her mid-twenties and transferred into Georgia State in 2018. "It's consistent about sending reminders, but not to the point where it's overwhelming. To me, that's saying: we care, we're trying to make sure you're on track. That's really it."

Over time, it became apparent that some students *preferred* talking to a chatbot than to a human being. When AdmitHub asked them why, they would say it was because Pounce didn't make them feel judged. In one sense, this was perfectly logical in the context of a university admissions process where students were quite literally being judged day in and day out. But there was also an illusory quality to it, because the chatbot was a creation of those same adult professionals—and everyone knew it.

The students' comfort in interacting with the chatbot became only more pronounced as AdmitHub was invited to extend Pounce to the entirety of the undergraduate experience. This new project, made possible by a grant from the Dell Foundation, presented complexities far greater than addressing summer melt alone. Now, Pounce needed to learn about different pathways to dozens of majors, the names and layouts of university buildings, the names of key contact people across a wide range of administrative offices, and so on. "If you're just dealing with enrollment you can largely stick to the highways," Magliozzi said, "but for retention and student success there's a lot more travel on the back roads."

From the students' point of view, though, the chatbot remained refreshingly straightforward. Twine was selected to participate in the pilot study and found that the prompts not only alerted her to important deadlines but also motivated her to meet them more efficiently. "Pounce encouraged me to beat the rush and see my academic advisor to help pick fall classes," she said. "I was going to wait a little bit, but then I thought, *Great, let me decide now what fall classes I want so when registration opens I'm ready.*"

For many students, Pounce acted as a campus friend and confidant, always there to lend an ear and offer help. Whatever troubles they were going through—money worries, a death in the family, depression—the chatbot would often learn about them first. That didn't mean the technology was replacing the university's counseling services. Rather, it alerted counselors to problems they might never have discovered otherwise and enabled them to help students overcome them. Again, this idea triggered waves of anxiety in some quarters. Was Pounce acting as a university spy, gathering otherwise unattainable data from students for some nefarious, un-declared purpose?

It didn't help that controversies about the data-collecting prac-tices of Facebook, Google, and Amazon were swirling at the same time, and the public was learning to grow more mistrustful of cell phones, laptops, and artificial intelligence devices like Siri and Alexa. Still, the anxiety was largely misplaced, because the univer-sity operated under strict federal privacy rules and was interested only in helping students, not in collecting or divulging sensitive personal information. "I don't think of our technology as being for broadcasting information but for listening," Magliozzi said, and the university concurred.

These were the issues that Georgia State's legal affairs depart-ment had weighed with great care at the start of the 2016 chatbot trial, and nothing had changed in the interim. Pounce served as a user-friendly interface with the administration, no more and no less. To the extent that it encouraged reticent students to speak up, it served as a useful icebreaker and a way of unearthing hidden problems the university might not otherwise have recognized or resolved. Renick drew a parallel with a similar anxiety that arose in 2012 about data collected for the proactive advising service. He had to spend time explaining that, no, we're not monitoring what time students are returning to their dorms or what they are or-dering from the cafeteria. "We believe there is a line between our role as an education institution . . . and an Orwellian world where every moment is controlled by the state, which is not our vision at all," he said.

It was not just the student success shop that saw the chatbot's potential. In 2018, a relatively new administrator, Wolfgang Schloer, found a way to apply the technology to one of his own ar-eas of responsibility, recruitment for study abroad. He won fund-ing for an initial year-long project to devise questions and answers for the chatbot—everything from course availability to passport and visa requirements—and integrate them into the Dell-funded pilot project. Target students received a weekly bulletin, together with entertaining trivia about overseas travel and alerts about study abroad fairs.

Even in the trial stage, the results indicated that the chatbot could significantly increase the number of student queries and, at the same time, free the study abroad staff from answering routine questions so they had more time to spend one-on-one with people already committed to going overseas. "This is like triage," said Schloer, whose title at Georgia State was associate provost for international initiatives. He found it particularly powerful that the chatbot was seen as judgment free, since students who had never traveled overseas were often afraid that human advisors would find their questions stupid.

One of the important lessons of the chatbot was that there *were* no stupid questions. Rather, the burden now fell on university administrators to have the imagination and foresight to anticipate what students needed to know—then remove themselves from sight so the machine could work at maximum effectiveness.

11

A HUNDRED YEARS FROM NOW

In November 2013, Mark Becker was in Washington, DC, to accept an award for Georgia State's student success initiatives when he received an unexpected phone call from Ceasar Mitchell, the president of the Atlanta City Council.

"I want to tell everybody Georgia State should get it," Mitchell said. "Do you want it?"

He had never called Becker before, and Becker had no idea what he was talking about.

"Get what?" Becker said. "What's going on?"

"You don't know?"

Becker had spent the day inside a cavernous conference hotel being feted by the Association of Public Land Grant Universities, and the big news had passed him by. The Atlanta Braves were leaving Turner Field, their baseball stadium less than a mile south of the state capitol, and that meant a vast parcel of land within spitting distance of Downtown Atlanta was up for grabs.

The area wasn't prime real estate, exactly, because it was depressed and had a troubled history stretching back more than half a century. But land of any kind around Downtown was hard to come by, and if the choice was between converting Turner Field into a college sports complex or a casino, Mitchell was in no doubt he wanted the sports complex. He had been pushing for years to breathe life into the neighborhoods around the stadium, and a university struck him as a far stronger long-term proposition than a commercial venture that might flail or go under at a moment's notice.

"Is it something you could be interested in?" Mitchell asked.

"Absolutely it's something we are interested in," Becker said.

He did not need to be asked twice.

Georgia State saw the Turner Field opportunity as little short of providential. Not only could the site serve as a permanent home for the university's football team, which had been sharing space with the Atlanta Falcons and would soon need to move on; it also presented an opportunity to consolidate the scattered pieces of Georgia State's athletics program in a single location. On top of that, six thousand students were parking at Turner Field every week—game times excepted—and taking a shuttle bus to and from class. The last thing the university wanted was to lose that access, because the Downtown parking structures were jam-packed and student numbers were increasing all the time.

The site also appealed to Becker's loftier ambitions—to integrate Georgia State more fully into the fabric of the city of Atlanta and enlarge the social mobility engine the university had already set in motion. Taking over Turner Field could mean reviving the neighborhoods of Summerhill, Mechanicsville, and Peoplestown, which had been hollowed out and cut off from the rest of the city when the highways were built in the 1950s and 1960s, and then neglected by various sporting ventures that had taken up residence since. It could mean jobs and educational opportunities for a new constituency of underserved Atlantans. It was, in Becker's mind, one more way to break the imaginative bounds of a modern-day university, one more way to establish Georgia State's reputation as a force for meritocracy in a vastly unequal society.

It was also a daunting challenge. For all the sporting glory the stadium had witnessed—the 1996 Olympics (when it was known as Centennial Olympic Stadium) and the nine consecutive times the Braves reached the baseball playoffs—the area was an asphalt wasteland with fetid, overheated air, sky-high asthma rates, and a drainage system prone to flooding with every new barrage of Southern rain. For decades, going back to the days of Atlanta-Fulton County Stadium and Hank Aaron's record-beating 715th major-league home run, the sports fans had treated the neighborhood with indifference or fear, dawdling only as long as it took to gun up their cars and join the slow crawl back to the interstate. "Outside this ballpark," Rebecca Burns wrote in a haunting piece for *Atlanta* magazine a few months before the Braves announced they were decamping to the suburbs, "there's nothing to do and nowhere to go but home."

Again and again, city officials and business leaders had promised investment dollars and redevelopment projects, but these proved illusory. In the run-up to the Olympics, some of the boarded storefronts along Georgia Avenue were renovated and made to look like the plausible beginnings of a revival, but the boards went back up as soon as the hoopla was over and the graffiti, weeds, and rubble soon returned, too. The Braves made a lot of noise about their $100 million-a-year impact on the Atlanta economy and gave local neighborhood associations a cut of the profits from the parking lots, but the money made no visible difference and the city showed only sporadic interest in partnering with the team to craft a more solid arrangement.

Georgia State wanted to set a very different tone, but it couldn't do it alone. To afford the sixty-seven-acre site, the university needed to team up with a commercial real estate developer. It needed to forge alliances with Fulton County as well as the city of Atlanta, because the public agency in control of the Turner Field site was controlled by a consortium of both. Then there was sporting history to consider. The old county stadium might have been razed, but the wall that Hank Aaron's record-beating home run cleared was still standing and considered a holy relic.

Becker worked fast and came up with a plan to split the property three ways, with Georgia State taking one piece outright and the chosen developer, Carter & Associates, buying one piece and leasing another. Between them, they formulated plans not only for an athletics complex but also for student housing, cafes, restaurants, a desperately needed grocery store, and a pharmacy; in other words, an entire community.

All this was music to the ears of Ceasar Mitchell, who had fought for the area for years and whose sister-in-law was president of the Summerhill neighborhood association. It also delighted Kasim Reed, Atlanta's mayor, who made a public show of entertaining at least two other proposals but told Becker early on that he was all in for Georgia State. "I know the difference that seeing a university, as opposed to a bunch of vacant parking lots, is going to do for kids," Reed said on the day the sale became official in 2016. "It is about reinventing the dense neighborhoods and walkable street grids that [this area] had before . . . Goodbye, asphalt eyesores. Hello, twenty-first century."

Such heady ambition and high-stakes political maneuvering would not have been possible without an earlier decision, made in the face of considerable skepticism and campus opposition, to start a football team.

The Georgia State leadership itself had resisted for a long time. Whenever Carl Patton was asked about it during his tenure, he would say: "Not in my lifetime." He knew that football was considered a religion in the South, the focal point around which many "real universities" organized themselves, but the way he saw it, Georgia State needed too many other things first. Some people remembered him saying: *Not over my dead body.*" But Patton was rarely that adamant about anything, and it was not what he meant. He meant only that he couldn't imagine a football program for as long as he was president. And he was almost—but not quite—right about that.

The key difference-maker was Tom Lewis, Georgia State's

political lobbyist, who believed football would win Georgia State love and respect that it couldn't otherwise get from the legislature and the business community. "It's all about university pride," Lewis said. "I'd see all these CEOs wearing Bulldog hats. Why not Panther hats?" Football, Lewis told the president, would bring unparalleled publicity and help give the campus the identity it lacked. It would encourage more students, particularly rural white students, to make Georgia State their first-choice school. It would redress Georgia State's gender imbalance, which at the time tilted 60–40 toward women undergraduates. "The alumni support it. The students are for it," Lewis told Patton at a 2006 meeting in which he, Jerry Rackliffe, and Edgar Torbert, the assistant provost for budget and facilities, orchestrated a full-court press. "They won't play their first game until after you retire. If it's a success, you started it. If it's a failure, you weren't here to see it through."

Patton agreed, reluctantly, as long as alumni and other donors were willing to front $1 million to get the ball rolling. Lewis raised the money in less than a month. Patton also insisted that the student government sign off on a $200 increase in fees that an outside consultancy had deemed necessary to fund the program. The students voted in favor without hesitation. As a last step, Lewis recruited Dan Reeves, the former head coach of the Atlanta Falcons who happened to be a customer at Lewis's neighborhood barber shop, to conduct a feasibility assessment of his own. Patton told Reeves that no was an acceptable answer, but Reeves came back with a resounding yes. And Patton finally stopped fighting.

By the time the first game was played in September 2010, to a sell-out crowd including several of Georgia's top business and political leaders, Patton was no longer president. But he told Lewis: "We made the right decision." Admittedly, it didn't always look that way over the first few seasons, as the team struggled and attendance scraped along at 50 percent of capacity. "Why were people surprised that nobody showed up to the games," one of the naysayers, Lauren Adamson, asked many years later, "when they know our students have to work on Saturday afternoons?" Still, Lewis stuck to the view that the program had value beyond gate receipts. "We didn't have to be successful at football, because it got us in the papers anyway," he said. "For forty-two weeks out of the year, it was a brilliant idea. The other ten weeks—well . . ."

The team eventually improved, as did attendance, to the relief of Mark Becker, whose competitive instincts would not let him have it any other way. But Lewis was correct in saying that success on the field was not what mattered most. Football made Georgia State a player with the board of regents and with the city, county, and state governments. It might seem hard, in a less football-obsessed part of the world, to fathom the extraordinary difference that a bunch of burly guys tossing a stitched leather ball could make to a university. But other Georgia schools without a foot-ball program had tried to earn respect by other means—growing bigger, for example—and almost never succeeded. "The only way you are important in the University System of Georgia," said Jeff Portnoy, an outspoken faculty leader at the Perimeter network of community colleges in the Atlanta suburbs, "is if you have a foot-ball team."

Not only did the advent of football inspire Ceasar Mitchell to lobby Mark Becker to take over Turner Field; it also spurred the state into approving tens of millions of dollars in capital projects, greatly widening the university's footprint on Downtown Atlanta even before it started sending bulldozers south of the interstate. In many ways football was the key that unlocked the vision that Becker had brought to Atlanta: to tie the university's educational mission to a wholesale reinvention of the twenty-first-century city.

There was a time, not so long ago, when the area around Down-town appeared destined for a very different fate. The banks and insurance companies bailed out in the 1980s and 1990s, and so did big retailers like Rich's, once the biggest department store in the South. The elegant Art Deco Fairlie-Poplar neighborhood was left all but derelict. Sweet Auburn, previously known for its thriving black business community, was reduced to boarded store-fronts, churches bereft of congregations, and abandoned relics of the civil rights era. What saved it all was the university, which started expanding in earnest just as the business community was jumping ship, filling many of the vacant buildings with class-rooms, administrative offices, performance spaces, and student residences. "This part of town would fall apart if we weren't here," said Jerry Rackliffe, the university's finance chief who oversaw many of the key redevelopment projects. "We are the anchor. We generate everything."

The transformation began under Carl Patton, with the pur-chase and restoration of the Rialto theater, followed by a flurry of other projects that expanded the university's boundaries west of Peachtree Street, Atlanta's principal artery, for the very first time. Two buildings next to the Rialto became the music school, and a third building, the former headquarters of the Citizens & Southern National Bank, fell into Georgia State's lap thanks to a series of bank mergers and the generosity of the outgoing chief executive whose son was a business school alum. A grateful Geor-gia State moved its business school into the upper floors of the grand, fourteen-story Art Deco palace and leased the ornate lobby back to the newly merged bank—first NationsBank, then Bank of America—for its Downtown branch office.

These first stirrings inspired a business development consor-tium, Central Atlanta Progress, to renovate a dilapidated park along Peachtree Street as a way of encouraging others to follow Georgia State's lead. And it worked. Woodruff Park, named af-ter the long-serving president of Coca-Cola who had been instru-mental in pressuring the Atlanta business community to embrace Martin Luther King, became the hub of a cluster of new teaching buildings, as well as coffee shops, art galleries and, eventually, a row of eclectic student-friendly restaurants along a pedestrian-ized stretch of Broad Street. "The return of students walking the streets was huge," said A.J. Robinson, president of Central Atlanta Progress, "a throwback to what Downtown Atlanta was fifty or sixty years ago."

Soon, Georgia State was in the throes of a property buying spree. Some of its purchases, like the car dealership that became the Commons, were bargains pure and simple. Others relied on Tom Lewis's singular ability to lobby politicians and state agencies, and on Jerry Rackliffe's financial savvy. In the late 1990s, for example, Lewis and Rackliffe took an interest in an abandoned city jail on the corner of Piedmont Avenue and Decatur Street, thinking it would be ideal for a new science center. Lewis learned that the property belonged not to the city, as was widely assumed, but to the state, and he asked Zell Miller, then the governor, if Georgia State could have it. For years, Miller and his successors blew hot and cold, largely out of fear of Tom Murphy, the septuagenarian speaker of the Georgia House, who was known to be looking for extra parking for the legislature and was likely to claim the site for himself if he ever learned it was available. By the time the deal was struck—after Murphy was voted out of office in 2002—Georgia State acquired the land only by agreeing to take over management of the state capitol's day care center. Lewis and Rackliffe privately called this the "land for children" swap.

The 2008 recession offered plentiful opportunities to acquire more buildings as businesses and commercial property prices collapsed. Georgia State had its own belt-tightening to contend with, of course, but it also kept separate ledgers for continuing budget items and one-time expenditures, which gave Rackliffe and his bosses some flexibility. If anything, the recessionary cutbacks freed up *more* cash, because every time someone was laid off it created a one-time saving that was split between the colleges (which claimed the unpaid salary) and the central administration (which claimed the unpaid health care, pension, and other benefits).

Often, it was a matter of being patient and seizing opportunities as they arose. When the Atlanta Life Insurance company, one of Atlanta's oldest and most venerated black-owned businesses, announced in 2007 that it was selling its building on Auburn Avenue, the asking price was $16 million. Rackliffe told them he could afford only $12 million, which they rejected. Two years later, in the midst of the recession, he offered $9 million, thinking they'd find the figure ridiculous, but they accepted. Georgia State repurposed the building to house its main administrative offices and welcome center, which opened in 2013, the university's centenary year, under the name Centennial Hall.

Another building, 55 Park Place on the east side of Woodruff Park, was financed by what Rackliffe called "a weird geeky accounting thing." The state auditors told him one year that Georgia State's $26 million revenue from summer tuition, normally entered into the books as a single item, now needed to be split between June, the end of the fiscal year, and July, the start of the new one. Immediately, Rackliffe asked: "Can I wait just one more year? I want to buy a building." When the auditors agreed, he took advantage of having $39 million in summer revenue for one freak year—the usual $26 million, plus half of the next year's—to make his purchase. As he often did, he leased out a portion of the building so the one-time expense would translate into steady revenue going forward.

Over time, an institution that had been close to invisible as a commuter school became impossible to miss, its logo emblazoned on building after building and stamped into the sidewalks beneath people's feet. The revenue that came with such visibility only increased as Downtown Atlanta became more desirable—not just to students, but to businesses, tourists, and Hollywood filmmakers. Parking spaces became a hot commodity, and Georgia State controlled a ton of them—the ubiquitous parking decks the university had owned for a couple of decades, and also the spaces that came with many of Rackliffe's building purchases. The buildings were attractive to film location scouts, whether they wanted a skyscraper for Spider-Man to scale (in the 2017 movie *Spider-Man:*

Homecoming) or a plausible office building for Ben Affleck (in *The Accountant*). Perhaps the most delicious of these filming escapades was the 2017 heist movie *Baby Driver*, in which a number of buildings that Georgia State acquired were dressed back up as the banks they'd once been, and robbed at gunpoint.

The political class picked up on the fact that the university was becoming an economic as well as an academic powerhouse. Nathan Deal, who served as governor from 2011 to 2019, was soon chipping in with state funds for the building spree, including $60 million toward a new law school that opened on the east side of Woodruff Park in 2015. "Every year that Georgia State proposed a capital project, they had consistent growth," Deal's chief of staff Chris Riley remembered. In an administration anxious to expand business opportunities there could be no higher praise. Indeed, Riley felt that investing in Georgia State was not only worth it, but "paid off tenfold."

The building and purchasing frenzy became almost too much for city hall, which had no permitting control over the university since it was a state entity, and no power to raise property taxes. (It was one reason Ceasar Mitchell was happy to encourage Georgia State to pursue growth opportunities on the other side of the interstate—to leave room for other businesses to come Downtown, too.) The boom was very good for the university's academic profile, however, and specifically for the student success project. Rackliffe found gaps here and there at the back of buildings to create extra classroom and lab space. With input from Tim Renick he also came up with an entirely new design for residential housing, aimed at lower-income students for whom every dollar in unmet financial need made a crucial difference in their ability to stay in school. The first residence to open after Renick became associate provost, Freshman Hall (later renamed Patton Hall), dispensed with apartment kitchens, which had been standard at older buildings like the Commons, and gave each student less than 200 square feet of study and sleeping space instead of 450 square feet. The cost was roughly the same as at the Commons, but the price tag included a meal plan and on-site cafeterias that stayed open twenty-four hours a day. That was not just a money saver, it also created an instant sense of community. "You go in there at two or two-thirty in the morning," Rackliffe said, "and two hundred people are in there, eating and studying and talking."

When the bill came due on Turner Field, Rackliffe had rent money coming in from businesses all over campus, plus film permit revenue, parking revenue, even a fund from commissions at the university bookstore. Georgia State's share of the tab was $22.8 million, plus another $20 million for the final renovation plan. The baseball field was converted for football—not rebuilt as originally envisaged—and a new baseball facility went up next door, incorporating the Hank Aaron wall.

In many ways, the logistics and financing turned out to be the easy part. Anti-gentrification demonstrators set up an encampment of about twenty tents outside Turner Field over the winter and spring of 2017, and many of them made noisy incursions into city hall and the lobby of Centennial Hall, five floors below Mark Becker's office. Ostensibly, the grievance was that the project could end up pricing long-term residents out of their homes. More immediately, the protesters were upset about the loss of what was known as the "community benefit agreement," the official name for the cash that the Braves had doled out each year from their parking revenues without worrying too much about what happened to it. Continuing the agreement was not an option, because Georgia State was a public entity and as such precluded by the gratuities clause of the Georgia constitution from offering handouts. Instead, the university, along with Carter, the developer, had been working with neighborhood groups on a variety of community support programs that, as they saw it, were likely to have a far greater impact.

This was no fig leaf operation. For years, Georgia State had made it a mission to foster good relations with the lower-income neighborhoods to the south and west of Downtown, making them both the subject and the beneficiary of urban research studies and a landing spot for graduating teachers from Georgia State's College of Education. Starting under Carl Patton's presidency, the university had also pioneered programs to bring college-level courses to the area's traditionally underperforming high schools, including Carver High in Peoplestown, less than a mile south of Turner Field. This was very much in keeping with the student success philosophy Tim Renick later elaborated—that when challenged, as one academic study of the program put it, "the underrepresented populations in higher education—first-generation, low SES [socio-economic status] background, students of color and black male students—will rise to the challenge." Graduation and college admission rates at these high schools soon increased dramatically.

Once the Turner Field project was underway, Georgia State reached out to the presidents of all the local neighborhood associations and sent representatives to public meetings to answer any and all questions—about public safety, traffic plans for football game days, rebuilding streets erased during the "slum clearances" of the 1950s and 1960s, and any number of other nuts-and-bolts issues. Bharath Parthasarathy of the university's legal department gave dozens of presentations to explain Georgia State's intentions, and he became personally involved in the neighborhood by joining the governance team of a local elementary school. Parthasarathy was consistently struck by how well attended, vibrant, and friendly the neighborhood meetings were. He got along with the neighborhood presidents and never doubted that they understood Georgia State's intentions to be with them for the long haul.

The protests appeared to be the work of a limited number of disgruntled residents out of sympathy with their own local leaders, joined by some well-known outside anti-gentrification protesters. Still, their indignation generated headlines, and put the university on the spot to find a response. Georgia State and Carter published the community engagement agreements they had signed, and the city of Atlanta, at Ceasar Mitchell's urging, set aside $10 million of its own for further community development. That did the trick; by the time the refurbished Georgia State stadium complex opened in August 2017, the protests had fizzled to nothing.

Two years later, a residence hall for 680 students opened directly across from the stadium, and a cluster of restaurants—a barbecue joint, a brew pub, an ice cream parlor, a hot dog outlet—popped up along Georgia Avenue. By then, the community response was more unambiguously positive. Students from the area were enrolling at Georgia State, the number of residents working for the university was increasing, and the crime rate was down markedly. Some attendees at neighborhood meetings expressed impatience that the changes were not coming fast enough, but Parthasarathy reminded them that Georgia State was not going anywhere and it was important to take the time to do things correctly.

That was Mark Becker's vision, too. "Baseball teams can move, but universities don't have a history of moving," he said. "We'll be here a hundred years from now." In his mind, the neighborhoods weren't just an interest group to placate; they were integral to the widening of Georgia State's circle of influence. Peoplestown and its neighbors didn't just need to be part of the solution. They needed to be part of the broader conversation.

One final piece Georgia State was anxious to put in place was a university convocation center, a single indoor facility that could host year-round graduation ceremonies, basketball games, concerts, and conferences. The university leadership saw a perfect spot for it: a lot just a few hundred yards from the stadium, almost exactly at the point where the Atlanta Connector and Interstate 20 intersected. A sorry-looking Department of Driver Services trailer had once sat there—it was where Mark Becker picked up his driver's license when he moved to Atlanta—but the land now lay vacant. This was nobody's idea of a scenic beauty spot, but the location was unbeatable, with plenty of space for parking, and the noise and the traffic fumes could easily be blocked out with the right building design.

Securing the site was far from straightforward, however. It already belonged to the state, which simplified things, but it was just a couple of highway overpasses away from the capitol and had attracted the interest of a number of other players. Foremost among these was the Georgia Building Authority, which was in charge of all state properties around the capitol and acted as both gatekeeper and potential bidder, because it was always looking for opportunities to acquire extra land and generate revenue through lease agreements. The GBA was certainly open to cutting a deal with Georgia State—it proposed acquiring the university's old football practice ground in exchange for the vacant lot—but it was also in no hurry. In 2014, Jerry Rackliffe offered $6.5 million for the lot, only to be informed that the GBA wasn't making any decisions until it saw what would happen to Turner Field. Once the Turner Field sale went through, GBA still wouldn't commit, because the governor's office was now thinking of using the land to build an office tower for community health and human services workers.

This was, in the end, a test of Georgia State's political clout. Had the university reached the same level of respect as Georgia Tech and the University of Georgia? Mark Becker and Tom Lewis thought it had, but this deal was the ultimate proof and it was eluding them. It wasn't until November 2017, after the Panthers had played their first game in the new stadium, that things moved decisively in their favor. Becker and Lewis sat down with Chris Riley, the governor's chief of staff, to remind him that they had been after the driver services land for a long time. And Riley stunned them by saying the land was theirs for the taking.

Riley didn't mention a price, and it became apparent as they talked that he meant Georgia State to have it for free. The office project was now off the table, he said. Georgia State's integrated vision was clearly the best fit for the neighborhood, and with the Turner Field project taking shape everyone could see the vision for themselves. The only thing the governor would ask in return was for permission to park construction vehicles on the site while a new judicial complex near the capitol was being completed.

"Tom and I looked at each other and thanked him," Becker remembered. "Once we were out of earshot, I said, 'Tom, I think he just gave it to us.' And Tom said, 'That's what I heard, too.'"

The GBA was blindsided. Steve Fanczi, the GBA's deputy executive director who had led the negotiations with Jerry Rackliffe, became convinced the fix was in. Georgia State, which he had regarded as an ally, was now a "monster" in his eyes. "This feels like a betrayal to me," he raged. "It sure seems like one of those backroom deals where someone tells you one thing and then goes and does another."

Rackliffe tried, in vain, to assure Fanczi that the news had come as just as much of a surprise to him. What he *wanted* to say was that the GBA had been foolish not to take the money while it was still on the table. But Fanczi was no longer listening.

Other university administrators were similarly flabbergasted, only in their case it was out of envy, not anger. "How come they give you land, and I have to buy it?" one vice president at Georgia Tech asked Becker. Becker had no real answer to that. He could take some pride in the years of hard work he and Tom Lewis had put into convincing the state government to take them seriously. But he was also keen to move on to the next task: lobbying the governor and the legislature for $60 million to get the convocation center built and to open it as quickly as possible.

12

ROGUE COWS

While Georgia State thrived, the five community campuses in the Atlanta suburbs known collectively as Georgia Perimeter College teetered on the brink of insolvency. These were institutions dedicated to many of the same things that Renick and his team at Georgia State believed in: providing an education to a large body of lower-income students, giving them the tools both to understand what that education was for and helping them navigate their way through. Morale on Perimeter's teaching staff, however, was close to rock bottom. After two decades of what one prominent faculty leader described as "abysmal leadership," they felt underpaid, under-resourced, and overworked. As a final kick in the pants, the board of regents discovered in the spring of 2012 that Perimeter was days away from running out of cash and would need an emergency infusion of $6 million just to make it to the start of the new fiscal year on July 1.

When system auditors looked closer, they discovered that for years Perimeter had been improperly drawing on its reserves to maintain unsustainable operating expenses. The regents had granted permission to dip into those reserves on an emergency basis in the depths of the recession, but Perimeter had abused the practice so badly that the $6 million cash deficit—covered on a temporary basis by Georgia State as a favor to the system office— was only the tip of what would become a $25 million debt mountain by the time the auditors finished their investigation just a few months later.

Most of Perimeter's top leadership was forced out, including its president, Anthony Tricoli, who would soon claim to have been the victim of a conspiracy involving his own finance chief and members of the system office who, he said, had deliberately kept him in the dark about the gravity of the situation. Tricoli spent the next several years suing everyone in sight for a colorful array of perceived offenses including breach of contract and racketeering, only to lose in every court that heard his case. The auditors, meanwhile, concluded that while Tricoli may have been correct to say he was not adequately briefed, he also "did not perform the necessary financial due diligence" that might have involved, for example, looking through the accounts for himself when they were presented to him for signature.

Such mismanagement would have been disastrous anywhere, but it was particularly tough on Perimeter's twenty thousand students who, lacking adequate campus support outside the classroom, struggled with low morale of their own and earned associate's degrees at only a 6 percent clip. Hank Huckaby made the best of a bad situation, turning to Rob Watts, an experienced and widely respected community college veteran who had ridden to Perimeter's rescue once before, to act as interim president. Together, Huckaby and Watts managed to turn Perimeter's finances around in a single academic year. Watts laid off almost 10 percent of the staff, restricted library and computer lab hours, and cut back on access to remedial tutoring. But he did not touch the core academic programs. Rather, he rallied the faculty to work harder and teach more, and he led by example by taking on two freshman composition classes a week himself.

That was the short-term solution. Longer term, Huckaby understood that Perimeter could not rely just on a faculty dedicated to the mission of transforming young lives. It needed an entirely new management culture to support and expand that mission. Perimeter wasn't tracking students, so there was no way of knowing how many of the 94 percent who did not graduate were satisfied taking just a handful of classes—as some no doubt were—or enrolling in college elsewhere—as some no doubt were—and how many were simply giving up. The campuses had no peer-to-peer supplemental instruction, no learning communities, and nothing remotely resembling a proactive advising service. The overall ratio of students to advisors—most of them faculty members doing what they could after class—was north of 1,200:1.

There was only one place such a line of thinking could lead, and once the worst of the emergency was over Huckaby called Mark Becker to ask if Georgia State was interested in taking over. It was a big ask. Why would a large research university, just now finding its feet after decades in the wilderness, want to take on the headaches and challenges of the state's biggest community college network? In many parts of the country, research universities and community colleges were run under entirely separate management structures and the very idea of joining them would be unfathomable.

Becker told the chancellor: "We'll get back to you."

This wasn't the first time Huckaby had sought to merge institutions. Within months of taking office as chancellor, he'd pushed for the consolidation of several of the system's thirty-five universities and colleges, because they were clustered unevenly around the state and duplicated a lot of administrative functions. The way Huckaby saw it, integrating these functions could free up a lot of money to benefit students more directly. A number of institutions besides Perimeter were struggling financially, and a handful of presidents were on the verge of retirement, all of which presented Huckaby with opportunities he was anxious to seize.

Still, consolidation was a hugely controversial idea. A 2012 analysis by the Pew Charitable Trusts described it as a "last resort" and quoted one expert, Dennis Jones of the National Center for Higher Education Management Systems, as saying he didn't know of a single instance where merging campuses had actually saved money. Huckaby also faced fierce resistance internally, from campus employees worried about their jobs and from university leaders and alumni who had a strong attachment they didn't want to lose to their alma mater.

That said, it was hard to overlook the fact that Georgia's public university system had been designed for another time and a different target population entirely. At the outset, in the early 1900s, institutions were distributed evenly around the state, with one agricultural and mechanical arts college placed in each congressional district. But as rural areas emptied out and the Atlanta region asserted its primacy, this arrangement became increasingly unworkable, even with modifications here and there. Segregation did not help, creating distortions of its own as white-majority campuses sprang up right next to historically black ones and vice versa—a duplication that was as wasteful as it was morally disturbing.

Quickly, Huckaby decided he wouldn't *start* by merging institutions that traced their origins back to the race question, because that was likely to lead to a backlash and could kill off the whole idea. He also resolved not to close any campuses, because that could trigger damaging outcries of a different sort. Knowing he needed buy-in at the highest levels, he began by making the case for merging North Georgia State University, on the edge of the Chattahoochee National Forest, with Gainesville State College, twenty miles to the southeast, because Governor Deal and Lieutenant Governor Casey Cagle both had deep Gainesville roots and carried a lot of sway in the area.

The strategy worked, and the newly merged University of North Georgia soon became a regional powerhouse, with five separate campuses stretching from the Tennessee border to the eastern Atlanta suburbs. "If I can't support it in my own community," Deal told Huckaby, "how can I expect people to support it elsewhere?"

By the time Huckaby approached Georgia State about absorbing Perimeter, he had completed work on three other consolidations, with a fourth on the way. It was no longer a question of whether it *could* be done, only of whether Georgia State wanted to do it. Becker already had experience of running a research campus with two-year schools attached at the University of South Carolina; Penn State, where he'd earned his doctorate, had a similar arrangement. But he wasn't going to make any decisions without seeking the opinions of his most trusted advisors.

Jerry Rackliffe was unhesitatingly enthusiastic, not least because he'd started his own higher education at a community college—Clarkston—that was now part of the Perimeter network. To him, consolidation fit perfectly with Georgia State's desire to broaden its mission and its reach. "If a student applies to us and we say, no, you can't come right now, we can tell them we have five Perimeter campuses. Do well there, and two years later you can transition," Rackliffe said. "We're known for access and excellence. This could only expand that reputation."

Tim Renick was less effusive, because he knew that absorbing the Perimeter campuses would complicate, if not slow down, his existing student success efforts. But he also felt there was no choice. If Georgia State said no, it risked losing its most valuable pipeline of transfer students. (Perimeter alumni accounted for about a quarter of Georgia State's total undergraduate student body.) Renick had already noticed how students from Gainesville College stopped coming to Georgia State after they became part of the University of North Georgia. He couldn't countenance losing thousands more each year to Kennesaw, or Clayton State, or whoever else ended up running the five community college campuses. "It's not a blessing on us, but if they are bent on consolidating Perimeter, we have to be the institution," he told Becker.

This didn't address Becker's bigger concern, whether the consolidation was actually feasible. On that point, though, Renick had no hesitation. "I said yes, absolutely," he recalled. "Nothing we were doing was particularly mysterious." And he offered, in essence, the Frank Sinatra argument: if we can make it work here, we can make it work anywhere. In fact, Renick saw a unique opportunity to *prove* that point and use a transformed Perimeter to change the minds of university administrators around the country who professed to admire Georgia State's breakthrough achievements, but worried that their campuses were too different to risk a similarly bold approach of their own.

It became apparent that Huckaby was thinking along similar lines, because when the system office announced the consolidation at the beginning of January 2015, the press release made no mention of saving money or streamlining bureaucratic procedures. It talked only about student success. "Georgia State is a recognized national leader in improving student retention and graduation rates and will be able to apply its best practices," the release quoted Huckaby as saying.

This was, of course, a deep compliment to Renick, but it was also a way of letting him know that his workload was about to go through the roof. The atmosphere on the Perimeter campuses was close to rancid at this point—not least because the faculty heard about the consolidation from the media before they received an announcement email from Rob Watts. They were fearful for their futures and deeply suspicious of Georgia State's motives. They weren't even sure if their campuses would survive. Some imagined they would be forced to come downtown and pay for downtown parking out of their meager salaries as a condition of remaining employed at all. "It didn't make any sense to us," recalled Jeffrey Portnoy, an outspoken English professor who had fought faculty battles at Perimeter for twenty years. "Grand things may have come out of it, but the reasons why were bewildering . . . We were instructed not to call it a merger or a hostile takeover, but a consolidation. Still, many of us considered it a hostile takeover."

Peter Lyons, who was given the delicate job of bridging the two institutions and later ran Perimeter College as its first dean post consolidation, understood the misgivings and challenges on both sides. On the one hand, the Perimeter faculty "had been working their asses off for decades for not very much money and for very little respect, had been jerked around by several administrations and then dropped into this huge financial hole that none of them knew anything about." And, on the other hand, Renick was being asked to ride in on a white horse and save an institution that wasn't at all sure it *wanted* to be saved—not by Georgia State, anyway. "We all felt responsible," Lyons said. "But the brunt fell onto Tim's lap—or on Tim's head."

Lyons struck Mark Becker as the perfect candidate to reassure Perimeter that it was not, in fact, under threat of extinction. He had a soft touch, a reassuring, unpretentious manner, and a wicked sense of humor. On top of that, he had a strong stomach for problems big or small. "I'm a social worker," Lyons said. "I don't look at the world and think: that's working perfectly, let's go there. I see disaster and think: this is a great opportunity."

Many at Perimeter appreciated his personality and his approach, and believed him when he said Georgia State was there to stabilize their mission, not torpedo it. "You need social workers to solve this," said Adam Stone, a veteran history and government professor whose students down the years had included a certain Cary Claiborne. "Peter represented complexity and a breadth of knowledge . . . Some people thought his humor was not so funny, but I thought it was hysterical. He could be biting about social class. As a Brit, that was one thing he certainly got."

Understanding social class in a country with a history of believing itself to be unburdened by the problem was an essential part of dealing with the wide array of students attending Perimeter. They ranged from full-time workers, who used the Alpharetta and Dunwoody campuses primarily for professional development, to some of the poorest students in the urban South, struggling with food insecurity and the unceasing threat of homelessness. Some could be spotted sleeping rough near the bike path that wound through the woods behind the Decatur campus; countless others were at risk of dropping out because they couldn't afford the bus pass to come to class. The five campuses also varied widely in size. Dunwoody and Clarkston each had more than five thousand students, whereas Newton, out in the country, had just fifteen hundred, along with a few rogue cows who would wander in from the neighboring fields. Collectively, the campuses covered a vast geographical area on the rapidly growing east and north sides of Atlanta. That posed a logistical challenge not only to Lyons, who found himself driving all over the suburbs several times a week, but to many of the department heads seeking to set up uniform services in registration, academic advising, and other vital areas.

The first question posed by consolidation was how much to centralize and how much to preserve of Perimeter's existing structure. And, broadly, the decision was to merge the two administrations but to keep the faculties separate. Perimeter would exist as its own college under the Georgia State umbrella, much like arts and sciences, or public health. The teaching staff at Perimeter were paid less and had a heavier course load than their counterparts in Atlanta, so they had a natural tendency to see this arrangement as reinforcing a fundamental inequality. That, though, was not the rationale. Georgia State knew that professors at Perimeter had different qualifications, different rules for promotion and tenure, and an entirely different pay and career trajectory, so knitting the two faculty systems together was likely to become "messy and unpalatable," as Lyons put it, creating upheaval without materially improving anything. Since Georgia State did not have budgetary discretion from the system office to raise salaries and reduce course loads, it could well result in *more* unfairness and inequality, not less. North Georgia had merged faculties in its own consolidation, and the results had not been pretty.

From a student success perspective, it was also important to separate Perimeter from the Atlanta campus because the challenges were entirely different for two-year and four-year degree programs. The last thing Renick wanted was to see the dramatic progress in Atlanta slowed or reversed because the Perimeter campuses were lagging behind. Conversely, he was determined to show that meaningful progress was possible at Perimeter, and the best way to do that was to track its data separately and to assess the results on their own merits.

Theoretically, a lot of these issues were to be hashed out by a consolidation committee made up of equal numbers of representatives from Perimeter and the Atlanta campus. Really, though, the conversation started before the committee had a chance to hold its first meeting, thanks to Jeffrey Portnoy, the outspoken English professor and director of Perimeter's honors college, who circulated a document he called "Re-Imagining Georgia Perimeter College as a Part of Georgia State University" to set out his agenda for maintaining the integrity of the community colleges. Some of the proposals Portnoy listed were ones he'd been pushing without success for years, like reducing class size and cutting the course load for Perimeter professors from five units per semester to four; these did not come to pass. Others were the rhetorical equivalent of a defensive crouch to make sure, for example, that Perimeter faculty members would retain their rank and tenure privileges, which they did. And some were a call to action: urging Georgia State to do for Perimeter what it had done to retain and graduate more of its own students. "I think that if comparable resources were put in place to help our students here, they would do as well as Georgia State students," Portnoy said in a follow-up interview with *The Collegian*, Perimeter's campus newspaper.

Many people at Perimeter lacked Portnoy's courage to speak out, and they worried his frankness would prove counterproductive. But Tim Renick was grateful to him, because offering Perimeter the full range of student success programs was exactly what he had in mind and the document gave him hope he could count on some baseline support from the Perimeter faculty and staff. The Georgia State leadership generally was glad to learn what a lot of people were obviously thinking anyway and to engage with them on those ideas.

"Seventy-two people have sent me your 'Re-Imagining' document," Lyons told Portnoy when they shook hands at one of the first meetings of deans and department chairs. To which Portnoy replied, with a deadpan humor to match Lyons's: "It's the most widely read thing I've ever published." The two liked and trusted each other from that moment on.

In the long, hard slog of knotting two institutions into one, the potential for petty power struggles and getting bogged down in minutiae seemed almost limitless. Lyons looked to Penn State and the University of South Carolina for guidance and was horrified to find that they had carefully prescribed shared governance rules on everything from conference room rentals to the caliber of bullets used by campus police. He did his best to keep things moving, and as an early goodwill gesture he encouraged the consolidation committee to grant custodians at Perimeter a pay raise to put them at the same level as their counterparts in Atlanta. Economic justice for everyone earning under $40,000 a year was how he billed it, and it set exactly the tone he hoped for. The only near-insurrection was over Perimeter's playing fields and sports equipment, because the Perimeter committee members suspected Georgia State's athletics department, incorrectly, of playing a nefarious role in the decision to consolidate in the first place and did not want to cede control to them. Otherwise, people treated each other with respect and worked fast.

Things grew significantly tenser as faculty members on either side of the consolidation line met to streamline their lower-level courses and make sure the curriculum for algebra, or government, or intro chemistry was the same across all Georgia State campuses. While a lot of these meetings went smoothly, the Perimeter teams became alarmed when they were told that they had to teach the whole of U.S. history in one semester instead of two, and again when they had to cut a literature component out of English composition. Was this what student success meant, they wondered—that saving students time and money trumped the quality of what they were being taught? As it turned out, Tim Renick's office had nothing to do with these discussions, except to lay down the general principle that courses had to match. Nobody had run numbers and concluded that teaching literature was a waste of time; this was just English professors haggling with each other over schedules and course requirements. But the Perimeter people did not necessarily know that—or even care particularly who was responsible for what they felt to be a profoundly misguided decision.

Such ructions were surely inevitable. "It's not necessarily pretty," said Adam Stone, who as an associate social sciences chair at Perimeter was directly involved in the faculty negotiations. "But the fact is, we're doing it. I never would have thought that you could marry these two institutions. And it is a marriage—in all the good and bad that might entail."

The good certainly surfaced, too. It didn't take too long for students to see the upside of becoming part of a big, prestigious urban institution where a lot of them hoped to study once they'd completed their associate's degrees. They welcomed the Georgia State signage when it came to their campus and rushed to lay their hands on Georgia State T-shirts and sweatshirts that Becker and others distributed when they visited. They, along with the faculty and staff, appreciated the exposure they would now have to research opportunities and Georgia State's connections to the wider world. Perimeter had lurked in the shadows for too long, and there was an opportunity now to bask in a little prestige and attract more love from the regents and the state legislature.

Nobody, certainly, missed the way things used to be. When Lyons moved into the old presidential suite on the Decatur campus, he discovered portraits of past campus leaders lining the walls of the executive suite corridor—with the exception of Anthony Tricoli, whose picture had been shoved unceremoniously into a bathroom.

In the middle of consolidation, Becker learned from a headhunter that a prestigious university was interested in luring him away and wanted to send a member of its governing board to Atlanta to meet him. Becker said he wouldn't move for less than $1 million a year, and he also wanted a guarantee he'd have the resources to do the new job the way he saw fit. The headhunter said the salary would not be a problem; he'd get back to him about the rest.

When Becker told Hank Huckaby he was being recruited, Huckaby asked what it would take for him to stay, and Becker gave much the same answer he'd given to the headhunter: a million dollars a year. He knew this was a big number in a public university system where anyone earning six figures, never mind seven, was breathing rarefied air. But he had an idea he could cut a deal with Huckaby whereby he agreed, in exchange for the elevated salary, to commit to several more years at Georgia State.

Huckaby was disquieted by the request but not entirely surprised. It was common for successful presidents to push for a significant pay increase once they had established a track record. In fact, Huckaby had recently taken a call from Bud Peterson, the president of Georgia Tech, asking for a million *and a half*. So he listened to Becker's proposal, doing his best to forget that a million dollars was twice what he earned as chancellor.

Becker suggested deferring half of the million-a-year for four years, to make the figure more palatable and to reassure Huckaby that he was unlikely to leave before June 2019 because it would mean leaving two million dollars on the table. The truth was, he wasn't seriously interested in another college presidency; Georgia State was likely to define him in a way nothing else could. But he also thought it was important to be paid what he now knew to be his market worth.

Huckaby had his misgivings. Among other things, there was a problem of optics at an institution dedicated to some measure of economic justice. Yes, Becker was making sizeable personal donations to scholarships for lower-income students through the Georgia State foundation, over and above what he was doing to improve their prospects day in and day out. But a million a year was also roughly equivalent to the salaries of twenty entry-level academic advisors. Still, Huckaby didn't see a choice, not if he wanted to hold on to a man he regarded as essential to Georgia State, the Perimeter consolidation, and the health of the university system as a whole. "Some people on the board of regents had to swallow hard," he said. "The governor had to swallow hard. But they accepted it."

Bringing the student success mission to Perimeter wasn't conceptually difficult. Georgia State took $3 million in savings from the elimination of duplicate positions and used it to hire thirty-four new academic advisors and place extra admissions and financial aid officers on the five campuses. Renick never doubted that the model in and of itself would work. The logistics, though, were another matter.

Much as Georgia State had had to put its data house in order, Renick's office now had to create a uniform record of students across all campuses so they could be tracked and evaluated properly. State rules did not permit the university to identify students by their social security numbers, so staff had to conduct a painstaking name-by-name check to make sure that none of the seventy thousand students with similar names who had enrolled at the two institutions over the decades were confused with each other. This wasn't just a matter of accuracy. If any student accidentally gained access to the records of another, it would be a violation of federal privacy laws and a major liability for the university.

At the outset, the hope was to develop a full picture of every community college student's courses, credits, and area of study, so they would be ready for predictive analytics in preparation for their associate's degrees and could then transition seamlessly to the Atlanta campus knowing what courses they still needed to take for their bachelor's. Unfortunately, this didn't come close to happening in time for what Renick called "the Big Bang," the moment in the late spring of 2016 when Perimeter and Georgia State merged within the Banner database system. "We had huge problems with data for semesters after," he said. "We had no reliable date-to-date numbers, and students were getting lost or double counted as they moved between campuses . . . We materially lost momentum, because it was such a drag on our resources and energy."

Renick's staff had a particular problem dealing with foreign students who were either undocumented or had limited protected status under the Obama administration's DACA (Deferred Action for Childhood Arrivals) program. Georgia State and Georgia Perimeter College previously had different requirements under a board of regents policy adopted in 2010, and reconciling them meant stepping into uncharted territory on a politically sensitive issue. As an access institution, Perimeter had had permission to enroll students without full legal status as long as they paid out-of-state tuition fees. But Georgia State, along with the state's other research universities, was obliged to show that it had turned away no academically qualified citizen or legal resident over the previous two years before it could admit a single undocumented foreigner. Post-consolidation, the more stringent set of rules applied across the board.

The data and immigration headaches were soon compounded by an even bigger one as the expanded university prepared to admit seventeen thousand new students in the summer of 2016 and was overwhelmed by a rush of financial aid applications ahead of the new academic year. The processing of new students had been crazy enough pre-consolidation: Renick's staff would set up dedicated call centers, knowing that wait times to answer student queries could top ninety minutes right before payment deadlines. Now they didn't know quite what to expect, in part because their data systems were not yet running adequately so they couldn't track incoming students as they would have liked. At first, Renick and

Lyons were cautiously optimistic that the wait times would be no worse than what they were used to, because Perimeter had never suffered from the sorts of delays that were common at the Atlanta campus; the Perimeter financial aid office said it never had to deal with more than a few hundred phone calls a day in peak periods. What Renick and Lyons didn't know, and didn't find out until it was too late, was the less than pretty reason why. "What happened was, they unplugged the bloody phones!" Lyons recounted. Perimeter had got away with this when nobody was paying much attention. But now *everyone* was watching—the university administration, the system office, local media—and everything blew up in full view of all of them.

"It was a disaster, one of the least happy periods in my life," Renick said. "Our ability to respond to the demand for financial aid collapsed. And the students deserved better." Thousands did not have their money lined up before the first day of class, or even before the drop at the end of the first week. Renick let them begin their studies anyway—there was ample precedent for doing so when the university knew federal grant money was on its way—but did not dare ask for formal permission for fear that the system office would say no. Several hundred students never came up with the funds they needed, and Renick's office had to scramble to find them scholarships to cover the shortfall.

Renick commissioned an outside report from the National Association of Student Financial Aid Administrators to help him work through the problem, and it became clear that he was dealing with something bigger than anything he'd inherited from the old administration at Perimeter. His own financial aid office was not equipped to deal with the influx of 20,000 extra students and needed to be redesigned from top to bottom. The logistics were truly dizzying: 40,000 Georgia State students out of a total of 53,000 were eligible for federal grants, but only 40 percent of them were completing their forms in time to have a reasonable chance of receiving their grant money before the start of the fall semester. "We'd tried to institute best practices from peer campuses, but the conclusion was that we may not have been radical enough," Renick said. "None of those schools have the same kind of demand and volume we do."

Renick contracted with an outside call center, which eased some of the pressure, but a phone service alone was plainly insufficient. Better technology helped: the student success office acquired a program to process federal government requests for verification and an improved customer-relationship management system to prevent application forms and student data from going astray. This was also the year that the chatbot came online, one of the few bright spots of the whole experience, and it helped to answer tens of thousands of financial aid questions, with no wait time at all.

By the following summer, the picture had cleared up considerably. A revamped financial aid office set up tables in the student center ballroom in Downtown Atlanta to serve students—"like a lunch counter at a deli," as Renick described it—and cut wait times to around ninety minutes. That was still intolerably slow, but a lot less intolerable than what had come before. "In an ideal world, we would not be keeping students waiting," Renick said. "But this is part of what we need to tackle if we're going to address equity issues. It's all compromises."

Over time, the Tim Renick medicine started working. Perimeter introduced retention grants, supplemental instruction, learning communities, and proactive advising—though not all at once. It took a year and a half to hire new advisors and get EAB to iron out the data challenges so they could extend their software to the Perimeter campuses. Learning communities were not introduced until the fall of 2018, because it took the extra year to convince a skeptical Perimeter faculty to introduce a new block schedule and give students in the same meta major the opportunity to take classes together. Once launched, though, learning communities quickly proved their worth. About 60 percent of incoming Perimeter students joined one, and soon they were attempting and completing more credit hours than the rest of the student body. That, in turn, led to a 7-percentage-point bump in enrollment renewals the following semester.

Cary Claiborne, who was sent to Perimeter to oversee the new student success programs, played an important part in drumming up enthusiasm for learning communities and the more structured academic pathways they offered. When he first arrived, he found that a lot of students expected to fail, and not without reason: at the time, you couldn't put ten of them in a room and be sure even one would earn an associate's degree. When Claiborne started pushing them to register for more classes, he would hear the retort: "In my class, we're all failing. Why would I sign up for class again?"

Claiborne made it his business to make the students believe. He helped them get their heads around the new class schedule by telling them it was like a burger meal; they should imagine English, math, and other core courses as the burger and the bun, and electives as the tomato and lettuce. If someone said she dreamed of being a doctor, Claiborne would address her right away as "doctor." If someone was doing unexpectedly well in a math class, he would encourage him to look into becoming a peer instructor. When students struggled, he'd let them know it was not the end of the world and suggest the learning and tutoring center. "You've already paid for a tutoring service," he'd say. "You should use it."

One of Claiborne's more remarkable charges was Osman Saccoh, a shy and cautious student from Sierra Leone who had moved to the United States without his parents at the age of thirteen and started at Perimeter full of doubts that he truly belonged. He wasn't confident in his English and, while he loved the idea of becoming a petroleum engineer, he didn't think he was strong enough academically. Claiborne didn't hesitate to call him

"Engineer Osman" and talked to him three or four times a week to make sure he was on track. "Cary encouraged me to follow my passion," Saccoh said. "I used to feel I wasn't good enough to do most of the things I wanted to do. I even worried that my hair didn't look professional. Cary said: 'Hair has nothing to do with the person you are. Cutting it would make no difference. What matters most is what you have to say.'"

Saccoh was not a natural talker, but he started speaking up anyway—to his peers, to his advisors, and his professors. And he discovered not only that people listened, but that he had talents he never suspected. Soon, he was acing his classes, working as a supplemental instructor in English composition, and lining up possible scholarships to study engineering at Texas A&M. "Cary," he said, "gave me the information to believe in myself."

The intervention worked not just because of Claiborne's singular ability to charm and inspire others, but because an entire structure was taking root. Saccoh's support system happened to be particularly extensive because he was one of thirty-nine inaugural recipients of a State Farm Insurance scholarship designed to give kids from the impoverished southern half of DeKalb County an education at Perimeter and enough adult supervision to see them through it. Claiborne was just one part of that—just one part of proactive advising once it arrived on campus, and just one part of a campaign, organized through fairs with free barbeque dinners and other incentives, to get Perimeter students to plan their classes more thoughtfully instead of leaving it to the last minute to register for whatever was still available.

Still, Claiborne found consolidation to be the hardest thing he'd ever worked on—because so many students had a dauntingly steep hill to climb, and because he had to push against the perception that he was some big-city know-it-all. "It was rough," he said. "People get defensive. They said, 'You're from Downtown, trying to tell us what's wrong with us, but you don't know us.'"

The turning point came when he ran into Dennis Jones, one

of his old professors from Gwinnett who now worked in student services. (Gwinnett left the Perimeter system in 2006, but Jones never did.) When they'd last crossed paths, Claiborne's GPA had been sinking like a stone and he was looking at a career doing inventory in a car lot.

"Oh my God," Jones said in disbelief, "Cary Claiborne!"

The encounter caused some stir, because people couldn't quite believe that the Atlanta hotshot, as they saw Claiborne, could possibly be acquainted with a low-profile community college veteran. Claiborne told them: "I'm the assistant director of student success at a school I got kicked out of. That's why I'm here. I was one of those students."

Nobody ever questioned his credentials again.

13

SECURE THE BAG

In late 2018, Tim Renick's office began hearing that something weird was going on with new student orientation, the welcome session that freshmen and, often, their parents attended to familiarize themselves with Georgia State before the start of classes.

For as long as anyone could remember, orientation had been a fun-filled day-long information session, including scavenger hunts to introduce new students to key locations on campus, mini-lectures from some of the more engaging faculty members, and a freewheeling question-and-answer session. Since the consolidation with Perimeter, however, the format had undergone some perplexing revisions overseen not by Renick's student success shop but by student affairs, an entirely separate division whose vice president was a member of Becker's cabinet.

Word was, the fun had been bled right out of it. Students were no longer being told: congratulations, you are coming to special place, this experience is going to transform your life. Rather, they were beaten over the head with regulations, rules, requirements, and procedures that made Georgia State sound more like a soul-crushing police state than a place of inspiration and learning. True or not, complaints were pouring in, so Renick sent a trusted lieutenant, Heather Housley, to attend a session and establish exactly what was happening.

Housley, who worked predominantly with international students, was a soft-spoken Tennessean hardly prone to critical overstatement. Yet even she had difficulty believing what she was hearing. The session kicked off not with a celebratory bang, but with a detailed breakdown of the university's administrative hierarchy, and a particular focus on the student affairs division. Next came the university's code of conduct, including several minutes' discussion of sexual assault and harassment policies. Then crime— cocaine use on campus, and a recent stabbing. "The sense was, look to your left, look to your right, everyone's a thief," Housley said.

Thirty tables had been set aside for student groups to promote campus activities, but only one was occupied. The session was led by student orientation leaders, not staff. Indeed, no staff member was in evidence anywhere.

Renick and his colleagues listened aghast to Housley's report. They had a natural interest in ensuring that students started their Georgia State careers on the right foot. But they were also aware of a litany of problems plaguing the student affairs division and aware, too, that Becker had reached the limits of his patience. The head of student affairs, Doug Covey, was a straight-laced traditionalist whose staff had taken the view that new student orientation had become too loosey-goosey because it did not do enough to address the university's legal obligations. The new script they produced went so far in the opposite direction that the team leaders in charge of orientation soon quit, and so did their replacements. That was why students had been left in charge: there was nobody else.

The obvious solution was to have Renick's office run new student orientation instead. That was why Housley went on her reconnaissance mission. But Becker did not stop there. He handed Renick control of the entire student affairs division, an overnight doubling of the size of his operation that gave the student success office jurisdiction over everything from student clubs and activities to housing and the counseling center. The challenge was not just to reimagine new student orientation but to reconfigure large parts of the overall campus experience that had somehow resisted the university's student success ethos for years.

Yet another Herculean task had landed at Renick's feet. As he announced the president's decision at one of his regular weekly managers' meetings in December 2018, he took one look around the room and remarked: "We're going to need a bigger table."

From an outsider's perspective, it might seem perplexing that Georgia State should be beset by such a glaring—and glaringly public—problem so many years into its student success experiment. In almost all respects Georgia State was riding high, lauded across higher education as the institution nobody could afford to ignore and heralded on the front page of the *New York Times* as the crucible of a "moral awakening" and an engine of innovation and social mobility of national importance. The student success office now had programs covering the gamut of the undergraduate experience, starting even before students set foot on campus with the chatbot, through to the last-minute financial support they could draw on to complete their final degree requirements.

The data told the story of one landmark achievement after another. The number of African Americans graduating was up 47 percent from 2011, the number of Pell-eligible graduates up 46 percent, and the number of Latino graduates—a smaller cohort—up a staggering 89 percent. Students in all three historically vulnerable categories were earning degrees at a rate at or above the university average and had been doing so *for four years in a row*, a definitive closure of Georgia State's achievement gap that no other U.S. institution had come close to emulating. The overall six-year graduation rate now stood at 55 percent, 23 percentage points higher than it had been fifteen years earlier. That didn't mean the other 45 percent dropped out, either: 80 percent of those who started out at Georgia State had either graduated from one institution or another in the previous six years or were still working toward a degree.

Even Perimeter, where the work of Renick's student success team was still in its infancy, was showing signs of solid progress. The three-year graduation rate had climbed from 6 percent to 15 percent since consolidation (and would soon hit closer to 20 percent), retention rates were heading in the right direction, and there were signs, despite the painfully low numbers, that achievement gaps were closing, too. Of the thirty-nine lower-income high schoolers who won a State Farm scholarship in 2017, thirty-three would soon obtain an associate's degree and move on with their studies—an astonishing 85 percent completion rate.

And yet, for all this extraordinary progress and the single-minded pursuit of the goals enshrined in the strategic plan, the student affairs division had proved to be a persistent drag on Georgia State, a source of needless problems of varying sizes that served to deter, not encourage newcomers as they faced the multiple challenges of campus life.

New student orientation was just one case in point. Housing was another. In the fall of 2017, the university sold 10 percent more dorm rooms than were available, leaving hundreds of students with nowhere to live and obliging the university to send four hundred of them to a downtown Sheraton for a couple of weeks until it could complete arrangements to have them double- or even triple-bunk at a discount. The following year, housing administrators erred in the opposite direction: they were so quick to start a waiting list, and communicated so slowly with the students on it, that they ended up scaring off a lot of people and leaving beds vacant.

The underlying problem was not just administrative incompetence, although that undoubtedly played a role. It was also a mindset that could not get to grips with the university's student success mission or think creatively about imbuing mundane bureaucratic procedures with meaning for the end user, the students. For a long time, Becker valued Doug Covey because he was a reliably solid manager with a deft touch when it came to organizing student clubs and working with the student government association. But it also became apparent that Covey and his team were unwilling—or unable—to use data to improve their services. They could, for example, have crunched the housing data to anticipate demand more accurately. They could have arranged student dorm assignments by meta major so members of learning communities not only studied but also lived together. They could have integrated their first-year welcome efforts with the chatbot. Yet they did none of these things.

How could a university with an unswerving belief in the power of data have tolerated a division that, in Renick's diagnosis, was "almost oblivious" to it? The answer has something to do with the complications inherent in changing course at any large institution. Even in a dynamic environment like Georgia State's, many different factors can lengthen the distance between setting a goal and achieving it. Covey was no Fenwick Huss; he had no apparent *philosophical* objection to Renick's work. Rather, the underlying issue was that he was a traditionalist in a nontraditional environment. "Doug's line was always, this is the way we do things," Becker said after the dust settled. "But we don't stick to traditional models at Georgia State. If we did that, we wouldn't achieve anything."

When problems with student affairs first surfaced, Becker transferred two of the more dysfunctional areas to Renick: career services and a student support service known as TRIO. He imagined this would send a clear enough message about his expectations for change. Once Becker came to realize this wasn't going to be enough, consolidation was in full swing, which made it difficult to ask Renick to take on more. When Covey let it be known he was applying for a string of university presidencies, Becker wished him well and offered to help. Only when it became clear that Covey was not moving on and the student orientation disaster came to light did Becker conclude he had run out of room for maneuver.

That said, it always made sense to Becker to put Renick in charge of student affairs. At the University of South Carolina, the head of student affairs and the head of student success initiatives had been one and the same, Dennis Pruitt, and the combination worked well. Even before the orientation debacle came to light, Becker had promoted Renick to be one of three senior vice presidents—Risa Palm, as provost, and Jerry Rackliffe, as finance chief, were the two others—with the idea that Renick would take full responsibility for every aspect of the student experience outside the classroom.

The complicating question was how to fold student affairs into his portfolio when Renick was so busy and Covey's bailiwick so extensive. At first, Becker kept Covey in charge but had him report to Renick. That arrangement proved unsustainable, however, and Covey opted instead for a nontenured position at the College of Education & Human Development.

It was far from ideal to expand the student success operation so drastically when Renick's team had barely had time to recover from the birth pangs of consolidation. But after almost a decade at Georgia State, Becker knew one thing to be true above all others: that when he asked Tim Renick to do something, it got done.

To sit in on one of Tim Renick's weekly student success managers' meetings on the eleventh floor of the old Citizens Trust Building on Piedmont Avenue is to gain insight into the extraordinary complexity of running a large and ever-changing public university.

The agenda invariably starts with data—pages and pages of graphs, spreadsheets, and historical analyses that are distributed to participants at the start of the session. Those with trained eyes—you don't get into the room without them—can see from the first page whether enrollment is higher or lower than expected, whether the average number of courses students are taking is up or down, and which courses at which colleges are more or less in demand. All these data points have implications that ripple out across the university administration. Higher enrollments create pressure to hire more instructors, find more classroom space, and complete the latest student residence construction projects to meet the extra demand. Renick's team looks at the week-to-week comparisons and makes judgments on where it thinks the numbers are heading so everything is in place for the right number of students at the start of each semester.

Invariably, Renick will invite discussion on particular points that jump out at him: how to deal with students who keep taking and retaking intro math, say, when the data shows that after they've failed twice their chance of passing dwindles almost to zero. Or he will present new research developed by his data analytics team—for example, on the number of times freshmen have logged into university websites and portals and the likelihood that those who have fallen below average usage are in some kind of trouble.

One abiding concern in these meetings is the tension that flares on a regular basis between the University Advisement Center and the college advisory services who continue to oversee students over their last thirty credit hours before graduation. One issue that preoccupied Renick's team in late 2018 and early 2019 was that the college offices were poaching advisors from the central office by offering them a few thousand dollars extra a year—even though they and the human resources department had agreed they would do no such thing. Another was that the college offices did not always enter changes in course requirements into the EAB system but would wax indignant anyway any time the UAC failed to inform students about them.

These were good examples of the unintended consequences that would periodically arise as a result of Georgia State's rapid reform process, and it was far from clear what Renick's office could do about them. Some on his staff felt the original compromise with the college advising offices had been a mistake. But it was not one they could see an easy way to rectify. "We're supposed to do things in concert," Allison Calhoun-Brown said, "but we don't have a lot of ability to make them change the way they do things."

On the day Renick announced the student affairs takeover, the data package he distributed included an organizational chart of the top administrative positions in the student affairs division. He wanted his staff to familiarize themselves with the names they needed to get to know and to familiarize themselves, too, with the large number of administrative slots that were either vacant or being filled on an interim basis by part-time retirees. Some members of his team were already familiar with what they were taking on and had initiated meetings with their student affairs counterparts. The feeling that emerged from the discussion was that some veterans of student affairs were wary of what was about to happen to them, while others welcomed the prospect of new management and the many opportunities it afforded. This was of course familiar territory, because the student success office did almost nothing without attracting its share of skepticism and pushback.

The mechanics of the takeover were familiar for other reasons, too, because Renick's team had gone through a similar exercise two years earlier when they took their first bite out of the student affairs portfolio and assumed control of career services. That had struck them as a gargantuan undertaking all its own, not just because they were under pressure to identify and correct missteps that student affairs administrators had made in the years when Atlanta was emerging from the recession and the demand for skilled labor began to soar. Helping students find a job after graduation had in fact been a consistent weak point at Georgia State, one that long predated Doug Covey's tenure and reflected failings across the university, not just in the student affairs division.

The keenest problem, which had grown only more acute as the university's demographics changed, was that lower-income undergraduates rarely had access to a professional network through their families and friends. That meant they had to rely on whatever help the university could offer through career fairs, internships, and other opportunities. And, too often, they had been left on their own. The way the system worked, they did not typically seek out career counseling in significant numbers until their final year, which was too late to be of much use. This was the part of Fenwick Huss's critique of Georgia State that arguably came closest to the mark: that the university's improving retention and graduation rates meant little if those newly minted graduates couldn't extend the success out into the job market.

Renick, characteristically, did not just look for an answer to this critique. He and Becker made career development a top priority for Georgia State and set about engineering a profound shift in how the university thought about career readiness. Preparing students for the world of full-time work, they realized, required a similar degree of care and supportiveness as preparing them academically to obtain their degrees.

Just as the proactive advising service had systematized and scaled the sort of one-on-one work that Crystal Mitchell did with Gabriel Woods, Renick sought ways to scale and systematize what the most resourceful and independent Georgia State students had been doing for years without the benefit of a university support network.

One vivid example of that resourcefulness was Terrance Rogers, a star business student from 2006 to 2010 and enthusiastic fundraiser for his alma mater, who became so frustrated as an undergraduate at Georgia State's failure to lay the groundwork for Wall Street internships that he and a fellow student started their own weekend boot camp—six hours a day, for seven weekends—to give their peers the training they lacked.

Rogers had grown up in a modest single-parent African American household and knew from experience how hard it was for kids like him to overcome the social and economic barriers they'd grown up with. He happened to be a brilliant student with a magnetic personality who became a campus leader and mentor on financial literacy. That work attracted the attention of Sponsors for Educational Opportunity, a national nonprofit dedicated to diversifying Wall Street. And SEO, in turn, guided him to an internship with Deutsche Bank. Rogers knew in his bones that he wasn't the only one capable of going to New York and competing with the kids from Harvard, Yale, and Columbia. "The reason people weren't getting jobs is because people at Georgia State weren't doing their jobs," he said. "Our students had just as much talent, just as much grit. I felt they could go up there and do well. So we put a ton of students on Wall Street, and they would come back and talk to their classmates. It created a perfect storm."

Several years later Tyler Mulvenna, who came from an even tougher background than Rogers, found his own creative ways to work around the limits of what the university offered. At one point he talked himself into a last-minute internship with the Atlanta office of the Quebec provincial government, only to learn that Georgia State wasn't able to process his paperwork in time to give him course credit for the placement. Undaunted, he used his connections with the 1913 Society, the university's student ambassador program, to figure out exactly which administrator was responsible for internship credits and appealed to him directly. When that didn't work, he got the paperwork through to Risa Palm, the provost, whom he knew through his ambassadorial work. She ended up signing off on it personally.

Like Rogers, Mulvenna was a natural networker, and since the university could not provide him with the connections he needed, he looked for them elsewhere. His fraternity helped him land an internship with Siemens in Boston. His front-desk job at the YMCA put him face-to-face with the contact who would end up securing him an internship and, later, a full-time job with the IHG hotel group. "It's not just school that's going to get you a job," he reflected. "Internships are the biggest things, but they are barriers to a lot of people." If he had one wish going forward, it was that Georgia State would provide support to students who didn't find it as easy as he had to improvise, circumvent rules as necessary, and create their own luck.

That is exactly what Renick set out to do. Once his office took over the career portfolio, he made sure students learned about career counseling in their GSU 1010 orientation class and integrated career prep into every aspect of their campus experience. One important tool had long since been integrated into the EAB dashboard: students could not only view their options for classes and majors, but also the careers and Atlanta-area companies typically associated with those majors, and the average starting salaries they could expect to earn. Now, though, that tool was more than just a stand-alone, it was part of a coherent overall plan. In the three years from 2016 to 2019, the number of career consultations increased sevenfold, with freshmen accounting for the bulk of the increase.

Students were encouraged to seek work opportunities for credit—70 percent of them did so—and to compile an e-portfolio detailing their skills and experience. Faculty members, meanwhile, were given grants to highlight the marketable skills they were imparting in their classes, both vocational ones like computer programming and accounting, and more intellectual but equally vital ones like critical thinking and writing. All of this honed a sense of purpose and direction, inside the classroom and out.

Renick's team took advantage of the university's soaring reputation and the dynamic Atlanta economy to strengthen connections between students and employers and to forge new ones. Alumni were often pivotal, whether at large corporations or in boutique industries like film and television production. One of Renick's former students, now a state legislator, could be counted on to arrange internships at the capitol. Terrance Rogers and a number of his friends made sure they helped open doors on Wall Street. When the United Parcel Service opened a vast new processing center twelve miles west of Downtown Atlanta in late 2018, the company calculated it was likely to see a turnover of 150 managers (out of 3,000 total employees) every six months and came to Georgia State to establish a pipeline of graduates for those jobs. State Farm insurance formed a particularly close bond with the Perimeter campuses, thanks to a $20 million philanthropic gift it made to help lower-income students at the Decatur campus. The company launched a program to recruit Georgia State graduates for insurance jobs and also a program to run college classes out of the State Farm offices near the Dunwoody campus.

Georgia State was also attentive to emerging industries, especially ones that required interdisciplinary skills that the university was interested in developing. When Peter Lyons heard that Takeda Pharmaceutical was planning to manufacture plasma-derived treatments at a plant near Perimeter's Newton campus, he made sure to create a pool of qualified applicants to manage the robotics equipment. He, like Renick, understood what was at stake. "We need to be available to meet employers' needs," he said. "I'm not just feeding the capitalist mill. I'm interested in students getting a job."

One place plenty of students were interested in getting a job was Georgia State itself. One of the side effects of Renick's student success work was to foster a generation of young people passionate about education who wanted nothing more than to help extend the achievements of their alma mater. And, often, they would beat the door down to be let in. Stephanie Tran, who had been in the inaugural cohort of Summer Success Academy students in 2012, was so excited to come back to Georgia State to work with the supplemental instruction program in the spring of 2018 that she ditched a better-paying human resources job she had started only days earlier in the medical field. "I'd interviewed for the Georgia State job but thought it was a lost cause. When they called a month later, I said yes right away," she said. "I wanted to pave the way for other students the way Georgia State paved the way for me."

The story of Georgia State's success has had two distinct aspects: the inward-facing one, which is all about the hard grind of grappling with large, complex problems as they arise and forging solutions in the face of extraordinary logistical challenges and internal resistance; and the outward-facing one, which is all about trumpeting the university's achievements, sharing data and encouraging other institutions to follow suit. Becker, Renick, and a number of other top university officials have had to learn to switch seamlessly between these two operating modes, spending large amounts of time away from campus on the conference circuit while at the same time staying on top of the unceasing deluge of day-to-day minutiae.

This switching between modes came fairly naturally to Renick, because he'd been doing something like it his whole career: getting on with the work quietly, sharply, and efficiently regardless of the pressures, and then going out and making the case for what he'd achieved with charm, eloquence, and precision. Temperamentally, Becker might have been more of a behind-closed-doors problem solver than a public speaker, but he, too, came into his own as the accolades and invitations piled up. He shed much of the awkwardness that had dogged him when he first took on the Georgia State presidency and became adept at speaking off the cuff as needed. He also crafted a public image as a risk-taker and an adventurer, someone who loved to challenge himself in his personal pursuits in the great outdoors as much as he did on the job. Becker's office walls were covered with striking black-and-white photographs of university climbing trips he'd led to Mount Baker and Mount Rainier, and his desk was adorned with miniature mile markers from the Tour de France in acknowledgment of his taste for long-distance biking against dramatic overseas backdrops. What the university, and the wider world, came to understand about him was that he was daring without being reckless; self-controlled without lacking in imagination; an introvert who sought to be an extrovert if only for the purpose of bringing people along with him.

Certainly, there was plenty to be proud of, and many outward signs of Georgia State's success. Anyone approaching Downtown Atlanta, particularly at night, had to marvel at the sheer profusion of university signs and logos emblazoned across the tops of buildings. In late 2018—around the time that Renick took over student affairs and Princeton Nelson and Savannah Torrance crossed the graduation stage—construction cranes were clustered thickly downtown and in the area around Turner Field, working on behalf of either Georgia State or one of its private-sector partners. The university colors were all over the airport, too, on posters abutting the doorways of the trains that shuttled passengers from terminal to terminal. What the posters touted was the latest verdict from top university administrators polled by *U.S. News & World Report*— that Georgia State was now the second most innovative university in the country, behind only Arizona State, and the second best for undergraduate teaching, behind only Princeton.

Seven years after Georgia State made a conscious decision to spurn *U.S. News* and all that it stood for, there was some irony in the fact that *U.S. News* couldn't stop piling on the superlatives. Indeed, in the publication's 2019 rankings of national universities, Georgia State broke the top two hundred for the first time. There was a further irony in the fact that it did so because *U.S. News* was now racing to catch up *with Georgia State*, not the other way around. For the first time, the *U.S. News* number crunchers added two "social mobility" indicators, one to measure the graduation rate of Pell-eligible students and the other to measure the gap between these lower-income students and their more affluent peers. That acknowledgment of Georgia State's pioneering work and its knock-on effect on other institutions was arguably the biggest accolade of all.

Seven months after Heather Housley sat in on the most unfathomably depressing of new student orientation sessions, she was standing in a Panther-blue dress in bright sunshine outside Georgia State's student center, welcoming hundreds of rising freshmen and their parents to an entirely different sort of reception, with banners, balloons, and a Hollywood-inspired blue carpet. Orientation was her baby now, and she had transformed it not only into a joyous occasion designed to inspire and excite the incoming class and their families but a practical one, too. She and her staff and guest speakers did not merely *explain* Georgia State's student success programs and why they were setting a standard for the entire country; they had turned the day into an *enactment* of them.

The students who signed up for orientation had been asked to provide some basic information about their academic strengths and interests and the health of their finances, and Housley's team used that information in ways the students weren't even aware of at the start of the day. Already, as they listened to the opening speeches, chanted along as members of the cheerleading crew taught them the football cheers, and applauded the inspiring stories of students who described how they had found their niche and their confidence at Georgia State, they were grouped at tables by meta major. During breaks, they had a chance to discover their common interests and bond over them as they helped themselves to bagels and donuts hanging from a pegboard at the back of the room. Later in the day, they would have lunch together as a mini-learning community and go on a university tour with a guide who was also a specialist in their subject area. In the afternoon, after helping themselves to a slice of Panther-themed cake, each of them would sit down first with an academic advisor who produced three draft class schedules to consider, then with a housing and financial specialist who would either sign them up for a residence hall or discuss the reasons why they might be better off saving money and living at home.

Housley and her team had turned the occasion into a one-day

version of the Summer Success Academy. Why wait until the first day of fall semester to guide students around the complexities of campus life when a golden opportunity existed to give them a head start? Even the career preparation piece was hammered home, as participants learned about the opportunities for résumé coaching, networking, and promotion via a student version of LinkedIn called Portfolium.

Every speaker reinforced the same set of messages. Cary Claiborne impressed on the students that college was both a marathon *and* a sprint. Yes, four years was a long time, but they couldn't afford to waste any of it because their job was to get out as quickly as possible and move on. The mantra Claiborne wanted them to remember: "Everything I do matters." To remind them of what mattered, each of them was given a checklist for their time at Georgia State: to be engaged; to be active and well; to give, learn, and lead; and, perhaps most important, to "secure the bag"—in other words, to stay afloat financially. Ways students could secure the bag included taking advantage of the scholarship resource center, or finding a campus job, or talking to a counselor at the student financial management center. The lesson was clear: if they ever found themselves in trouble—and many of them would—they would not be alone.

To emphasize the point, one of the session leaders started another chant, encouraging participants to shout along with him: *I'm in my bag.*

"I'm in my bag!" they echoed gleefully. "I'm in my bag!"

14

REPRODUCIBILITY

In the summer of 2017, Bill Gates paid a quiet visit to Georgia State to see for himself how the university had broken through barriers that other institutions still found insurmountable. He didn't want crowds or fanfare, just a chance to meet the architects of the student success program and some of the students who had benefited from it. He was in town anyway, as the keynote speaker at a global health convention, and one afternoon he opened the door of his SUV on Decatur Street like any other visitor and, with an ease that belied weeks of meticulous planning, walked into the Classroom South building in a distinctly professorial open-necked gray shirt and workaday black pants.

For Georgia State, receiving the founder of Microsoft was akin to a royal visit. Tim Renick's team worked exhaustively to select suitable students and make sure they were all free on a weekday—no easy feat since the visit was shrouded in secrecy and the students couldn't be told why they were being summoned. They shot footage of all four talking about their experiences in and around campus and introduced them to members of the Gates Foundation staff before announcing their special guest at the very last minute.

The Gates Foundation had been involved with Georgia State directly or indirectly for years, going back to its funding of Complete College America, and had provided seed money to establish the University Innovation Alliance. Renick had been invited to meet Gates in small, private settings on a couple of occasions.

But this was something else, an opportunity to promote Georgia State's achievements at a different level. Gates plainly felt the same way, because he later put out a blog post and a video to draw attention to what the university was doing to boost graduation rates and to encourage other institutions to "do some of the same."

That, in turn, raised some important questions. Could other universities replicate Georgia State's results? And, if so, what would it take to pull it off? The four students invited to meet Gates provided a snapshot of what was possible and, perhaps, the beginnings of an answer.

All four chosen students were campus superstars, but not in the conventional sense. They had come into the university with distinct disadvantages—because of their background, their ethnicity, their family's financial struggles, even because of questions about their academic chops. Their path, in other words, had been nowhere near as easy as it looked. And that was the point. They were brilliant kids who, in another institution, might have failed, or gone unnoticed, or never made it through the door in the first place.

Fortune Onwuzuruike found his path through the Summer Success Academy. He was a textbook candidate for it: a high school graduate from the suburbs with a strong grade-point average but indifferent SAT scores and a background that suggested he might not find it easy to adapt to college life. He was the eldest of four children of Nigerian-born parents who had sky-high expectations but also ran a strict and sheltered household. Georgia State, he said, was the first place where he had encountered large numbers of people unconnected to his parents' church and he appreciated the chance to learn about other ways of seeing and thinking. By the end of the seven-week summer session he was on his way, scoring a perfect 4.0 in his classes and making his first inroads into a social and political life thanks to a student government association mentorship program. A year later, he was himself a student government mentor at the success academy and working his way toward the SGA presidency. Onwuzuruike hadn't been sure, coming in, what he wanted to study and leaned heavy on the advising service, which steered him into a cutting-edge new field, health care informatics. He walked off the graduation stage straight into a full-time job with WellStar, the largest health care system in Georgia.

Kalif Robinson hadn't thought he'd go to college at all. He grew up in Virginia Beach, where his parents ran a modest music business—his father taught piano and voice, did some producing, and oversaw the music at his local church—and the recession hit them hard. They moved to Atlanta in Robinson's junior year of high school because their house was underwater and they urgently needed to go somewhere with a lower cost of living. Still, the move worked to Robinson's benefit, because he went from a small bubble of predominantly military families in Virginia to a multicultural high school in north DeKalb County, which opened up the world. He was a good student and qualified for the HOPE scholarship, which meant he wasn't quite as hamstrung as he might have been by his parents' money worries. Robinson wasn't just an example of what Cary Claiborne called a student in the net; he was specifically in *Claiborne's* net, because they bonded as soon as they met at a new student orientation session and later developed a close relationship. Robinson's mother told Claiborne: "We've just moved here. We want to make sure he's good." To which Claiborne replied: "That's your son? I'll make sure he's good." Later, Robinson landed himself a job in the student advising office, where Claiborne and his colleagues continued to keep a close eye on him.

Robinson worked unflaggingly—at a Nike store, as a waiter, at his campus job, and at his studies, including intensive Arabic courses that set him up for a study abroad opportunity in Jordan. At the end of his sophomore year, he realized he was in trouble because he needed $800 for a summer Arabic course. If he couldn't come up with the money he'd lose a semester and might not be able to stay in school long enough to graduate. Much like Tyler Mulvenna, he won a Panther retention grant even though he wasn't technically far enough along in his studies to qualify. And it saved him. He didn't just go to Jordan; he won a foreign service scholarship that took him to Washington for a summer, followed by a fellowship for graduate school at Georgetown. When Allison Calhoun-Brown invited him to Atlanta to meet with a mystery guest, he was working as an Africa policy fellow in the office of California congresswoman Karen Bass. Robinson made it look easy, but it was very far from that. "It seemed almost impossible at certain points," he said. "I was so tired for a lot of my time as an undergraduate."

Gabriella Salinas seemed, on the surface, to have had a much easier time of it. She came from a comfortable middle-class family and her father, an engineer with Delta Airlines, helped find her an internship in the airline's marketing department that she later turned into a part-time job. She, like Onwuzuruike, had been sent to the Summer Success Academy, in her case because she had both low SAT scores and a GPA below 3.0, putting her below the cutoff for HOPE. It didn't take her long, though, to win HOPE back and to work her way to a double major in marketing and managerial science.

Things changed in a hurry in her junior year. First her cousin, who had struggled with mental illness all his life, killed his parents, Salinas's aunt and uncle, in their home before turning the gun on himself. Salinas knew her cousin Eric had been troubled and had attempted suicide years earlier. But she also thought he was doing better, because he had his own apartment and was working as a chef and thinking of going back to college. Salinas was bereft. "You always hear of things like this," she said. "And then it happens to your family, who you think is so perfect that nothing can be wrong."

Then came another unwelcome announcement, that her father

and stepmother were separating. This time, the shock wasn't just emotional. Her father struggled with the extra expenses of living on his own and found himself unable to pay Salinas's bills the way he always had. Salinas's first instinct was to tell him she'd take care of it herself. "I took out all the loans I could, but still I had a remaining balance on my student account," she said. "I thought, where in the world am I getting that money from?" She, too, had a job in the advising office, and her champions there helped her win a Panther retention grant, without which she would have struggled to stay in school. "They knew what kind of student I was," she said. "I busted my butt." By the time of the Gates visit, Salinas had racked up $20,000 in debt and would end up with $10,000 more. But her straight-A grades never slipped.

Austin Birchell had also endured family loss and heartbreak, in his case a father who was diagnosed with Lou Gehrig's disease when he was ten and died five days after his sixteenth birthday. For the first half of his teenage years, Birchell didn't get to go out and have fun like his friends. Mostly, he was home helping to nurse his father through a long, painful decline and studying as hard as he could, because he knew he did not have the luxury of slacking.

The family had very little money. His grandparents owned a fruit stand, where Birchell spent long hours as a young child. His father, a navy veteran, worked at the stand himself before moving to a trucking parts company, while his mother had a job at a jewelry store. After Birchell's father was diagnosed, his mother stopped working to become a full-time care giver and they lived off disability checks from the Veterans' Administration. For a while, Brent Birchell got around in a wheelchair, showing up at the football practices he used to coach and teaching his son to drive. "To this day," Birchell said, "I make the smoothest stops in the car. When my dad was riding with me he couldn't control his neck, and I didn't want it to flop forward if I braked too hard."

The end was almost unbearably tough. Once his father was on morphine, Birchell stayed home and was boundlessly grateful to spend his last day with him. After the funeral, Birchell went straight back to school, feeling driven to do his father proud. A teacher put him in a side room so he could catch up on the work he'd missed.

If he hadn't thought much about college before—nobody in his family had gone before him—he thought hard about it now, because he and his mother were both in the job market and he was shocked to discover that even to be a part-time restaurant host he'd need a college degree. He ended up with a job at a movie theater, and on the side took paying gigs shooting video of baseball games for a recreational league. His mother lived off a widow's stipend for a while, then found work at a bank. Even with their pooled resources, Birchell was not going to be able to afford college unless he won a Zell Miller scholarship, the deluxe version of HOPE which offered full coverage of tuition and books to anyone with a high school GPA above 3.7. He finished with a 3.85. He and his mother battled their way through the student financial aid forms, and he was excited to start what he imagined would be a film studies major at Georgia State.

Then came a problem. Birchell kept waiting for the Zell Miller money to come through, but as the summer rolled on and three of his friends received notification of their financial awards, he was left without news. Birchell began to wonder if he'd failed his last high school statistics test, or if he'd made a mistake filling out an application form. He didn't want to burden his mother with this right away, so he turned instead to a new technology that Georgia State had invited him to use on a trial basis. It was, of course, the chatbot. He fired off queries during breaks from his movie theater job, and Pounce responded within seconds. At first the advice was: give it a couple of weeks. Then, in July, even the chatbot agreed something was off and suggested Birchell make an appointment at the financial aid office. It turned out there had been a mechanical error in reading one of the digits in his social security number, even though Birchell had written it down correctly, and his access to state funding had been blocked as a result. Luckily, he'd brought his social security card as one of two forms of government ID that Pounce said he'd need, and a clerk was able to fix the problem on the spot.

The impact on a low-income student like Birchell was profound. Had the problem not been caught, he would have lost at least a semester, complicating not just his timeline toward a degree but also the financial arrangements he'd need to get there. "I would have fallen victim to summer melt," he said. Instead, a year later, he was a thriving political science major—he switched from film studies right after the 2016 presidential election— and he was showing Bill Gates, of all people, how the chatbot worked. "It's extremely humbling," he told Gates, "to teach you how to use a software."

The lesson of these narratives was not lost on Gates. Yes, these were all remarkable individuals, but the university had also given itself the tools to recognize and nurture their potential. "GSU's key insight," Gates later wrote, "was that there isn't a single, big reason that leads to students dropping out. It's dozens of smaller things that disrupt their journey to graduation." It's worth remembering that if Fenwick Huss and Risa Palm had won the argument about using SAT scores to shape the applicant pool, Fortune Onwuzuruike and Gabriella Salinas might not have been admitted to Georgia State at all. It's worth remembering, too, that academic ability is almost never the factor causing lower-income students to drop out. A few hundred dollars here and there could have spelled the difference between Kalif Robinson being fast-tracked toward a State Department career and becoming just another young black college dropout struggling to get by in a city that does not easily forgive missed opportunities. A mistranscribed social security number could have doomed Austin Birchell's college career before it started.

Each of the four benefited from programs that have been proven to work at scale—both on the Atlanta campus and at Perimeter.

That suggests they should be easily transferable to other institutions. Yet the record on that has been mixed, at best.

The technology that Georgia State has pioneered along with its outside partners has certainly spread. AdmitHub now has dozens of chatbot clients around the country, and the Education Advisory Board has sold hundreds of versions of its interactive student data dashboard. The difficulty has come in convincing universities to embrace the leadership strategies that have enabled Georgia State to make a success of these technological tools, whether that is centralizing academic advising, or showing faculty departments the benefits of reordering and reorganizing their class schedules, or abandoning traditional teaching techniques in favor of adaptive learning.

Plenty of other institutions are hungry for the *results*. "Georgia State," one visitor told Mark Becker in 2019, "is what we want to be when we grow up." What gives them pause is the work required to get there. Too often, they have contented themselves with dipping a toe in the water of student success and have not mustered the courage to plunge all the way in. Technology becomes a prop, not a strategy, a shiny object that gets stuck in the corner of a room and is either underused or neglected altogether. Sometimes, institutions imagine that technology alone will get them where they want to go. And, sometimes, the technology becomes a foil for the underlying truth that they aren't all that interested in changing their ways, only in giving the *appearance* of doing so by purchasing a software package. Bridget Burns of the University Innovation Alliance recounted how one of her members—an institution ostensibly more committed to radical change than most—canceled its contract with EAB because its advisors simply weren't using the predictive analytics dashboard. "We gave them this platform, and trained them, but it wasn't good enough for them," she said. "Unfortunately, not figuring out how to get your advisors to do something is a really common thing."

When university delegations come to Atlanta for one of the

informational tours that Georgia State organizes dozens of times a year, they are frequently blown away by the presentations put on by Renick, Calhoun-Brown, and their colleagues, and filled with excitement by all the ways they can see to help their own student populations. These are institutions that generally share the underlying premise that higher education has been failing too many of its students by sending them off with a lifetime's load of debt and no degree. Yet the initial enthusiasm can soon give way to a cold blast of reality. *The faculty will never accept this*, they say, sometimes out loud. *Our state board of regents exercises too much control. We're not a big research university, so we don't have Georgia State's clout.* Whatever the reasoning, it causes many delegations to walk away as daunted as they are inspired. As a visiting Californian vice president of student affairs, William Franken, said during a question and answer session on a December 2018 tour: "The question is not: are the students ready for college? But: are we ready for them?"

One of the more visible institutions on that tour was California State Polytechnic, Pomona, a public college twenty-five miles east of Los Angeles. It sent no fewer than eleven representatives—essentially, its top campus leadership—to learn everything possible about the Georgia State model and to assess how much it could reasonably adapt. The university, which despite the name offers a full range of courses to 25,000 predominantly lower-income undergraduates, seemed to have every advantage: a dynamic president, Soraya Coley, with a deep-seated commitment to improving the lives of her students, a student success team fully invested in technology to introduce novel classroom teaching methods and eliminate needless administrative procedures, and a California State University system determined to double graduation rates and close all achievement gaps by 2025.

And yet *everything* has proven to be a challenge, even in the wake of the Atlanta visit. Not only has Georgia State's example failed to serve as proof of concept to speed up the reform process,

Cal Poly has had to rehash many of the issues Georgia State did a decade ago—and has added a few extra of its own.

To give an example: In 2019, the university appointed a chief data officer (who happened to be an alumna of Georgia State's College of Education), because it understood that the push for meaningful reform would stand or fall on the collection of reliable information about its students. The university, though, had just switched from a quarter to a semester system, and the data was not transferable. Instead of being able to draw on ten years of grades to develop predictive models, Cal Poly and many of its sister institutions making a similar move were starting from scratch. Worse, Cal Poly had a long-standing experimental approach to education that sought not to overburden students with tests and exams for credit. It could not collect and analyze midterm results, because it didn't *have* midterms.

The data problem has radiated out into a panoply of other areas. When the CSU system sought to streamline its intro courses and make sure first-year students were taking subjects that would best serve them regardless of their choice of major, it provoked howls of protest and, on the campus of Cal State Northridge in the northwestern Los Angeles suburbs, a vote of no-confidence in the chancellor. One of the arguments behind the no-confidence vote was that the data to justify the changes wasn't there. On the Cal Poly Pomona campus, the lack of solid information made it harder to press what was already a difficult case for centralized advising. According to Terri Gomez, the university's associate vice president of student success, the faculty union saw it as an affront to its members, who had previously done the bulk of academic advising themselves and worried that predictive analytics would encode assumptions and prejudices about minority students instead of helping them. In the face of such resistance, Cal Poly Pomona was able to hire only nine full-time advisors in the first instance, bringing the student–advisor ratio down from 1,300:1 in 2016 to about 1000:1 three years later, far short of the target Gomez and her team had set. "We haven't worked out the relationships around data," Gomez acknowledged. "It's a big challenge for us."

The power of campus unions is frequently cited across the country as an impediment to change, not least because the states recognized as having made the most progress on retention and graduation rates—Georgia, Tennessee, Florida, Arizona, parts of Texas—do not have campus unions with collective bargaining rights. It is, however, an argument resisted by many of the leaders of the student success movement, because it implies that union reps are intrinsically hostile to the idea of retaining and graduating students, which is rarely the case, and because in an arena of maddeningly slow progress it can sound like one more excuse for inaction. It is certainly true that unions represent an extra layer of negotiation, one more campus constituency to win over. That can slow things down, particularly when institutions do not have their arguments and data pinned down with Renick-like precision. At the same time, there is nothing insuperable about unions. The University of Illinois, Chicago, for example, is a unionized campus that has made significant progress on college completion.

It may be more accurate to say that university campuses are riddled with vested interests, of which unions are just one, and that these interest groups have an unfortunate tendency to defend their own turf first and to work together in the students' interest a distant second. Any campus leader who wants to push back against these territorial instincts has to be willing to break heads and lose some friends, and many are not. Their gut instinct, shaped by decades of institutional practice, is to be collegial and to govern by consensus. And that tends to perpetuate problems they may have set out to solve, and to normalize what should be intolerable patterns of institutional failure. "In too many ways," Tim Renick observes, "universities were not designed with students in mind."

————

Still, the positive examples of institutions that have successfully replicated aspects of Georgia State's work—or found their own way to similar conclusions—are starting to emerge with a consistency suggesting that reproducibility may not so elusive after all. The University of Houston has not only embraced the consolidation ethos but has greatly extended it to encompass five four-year institutions and eight community colleges within the greater Houston metropolitan area. And the results have been remarkable. All students are exposed to a suite of support programs that include advising, peer tutoring, and services tailored to first-generation students and to those with undeclared majors. As of 2018, the six-year graduation rate was close to 60 percent and climbing rapidly.

In Baltimore, Morgan State University, a historically black college, has seen a jump of more than 10 percentage points in both its retention and graduation rates over the past decade thanks to a formula closer still to Georgia State's: early alerts, proactive advising, a summer program for incoming freshmen, and peer tutoring. Indian River State College, on Florida's Atlantic coast, won the 2019 Aspen Prize for Community College Excellence because of its impressive record of preparing students for bachelor's degrees and for successful careers thereafter. Both institutions consulted Renick and sent delegations to Georgia State while in the thick of their work.

What makes these and other institutions stick out is not that they have been pioneers, necessarily, but that they have had the courage to recognize good ideas when they see them and to develop the institutional will to implement them. "We're not building the space shuttle here," said Rick Sluder, the vice provost for student success at Middle Tennessee State University outside Nashville. "It's about paying attention to the basics and making sure they are done."

Middle Tennessee saw firsthand what Georgia State was doing in 2013 and decided it wanted to do something similar. By the time Sluder started his job the following year, the university had already signed on with EAB and hired forty-seven new advisors, bringing the student–advisor ratio down to 260:1. His challenge: to launch the system and make sure the university's retention and graduation rates went up.

And they did. When Sluder attended EAB's annual conference a few months later, he saw Tim Renick receiving a Data-Driven Impact Award and said to himself: "I'm going to get that award next year." That, too, came to pass.

Sluder understood very quickly that all the technology in the world was no substitute for the hard work that Renick and his team had put in. "It's 70 percent people, 15 percent technology and 15 percent process," he said. "Yeah, you can bring in that platform, but you've got to make sure people are using it and know how it works at the ground level."

Many in higher education think of this moment as a test period to determine whether the Georgia State model is really reproducible. Maybe, they think, it's just a one-off attributable to unique circumstances and opportunities in Downtown Atlanta. But that is not what the evidence shows. What the evidence shows is that universities are the primary obstacles to their own students' success, and the sooner they learn to get out of their own way the better. If they are not doing so, it is because we are still in a phase of hesitation or resistance or lingering denial, an intermediary period in which the way forward is clear but not everyone has found the resolve to put one foot in front of the other. As Rick Sluder put it: "We're ten years behind the corporate sector in using big data. This is an awakening."

Once again, baseball may serve as a useful point of comparison. For years after the Oakland A's first used sabermetrics to punch above their weight in the American League, managers and scouts pooh-poohed their achievement and sought to poke holes in the very notion that data could teach them more than their years of experience and the evidence of their own eyes. Fifteen years on, *everyone* is using sabermetrics, and the utility of the data models goes unquestioned.

Renick, for one, expects a similar pattern in higher education, but perhaps a shorter timeframe because of what the technology is now able to deliver. "There are certain things we're able to do at scale that were just not doable even four years ago," he said. "We're talking about personalized, day-to-day, on-time interventions to navigate the bureaucracy. If you give people better tools to make better decisions, you'll have better and more predictable outcomes."

University presidents are certainly feeling the pressure—from their peers, from system offices, from politicians and the public—and most of them now understand that the status quo will no longer do. "If you don't speak the language of student success, you just don't fit in anymore," said Tom Sugar, one of the co-founders of Complete College America, now spearheading a new initiative with EAB to expand student success programs nationwide. "Leaders today are much more focused. They understand their own reputations and career trajectories are pinned to these outcomes."

The calculus for many institutions is the same as the one Georgia State faced after the 2008 recession: the prospect, on the one hand, of declining state funds and the need to find alternative revenue streams, and the opportunity, on the other, to reap the financial benefit of higher retention rates and form partnerships with local employers crying out for large numbers of entry-level college graduates.

No two institutions are the same, of course, and the skeptics are not wrong to think that Georgia State's evolution from a sleepy, segregated commuter school to a dynamic and extraordinarily diverse research university with a remarkable track record of student achievement owes as much to idiosyncrasies and happy accidents as it does to rigorous pursuit of a scientific method. But other institutions do not have to navigate such a complex path to achieve results of their own, because the pioneering work has been done.

The models have been developed and scaled, and the results are in. What they need to do now is take the salient lessons and apply them.

Committed leadership is of course essential. So is embracing the technology, and understanding that despite the initial start-up costs student success initiatives pay for themselves many times over as universities reap the benefit of continuing enrollments and tuition payments. One argument that Renick believes may make the transition more palatable to many institutions is that a significant number of student success programs are about what goes on *outside* the classroom and thus unlikely to involve a clash with faculty. Who could object to the chatbot? Or retention grants? He also believes, based on his own experience, that there are ways to bring faculty around to the benefits of more intrusive ideas like inverted classroom models, or schedules rearranged around meta majors; they just need to understand that the programs are a tool, not a threat, and that the groundwork is there to show that they are effective. "We're not forcing faculty to do anything," he said. "We're creating a context in which faculty can embrace change."

Georgia State did not chalk up its achievements alone. It relied in different ways on the state university system, the legislature, the governor's office, and Georgia's congressional representatives, all of whom had reasons to want to reform higher education and claim a piece of the credit for doing so. The university was careful to stress the cost-effectiveness of its programs and the contribution that a larger pipeline of graduates could make to the economy, and these proved to be winning arguments, particularly in a red state. That isn't to say that Georgia State believed *less* in the moral argument about lifting long-oppressed minorities out of poverty. On the contrary: One of the most heartening aspects of the university's success is that it has cut across ideological lines, even in a time of deep partisan rancor. It has offered a solid return on investment *and* moral justice, economic growth *and* social mobility. One or both arguments are likely to be equally effective elsewhere.

There are other lessons. A strong statewide university system like Georgia's can make a big difference in overcoming pockets of resistance. So can a state government interested in setting its own education policies, as is the case in Texas, or states willing to experiment with budgetary formulas, like the ones in Tennessee, Indiana, and Ohio that tie a portion of higher education funding to graduation rates and other performance outcomes. It's not that these initiatives always succeed, or are always adequately funded, or come with the necessary follow-through. What they do, though, is send a signal about the urgency of improving college completion rates. They educate the public about ideas that are still too little known, and push the broader culture of higher education toward much needed reform.

When Kyle Stapleton left Georgia State with a marketing degree in 2009, he thought of his alma mater as "a place where things are possible for people who would find them impossible anywhere else." That was certainly true at the time. Georgia State was, and in many respects continues to be, a remarkable place where students from the most unlikely backgrounds have an opportunity to prove themselves and excel. But it is also time for that exceptionalism to end. In the words of Mark Becker: "This has to become a national movement. We have to show this is scalable across the country. We need other institutions to produce the same results."

The stakes are clear. This is about reversing an unsustainable trajectory, for universities and their students, and laying the groundwork for a brighter and more equitable future. Once, it seemed impossible. Now it has become impossible to ignore.

ACKNOWLEDGMENTS

This book began as an intellectual curiosity, about a university doing interesting things in downtown Atlanta, but it soon evolved
into a full-blown passion project as I learned about the extraordinary journeys that Georgia State's students have traveled and the
extraordinary impact of the people who have committed themselves to transforming their lives and changing the national conversation around higher education and social mobility. It became
not just a book I wanted to write, but one I *had* to write.

I wanted readers to be as moved as I was by the resilience,
talent, and strength of spirit of students from the toughest of
backgrounds who battled their way to a university degree when
many people—family, friends, and society at large—told them
they didn't stand a chance. I wanted readers to be awed, too, by
the imagination, tenacity, and unrelenting hard work of Georgia
State's administrators, staff, and faculty, who refused to accept
conventional wisdom and kept looking for new opportunities to
give undergraduates the support they needed and to remove the
obstacles in their way. Paying tribute to that achievement and telling the inside story of how it came about—also against daunting
odds—has been an unceasing privilege and pleasure.

My thanks, first and foremost, to Mark Becker and Tim Renick,
who were generous with their time and thoughtful about the complex, multifaceted problems they have sought to overcome. They
opened up the university, encouraging one and all to talk frankly
about the struggles as well as the triumphs. This is a unique, collaborative project. It originated with the instigation and support
of the Kresge Foundation; was shepherded by The New Press; and

was made possible by the extraordinary level of access and support afforded by Becker and Renick. They offered feedback and guidance on the manuscript in draft form. But they also had the guts to entrust the task to an independent writer, with a brief to follow the information wherever it led and to produce a narrative that dug into the difficult, uncomfortable issues as well as the straightforward, celebratory ones. As they have been many times down the years, they were gutsy enough to depart from standard university practice and plunge into the unknown for the sake of the students. Georgia State, under their leadership, has always been more interested in results than in what critics and detractors might have to say. And those critics and detractors were far from shy with me, as the book makes plain.

For several months Atlanta became my second home, and Georgia State—starting with the members of Renick's student success team—provided the warmest of welcomes. I ended up interviewing about a hundred people, most of them in Atlanta and a number of others spread across the country. Their names are in the text and in the endnotes, and I am grateful to all of them for the time they devoted and the intelligence, grace, and humor they showed in answering my many questions. I want to extend particular thanks to the ones who sat for multiple sessions—in person, on the phone, by email, or in some combination. Sometimes I had to go back because I learned things I hadn't known the first time. Sometimes I had to reconcile conflicting narratives from multiple sources. The following were all patient and insightful and unfailingly responsive: Allison Calhoun-Brown, Carol Cohen, Scott Burke, Tom Lewis, Jerry Rackliffe, Risa Palm, Paul Alberto, Peter Lyons, Tom Sugar, and Fenwick Huss.

In addition to their own narratives, Pamela Barr and Deborah Semans provided invaluable documentation relating to the 2011 strategic plan. Cary Claiborne and Crystal Mitchell happily tore up their day's schedule when my hourlong slot with each turned into a marathon of amazing and, at times, tear-filled storytelling.

Andrew Young gave me an unforgettable few hours. Erroll Davis and Hank Huckaby opened their homes and were generous hosts as well as terrific interviewees. Tim Crimmins not only shared the transcripts of his oral-history interviews with a variety of Georgia State luminaries past and present, he also offered valuable feedback on historical aspects of the manuscript.

My deep admiration as well as my thanks go to the many students and ex-students I got to know over the lifetime of the project: Princeton Nelson, Savannah Torrance, Brianna Cheek, Gabriel Woods, Joshua Okinola-King, Stephanie Tran, Sharon Sample, Tyler Mulvenna, Kyle Stapleton, Terrance Rogers, Jovan Paige, Jasmine Twine, Osman Saccoh, Fortune Onwuzuruike, Kalif Robinson, Gabriella Salinas, and Austin Birchell. They didn't just answer questions but opened up their lives and their souls, sometimes for hours at a stretch and sometimes in ways they never had previously. I can't overstate how honored I am by the trust they placed in me. The space I ultimately devoted to each was determined not by how fascinating or remarkable they were—they were all remarkable—only by the demands of the overall story. To my regret, some did not end up in the final manuscript but were an inspiration nevertheless. Equally heartfelt thanks to Tiffany Harvey, Phebe Philippe, Chelsea Moore, Brad Colwell, Amila Shake, and Carl McCray. I don't think I'll ever stop rooting for all of you. Neia Omer was not only an inspiration but moved me closer to the heart of the story at a vital juncture by connecting me to members of the advising office where she had worked as an undergraduate.

A number of other people were helpful behind the scenes or offered insights for which I didn't ultimately have space. A big thank-you to Andrea Jones, who I suspect did more for this project on a more consistent basis than I will ever know, to Holly Joseph, who was gracious and brilliant and acted as a gateway to some of the students whose stories moved me most, to Chandler Brown (ditto—and he also knew his way around Mark Becker's old speeches because he helped write them), to Shelby Frost, who does deeply impressive work with cutting-edge classroom teaching methods, to Kerry Heyward, Georgia State's delightful and razor-sharp chief legal counsel who dotted my *i*'s and crossed my *t*'s on a number of important issues (especially in the endnotes), to Randy Trammell, who led me to Princeton Nelson, to Emily Buis, Joshua Reaves, Julie Kerlin, Megan Tesene, Sutandra Sarkar, Lee Webster, Jennifer Stephens, Angela Turk, Lance Wallace, Jen Ryan, Jennifer Spann, and Richard Chambers. Georgia State's Office of Institutional Research came through multiple times with data not available through other means. Meg Buscema, Carolyn Richardson, Steve Thackston, and Laurel Bowen worked with dedication and enthusiasm on the photo insert. Thanks also to the university support staff who smoothed my visits to Atlanta and made sure busy senior administrators were available when I needed them: Jazmine Glasper, Wanda Taylor, Joyce Presswood, Susan Feuerzeig, Ethel Brown Wright, and Julie Lawson. There's a reason they call it Southern hospitality.

This project was possible only thanks to the generous financial backing of the Kresge Foundation and the enthusiasm and commitment of Bill Moses, the managing director of Kresge's education program. As was appropriate, Bill kept his distance once the project was in motion, but his belief in Georgia State's work and his determination to see it celebrated and analyzed in book form for the benefit of the widest possible audience inspired us all.

At The New Press, I had an ideal editor in Marc Favreau, who put great faith in me and gave the manuscript the benefit of his fine editorial judgment. Carl Bromley demonstrated, yet again, that I have no stauncher friend and ally in the publishing business. The team as a whole treated me like family, starting with Ellen Adler, the publisher. I'm particularly grateful for the hard work of Brian Ulicky, Maury Botton, Emily Albarillo, Sarah Scheffel—my outstanding copyeditor—Laura Starrett, David Shoemaker, and zakia henderson-brown.

Dana Newman untangled some unexpected legal knots with her usual grace and intelligence. The brilliant Joe Donnelly was an invaluable early reader and a true mensch. My equally brilliant wife, Naomi Seligman, spotted a problem in the first draft that had escaped others' attention, inspiring a comprehensive (and much needed) rewrite.

Naomi developed a love for this material to rival mine, and threw herself heart and soul into supporting the book, in the same irresistible way she throws herself into everything and everyone she believes in. She rooted for me when I was in Atlanta and she was home solo parenting, and she rooted for me just as hard when I was writing the manuscript and living night and day in the Georgia State University inside my head. I feel incredibly fortunate to have had so much support from her and from the rest of my immediate family—Max, Rara, Sammy, Tonka the tortoise (who made sure I thought about something else occasionally, if only romaine lettuce), and Muffin the cat (a lousy typist but a soulfully meditative purrer).

This book navigates a lot of previously uncharted territory, and much of the narrative relies on personal recollections, some of them a decade old or older. I did my best to corroborate those recollections through documentation, by conducting multiple interviews with as many people as I could think of, and by seeking to reconcile conflicts and contradictions. I went back to a large number of my sources after the first draft to double-check that I had rendered their accounts accurately and fairly. Ultimately, I had many allies invested in making this as readable and as accurate a book as possible. That said, not everyone is going to agree with my judgments and interpretations in every instance, and some of that will be due to my own imperfections. There may be people I should have thought to talk to but didn't, or questions I should have asked but didn't. For any oversights or inadvertent errors, I of course take full responsibility.

NOTES

Interviews were conducted in person in Atlanta, except as otherwise indicated. Dates of interviews are not repeated except in cases where subjects gave multiple interviews.

Introduction

Interviews for this section include Princeton Nelson (January 29, 2019); Savannah Torrance (November 12, 2018, in Dacula, GA); Tim Renick (May 21, 2018); Mark Becker (September 18, 2018); and Andrew Young (February 1, 2019).

Nelson and Torrance graduated in December 2018; Greyson Walldorff and Larry Felton Johnson in May of that year. Video of commencement ceremonies including speeches can be seen at commencement.gsu.edu. Walldorff's story is from the Robinson College of Business website; for more on Johnson's story, see Dakin Andone, "He wanted to graduate from college before he was 100. He just did it at 66," *CNN.com*, May 10, 2018.

Graduation figures, demographic breakdowns, and numbers of low-income students come from Georgia State's annual Complete College Georgia reports to the board of regents and from data compiled by the university's Office of Institutional Research. The exact figures are as follows. In the 2017–18 academic year, 4,990 people earned bachelor's degrees, of whom 32 percent were white, 41 percent were black, and an astonishing 70 percent were low enough on the income scale to be eligible for a federal Pell grant. In the 2010–11 academic year, 4,222 people earned bachelor's degrees, of whom 44 percent were white, 33 percent were black, and 57 percent were Pell-eligible. In the 2002–03 academic year, 2,885 people earned bachelor's degrees, of whom 51 percent were white and 31 percent were black. There is no data on income levels from that period.

On Ludacris: The Georgia State law school established a firm connection with the rapper in fall 2019 by offering a course on his work contracts as a case study in entertainment-industry legal affairs. Places for "The Legal Life of Ludacris" filled up quickly, and Ludacris himself showed up on campus to launch the course, taught by Mo Ivory, a well-connected former attorney, radio host, and candidate for the Atlanta City Council.

On two-thirds of all jobs in America require postsecondary training: this is based on a projection for 2020, made in 2013 by Anthony Carnevale and his team at Georgetown University in their report "Recovery: Job Growth and Education Requirements Through 2020." On inequality and its impact on higher education, see William G. Bowen, Matthew M. Chingos, and Michael S. McPherson, *Crossing the Finish Line: Completing College at America's Public Universities* (Princeton, NJ: Princeton University Press, 2009), 1–9; Sara Goldrick-Rab, *Paying the Price: College Costs, Financial Aid, and the Betrayal of the American Dream* (Chicago: University of Chicago Press, 2016); and Richard V. Reeves, *Dream Hoarders: How the American Upper Middle Class Is Leaving Everyone Else in the Dust, Why That Is a Problem, And What to Do About It* (Washington, DC: Brookings Institution Press, 2017), especially 37–57. King quotes are from his essay "The World House," collected in Martin Luther King, Jr., *Where Do We Go from Here: Chaos or Community?* (Boston: Beacon Press, 1967), pp. 177–202.

Chapter 1: Fishing Village

Chapter based on interviews with Mark Becker (May 23, 2018, January 31, 2019, by phone March 13, 2019); Michael Eriksen (by phone October 15, 2018); Allison Calhoun-Brown (by phone July 10, 2018); Harris Pastides (by phone March 5, 2019); Erroll Davis (September 20, 2018); Paul Alberto (by phone June 21, 2018); Bob Smith (by phone April 19, 2019); Tom Lewis (November 15, 2018, by phone January 29, 2018); Carl Patton (December 5, 2018); Jerry Rackliffe (September 21, 2018); Risa Palm (September 21, 2018, by phone May 31, 2019); Lauren Adamson (by phone August 1, 2018); George Rainbolt (by phone February 26, 2019); Hugh Hudson (by phone February 28, 2019); Fenwick Huss (November 27, 2018 in New York); and Tim Renick (by phone August 8, 2018).

Becker provided a copy of his PowerPoint presentation, which he delivered on February 23, 2010. General MacArthur's speech to the cadet corps at West Point was delivered on May 12, 1962, and is widely available online in both text and audio formats. Duderstadt's thoughts on the future of universities are from James J. Duderstadt, Daniel E. Atkins, and Douglas Van Houweling, *Higher Education in the Digital Age* (Westport, CT: Praeger, 2002), 228; see also Duderstadt's solo book *A University for the 21st Century* (Ann Arbor, MI: University of Michigan

Press, 2000). For Rhodes's views, see Frank H.T. Rhodes, *The Creation of the Future: The Role of the American University* (Ithaca, NY: Cornell University Press, 2001), 223–24, from which the quote is taken. On Richard Florida, see, e.g., Florida's *The Rise of the Creative Class . . . and How It's Transforming Work, Leisure, Community, and Everyday Life* (New York: Basic Books, 2002). For more on the Charlotte to Atlanta corridor and other urban corridors, see, e.g., Richard Florida, "The Dozen Regional Powerhouses Driving the U.S. Economy," *CityLab*, March 12, 2014. (Florida started writing about this years earlier, but the CityLab piece is a succinct summary.)

On Bob Smith not having a soft spot in his heart for Georgia State: Smith, invited to comment, denied causing any sort of trouble for the university ("If we were a roadblock, how did they double their student population?"), but he did not refute Patton's underlying premise. He and two of his children went to UGA, while a third attended Georgia Tech. Tom Lewis said in an email (April 19, 2019) that Smith "was kinder to us than others at the time," but Smith did not reciprocate the good feelings. In fact, he denied ever meeting Lewis for breakfast, or a number of other interactions and kindnesses that Lewis itemized and that others recalled independently. Rather, Smith called Lewis's interactions "perfunctory," with a soft *n*. "I saw him," he said, "but there was no camaraderie."

The numbers behind the fallout from the 2008 recession come from Jerry Rackliffe and from Georgia State's annual financial reports; some of the figures quoted here do not line up exactly with those reports because of overlap between years and other accounting minutiae. Becker's 2009 State of the University speech is not available on the university website but was provided by his staff. Bob Morse and Enxhi Myslymi of *U.S. News & World Report* provided historical data on Georgia State's placement in the ranking of national universities. The Tom Wolfe quote is from *A Man in Full* (New York: Farrar, Straus and Giroux, 1998), 26.

The apple-cart line came from George Rainbolt, then chair of the philosophy department and of the university senate committee on admissions and standards. Hugh Hudson resigned as history department chair in 2011. Palm did not refute most of the stories told about her. In many cases, she said she didn't remember. In response to Hudson's account of her expressing a low opinion of a number of the deans, she said: "That's so out of character for my brain that I find it hard to believe I did it. Honestly, I think I know how to talk to faculty committees. This is something you don't do, and I don't think I did."

Chapter 2: Admit Them

Chapter based on interviews with Tim Renick (May 21, 2018, May 22, 2018, by phone August 8, 2018, by phone September 5, 2018, January 30, 2019, by phone March 14, 2019, by phone July 31, 2019); Matt Lyons (by phone November 19, 2018); Matt Hinton (March 18, 2019); Anthony Petro (March 22, 2019); Stephen Prothero (by phone June 11, 2018); Ron Henry (by phone March 5, 2019); George Rainbolt (by phone February 26, 2019); Lauren Adamson (by phone August 1, 2018); Mark Becker (May 23, 2018, September 18, 2018); Brianna Cheek (July 26, 2019); Allison Calhoun-Brown (May 22, 2018, by phone August 8, 2018, February 1, 2019), Risa Palm, Fenwick Huss (November 27, 2018, in New York) and Jerry Rackliffe. Note: Matt Lyons is the son of Peter Lyons, a Georgia State professor of social work who served as associate provost for institutional effectiveness before becoming the inaugural dean of Georgia Perimeter College following the 2016 consolidation (see chapter 12).

The quote from F. Scott Fitzgerald's *The Great Gatsby*, first published in 1925, is from page 5 of the 2004 Scribner edition. The New Hampshire congressman Renick interned with was Norman D'Amours, who entered Congress in 1975 in the post-Watergate Democratic wave and served five terms. Additional material on Renick comes from his CV, available at the Georgia State website, and from a teaching statement, also available at gsu.edu, that Renick delivered in 2002 on receiving his state teaching award. The Aquinas peanut butter riff is reproduced in Renick's entertaining book, *Aquinas for Armchair Theologians* (pages 147–49), published by Westminster John Knox Press in 2002. The quote from Renick's writings is from an article in the Association of American Colleges and Universities house magazine, *Liberal Education*, "The Religious Studies Major and Liberal Education," which appeared in the Spring 2009 issue. Renick, who is not credited, wrote it on behalf of the American Academy of Religion.

The data models for Keep HOPE Alive, and all Renick's subsequent projects, were developed by Renick's office in association with the Office of Institutional Research. The criticism of aptitude tests from the 1940s is based on a 1948 study published in *Scientific Monthly*. Lemann's book is *The Big Test: The Secret History of the American Meritocracy* (New York: Farrar, Straus and Giroux, 2000); see especially 66. The data on SAT and ACT scores and how they compare with high school GPA as a predictor of student success comes from Bowen et al., op. cit., 113–22.

Georgia State's place in the *U.S. News* list of national universities went up in the two years it was controlling more stringently for SAT scores. It was number 202 in the 2011 list (issued in 2010) and number 206 the following year, before sinking back to 214 in 2012 and 216 in 2013. In 2017—a year when Georgia State was attracting national media attention for its groundbreaking work in student success—it was ranked 236th.

Chapter 3: Who Are We? Where Are We Going?

Chapter based on interviews with Ken Bernhardt (by phone October 24, 2018); Risa Palm, Mark Becker (May 21, 2018, September 18, 2018, by phone October 23, 2018, November 2, 2018, by phone March 13, 2019, July 8, 2019); Jorge Martinez-Vazquez (September 20, 2018); Maury Cotter (by phone February 5, 2019); David Ward (February 11, 2019, in Manhattan Beach, CA); Michael Eriksen, Allison Calhoun-Brown, Harris Pastides, Bob Smith, Tom Lewis, Andrew Young, Peter Lyons (November 13, 2018); Fenwick Huss, P.C. Tai (by phone March 7, 2019); Pamela Barr (by phone, June 19, 2018); Paul Alberto, Tim Renick (September 19, 2018, by phone March 14, 2019); Debra Semans (by phone December 18, 2018); and Hugh Hudson.

Becker's stated goal of creating a plan that would "provide direction for at least twenty years" comes from the minutes of a November 4, 2009, administrative council meeting. Risa Palm's provisional agenda for undergraduate teaching comes from the minutes of a special meeting of the planning and development committee held the same day.

Michael Crow material is taken from a speech Crow gave at Georgia State on the day the strategic plan was approved in 2011, available on YouTube; from an Aspen Institute report, *Connecting the Edges: A Report of the 2012 Aspen Institute Roundtable on Institutional Innovation*, by Richard Adler (Washington, DC, Aspen Institute, 2013), 2–3, 30–32; and from a profile by Steven Beschloss, "The Velocity of Change" (*ASU Thrive* magazine, Vol. 20, No. 4, September 2017). The handbook he likes is *High Velocity Culture Change: A Handbook for Managers*, by Price Pritchett and Ron Pound (Dallas: Pritchett Publishing Company, 2007).

Details of the budget crunch that led to the Hildreth controversy are taken, in part, from Maria Saporta and J. Scott Trubey, "Andrew Young School dean says he was asked to resign," *Atlanta Business Chronicle*, March 10, 2010. The Hildreth memo is cited in Jack Stripling, "Deanship 2.0," *Inside Higher Ed*, September 15, 2010. On March 9, the day Hildreth's resignation became public, Scott Trubey of the *Business Chronicle* emailed Georgia State to ask for comment on possible changes that he'd been told about "by folks" that "might be in store related to the makeup of the Andy Young school and its relationship with the Robinson College [of Business]." Hildreth, in an email dated March 1, 2019 (at which point he was still a tenured faculty member at Georgia State), expressly denied that he contacted the media before his resignation as dean but otherwise declined to comment. He did not challenge Becker's account of their conversation.

The Education Trust report, published on January 28, 2010, consisted of two parts written by Jennifer Engle and Christina Theokas. They were titled "Top Gainers: Some Public Four-Year Colleges and Universities Make Big Improvements in Minority Graduation Rates" and "Top Gap Closers: Some Public Four-Year Colleges and Universities Have Made Good Progress in Closing Graduation-Rate Gaps." A press release issued by the Education Trust the same day listed Georgia State first on a short list of universities singled out for praise. The others were the University of Wisconsin–Madison, Western Oregon University, and the Richard Stockton College of New Jersey.

Early drafts of the strategic plan were provided by Pamela Barr. Focus group feedback is from a written report by Debra Semans, a former graduate student of Bernhardt's then working for Polaris Marketing Research. She conducted phone interviews with forty people—"alumni, GSU Foundation and Board of Visitors members, state and city legislators, foundation executives and business and community leaders"—and presented her findings to the committee on November 8, 2010. Semans provided a copy of the written report, which did not name any of the respondents.

Chapter 4: The Path to Destruction

Chapter based on interviews with Gabriel Woods (January 28, 2019, in Savannah, and by phone March 18, 2010); Duane Carver (by phone March 12, 2019); Maria Gindhart (by phone February 14, 2019); Allison Calhoun-Brown (February 1, 2019); Tim Renick (May 22, 2018); Fenwick Huss (November 27, 2018, in New York, and by phone September 5, 2019); Ron Henry, Kyle Stapleton (October 11, 2018, in Santa Monica, CA); Terrance Rogers (by phone December 14, 2018); Jovan Paige (December 5, 2018); Jorge Martinez-Vazquez, Elisha Jarrett (January 30, 2019); Carol Cohen (November 14, 2018); and Crystal Mitchell (November 13, 2018, in Decatur, GA).

Gabriel Woods's email to the assistant director of the music department was written on August 20, 2008. Woods has kept copies of that email and the response, which he read out during the interview. The General Classroom Building has since been renamed Langdale Hall. For more on the winter storm of January 9–11, 2011, see Greg Bluestein, "Should Atlanta Have Been Better Prepared for Snow?" *Associated Press*, January 13, 2011. Details of the university closures were still viewable as of March 2019 at the Georgia State library blog.

Chapter 5: Multidimensional Chess

Chapter based on interviews with Tim Renick (May 22, 2018, September 19, 2018, by phone March 14, 2019); Joshua Okinola-King (May 22, 2018); Ron Henry, Allison Calhoun-Brown, Carol Cohen (May 22, 2018, November 14, 2018); Elisha Jarrett, Mark Becker (May 23, 2018, by phone October 23, 2018, November 16, 2018); Peter Lyons, Hank Huckaby (November 12, 2018, in Athens, GA); Chris Riley (by phone May 10, 2019); Jerry Rackliffe, Fenwick Huss, Lauren Adamson, and Risa Palm.

National research into the "murky middle" was led by Ed Venit of the Education Advisory Board, starting around 2010, and eventually published in Venit, et al., "The Murky Middle Project—Preliminary Findings," Education Advisory Board/Student Success Initiative, 2014. More on Venit in chapter 6.

NACADA, based at Kansas State University in Manhattan, KS, began recommending a student–advisor ratio of 300:1 in 2004. It later fine-tuned this recommendation, first in 2011 when it noted that it might be appropriate to assign larger advising loads in specialist fields of study like business, and again in 2013, when it noted that student loads tended to be higher in larger institutions, which made it shy away from a specific recommendation because "meaningful case load comparisons remain elusive." See Debra Y. Applegate and Gayle Hartleroad, "Effective Ways to Deal with Large Advising Loads" (Academic Advising Today, March 2011) and Rich Robbins, "Implications of Advising Load" (National Academic Advising Association, Monograph No. 25, 2013), both available via NACADA's website.

The text of the University of Georgia System's 2007 strategic plan provided by the UGS communications team. Information on Complete College Georgia available at completega.org. For an example of the less-than-stellar education headlines Deal garnered in 2011, see Nancy Badertscher, "Deal unveils cuts for HOPE, pre-K," *Atlanta Journal-Constitution*, February 23, 2011.

One reason for the cautious approach taken by Georgia State's office of legal affairs was a high-profile lawsuit filed against the university by three academic publishers who argued that they were not being fairly compensated for the electronic distribution of their materials through the Georgia State library's e-reserve system. When the case started in 2008, it was seen as an important test case to define fair use of educational materials. But it also turned into higher ed's very own version of *Jarndyce v. Jarndyce*, dragging on for more than a decade to the point where almost nobody understood the stakes anymore and many institutions resorted to negotiating fair use on a case-by-case basis. See Lindsay McKenzie, "An Unending Copyright Dispute," *Inside Higher Ed*, October 30, 2018. The case, which started out as *Cambridge University Press v. Patton* and morphed into *Cambridge University Press v. Becker*, is also usefully summarized by Georgia State's own law school at libguides.law.gsu.edu/gsucopyrightcase.

Chapter 6: Moneyball on Campus

Chapter based on interviews with Ed Venit (by phone October 15, 2018); Allison Calhoun-Brown, Tim Renick (September 19, 2018, November 15, 2018, July 8, 2019); Mark Becker (November 16, 2018); Rich Staley (by phone October 16, 2018); Carol Cohen, Crystal Mitchell, Elisha Jarrett; Cary Claiborne (November 13, 2018, in Decatur, GA), Savannah Torrance, Risa Palm, Hank Huckaby.

The piece written by Capaldi (with John V. Lombardi and Victor Yellen) appeared in *Change* magazine in July–August 2006 and was titled "Improving Graduation Rates: A Simple Method That Works." Capaldi died in 2017. An insightful piece on her contributions is on the ASU website, "'Transformational' former ASU provost dies," ASU News, September 24, 2017.

Starfish, founded by former Blackboard ed tech executive David Yaskin in 2007, was acquired by Hobsons in 2015 and now offers a product that incorporates some of the features of EABs, including alerts, predictive analytics, and other features pioneered by Venit and his team.

The three earliest clients of EABs were Wright State University in Dayton, Ohio, Northern Illinois University in the Chicago suburbs, and Roosevelt University in downtown Chicago. They were soon joined by Florida International University in Miami.

On the political uses of data technology, listen to Jody Avirgan's podcast "A History of Data in American Politics (Part 2): Obama 2008 to the Present," published by FiveThirtyEight.com on January 21, 2016. For a more detailed account of how the Republican Party leveraged new data technologies to redraw district boundaries to their advantage in North Carolina and other states in 2011, see

Andrew Gumbel, *Down for the Count: Dirty Elections and the Rotten History of Democracy in America* (New York: The New Press, 2016), 207–209.

Mauriello quoted in Michael Lewis, *Moneyball* (New York: Norton, 2003), 131. In his introduction (page xiv), Lewis writes: "Baseball—of all things—was an example of how an unscientific culture responds, or fails to respond, to the scientific method." The "silent shrieks" line later in the chapter is from page 99.

The data on the first year of proactive advising comes, in part, from the presentation Renick made to the board of regents on August 14, 2013—one that earned him a standing ovation. Slides from that presentation are available at the University System of Georgia website, dated October 22, 2013, when they were submitted to Complete College Georgia. Other data is derived from the Georgia State's 2013 Complete College Georgia Status Report, which Renick submitted to the board of regents.

Chapter 7: This Is Not a Scam, Do Not Hang Up

Chapter based on interviews with Mark Becker (May 23, 2018, by phone October 23, 2018, November 16, 2018, by phone March 13, 2019); Tim Renick (May 22, 2018, by phone September 13, 2018, November 15, 2018); Jerry Rackliffe, Hank Huckaby, Princeton Nelson, Sharon Sample (November 13, 2018, in Stone Mountain, GA); Allison Calhoun-Brown (May 22, 2018); Tyler Mulvenna (December 4, 2018); Crystal Mitchell, Risa Palm, Peter Lyons, Fenwick Huss, and Jorge Martinez-Vazquez. Some of the material from Huss is from an email dated January 10, 2019.

Rackliffe's figure of a $5,000 return on a $500 investment is a hypothetical based on his initial reaction to Renick's idea. The actual amounts, as listed, come from a 2018 analysis of Georgia State's retention grants by the Boston Consulting Group. In chapter 22 ("Milo the Mayor") of Joseph Heller's *Catch-22*, Yossarian asks Milo how he can buy eggs at seven cents each in Malta and make a profit selling them at five cents each on Pianosa. Milo answers: "Because I'm the people I buy them from." The Panther Retention Grants have a not dissimilar explanation. See the fiftieth-anniversary edition of *Catch-22* (New York: Simon & Schuster, 2011), 241.

Senator Isakson described the Panther Retention Grants and the proactive advising system at a hearing of the Senate Committee on Health, Education, Labor and Pensions on July 24, 2014. He said of Georgia State: "They are a majority minority university that has done a great job of addressing the disparity in terms of income and giving their students access to a quality education, and I'm very proud to brag about them." (Senate hearing 113–861, transcript available via govinfo. gov.) In his remarks at the College Opportunity Day of Action on December 4, 2014, President Obama said: "Georgia State University, just to cite one example, is developing a new system to give small grants to students who might be a little behind on their bills." (Transcript available via the White House website.) Georgia State and the retention grants were featured in eleven national news articles in 2014—the beginning of what would turn into a cascade of media interest in the university and its student success initiatives.

The details of Georgia State's short-lived experience of deferring weaker students to January were confirmed by Renick in an email dated April 25, 2019. Calhoun-Brown's "pitiful, poor and at risk" line was not from an interview but from a presentation made to visiting university administrators on December 7, 2018. The 30 percent drop in freshmen switching majors was from 2013 to 2015. The meta majors offered by Georgia State are: business, education, STEM (science, technology, engineer, and math), humanities and arts, health professions, public policy/social science, and—for those who arrive at the university undeclared—exploratory.

Renick continued to report directly to Risa Palm until 2014, when he was appointed vice president for enrollment management and student success and vice provost; the former role had him reporting to Becker and the latter role to Palm. In January 2018 he was appointed senior vice president for student success, making him fully Palm's equal (she, too, was a senior vice president), with each reporting to Becker only. Regardless of title, it was clear from quite early on that Renick had the president's ear and Palm recognized and respected that. "We worked as a team," was her way of describing the arrangement.

Risa Palm first adopted her military-style morning meetings at SUNY and they were inspired, in part, by Patrick Lencioni's book *Death by Meeting: A Leadership Fable About Solving the Most Painful Problem in Business* (San Francisco: Jossey-Bass, 2004).

Chapter 8: A Well-Managed Plantation

Chapter based on interviews with Carl Patton, Tim Crimmins (September 17, 2018); Jorge Martinez-Vazquez, Ken Bernhardt, Stephen Portch (by phone April 18, 2019); Hank Huckaby, Andrew Young, 1990s-era student Brad Colwell (October 23, 2018, in Santa Monica, CA); and Kyle Stapleton.

The material on the 1992 sit-in and its aftermath is based on contemporaneous accounts in *The Signal*, the Georgia State newspaper, as well as Patton's memories and an oral history interview that Ahmed Abdelal gave to Georgia State history professor Tim Crimmins on May 20, 2015, transcript kindly provided by Crimmins. One retrospective piece that provides a useful summary is Victor Sledge, "How a protest led to the creation of African-American studies at Georgia State," *The Signal*, February 20, 2018.

The story of Georgia State's integration in the 1950s and 1960s is taken largely from Merl E. Reed's *Educating the Urban New South: Atlanta and the Rise of Georgia State University, 1913–1969* (Macon, GA: Mercer University Press, 2009), 199–214, from contemporaneous articles in *The Signal*, and from Calvin Trillin's book, *An Education in Georgia: The Integration of Charlayne Hunter and Hamilton Holmes* (New York: Viking Press, 1964). Marvin Griffin's "hell or high water" line is from an interview he gave to *Time* magazine in a piece entitled "The Strategists" (July 12, 1954). Some of the details about Barbara Hunt and Annette Lucille are from a Liz Babiarz piece for GSU magazine, "Quiet Courage" (Fall 2009). The Jesse Hill quote about sparing seventeen-year-olds is from Trillin's book, 10. The account of Hunter and Holmes visiting Georgia State comes from Charlayne Hunter-Gault's autobiography, *In My Place* (New York: Farrar, Straus and Giroux, 1992), 126–27. The two cited editorials from *The Signal* are "Four Negroes Acting Unwise?" unsigned, July 12, 1957, and "In Education Today, Many Fleas Come with the Dog," written by *The Signal*'s editor in chief Rod Spicer, February 6, 1959. Spicer went on to be a sports columnist for the *Atlanta Journal-Constitution* before switching to public relations.

Horace Ward had a long and distinguished legal career and was elevated to the federal bench by President Carter. Hamilton Holmes was not the first trailblazer in his family: his grandfather and uncle campaigned successfully to desegregate Atlanta's public golf courses in the mid-1950s. After UGA, he enjoyed a successful career as an orthopedist and Emory University medical school professor before dying of a heart attack at fifty-four. Charlayne Hunter didn't wait to leave UGA before incensing the white establishment all over again by marrying a white fellow student in defiance of Georgia's law against interracial marriage. Later known as Charlayne Hunter-Gault, she went on to distinguish herself in journalism including stints with the *New York Times* and NPR. In 1988, on the twenty-fifth anniversary of her graduation, she gave a remarkable commencement speech at the University of Georgia, the text of which is reproduced in her book.

Part of Suttles's motivation for starting the law school in 1982 was that he believed a number of otherwise deserving white students would be turned away from the University of Georgia's law school because of affirmative action policies, and that Georgia State thus had an opportunity to offer those students an alternative. Georgia State also hoped to start minting lawyers who would run for the state legislature and increase the university's visibility and influence there. The Georgia House speaker in the inaugural law school graduating class was Glenn Richardson, who ended up resigning in disgrace. See the *Associated Press* story, "Georgia's Speaker of the House resigns after suicide attempt, claims of affair with lobbyist," December 4, 2009.

The Langdale family history is chronicled in John E. Lancaster, *Judge Harley and His Boys: The Langdale Story* (Macon, GA: Mercer University Press, 2002) and Noah Jr.'s part in it is on pages 263–64. Noah's cousin John W. Langdale was a longtime state legislator who went on to serve on the university board of regents while Noah was president of Georgia State. The stories about Langdale and Suttles on campus come from interviews with Crimmins, Bernhardt, and Martinez-Vazquez, and from oral history interviews conducted by Crimmins with Harvey Newman (October 24, 2014) and Ahmed Abdelal (see above). At some point in the late 1970s or early 1980s, Langdale was persuaded to stop interviewing prospective faculty himself, and Suttles did it instead; Tim Renick, for example, was interviewed by Suttles in 1986. The "yard wide, bull-necked, granite block" line about Langdale is quoted in Kay Powell's obituary of Langdale ("Georgia State's Langdale dies at 87") that ran in the *Atlanta Journal-Constitution* on February 25, 2008. The department chair whom Langdale spun around three times was John Wright of the business school, who retired in 1990. The Henry Ashmore story comes courtesy of Tim Crimmins.

For more on the Albany State flood, see Terry Lewis, "Flood of 1994 spurred building boom at Albany State University," *Albany Herald*, June 26, 2014. With vigorous support from Governor Miller, the university not only did not close but was back open for classes, many of them held in makeshift trailers, in time for the fall semester.

On the costs of education versus incarceration, see Andrew Young's autobiography, *An Easy Burden: The Civil Rights Movement and the Transformation of America* (New York, HarperCollins, 1996), 516, 524. Georgia's prison population continued to skyrocket in the 1990s and remains at or near the top of the list of U.S. states. (See, for example, the state report at the Prison Policy Initiative website.) On the impact of the HOPE scholarship on access to higher education and outcomes by race, see Susan Dynarski, "Hope for Whom? Financial Aid for the Middle Class and Its Impact on College Attendance," *National Tax Journal*, Vol. 53, No. 3, September 2000. The enrollment figures for Georgia State in the 1990s and 2000s are taken from the university system's data archive, available at the USG website under "enrollment reports."

Chapter 9: Birth of an Idea

Chapter based on interviews with Ron Henry, Carl Patton, Larry Abele (July 31, 2018); Tim Renick (May 21, 2018, November 15, 2018, January 30, 2019, by phone March 14, 2019); Tom Sugar (by phone October 29, 2018); Dennis Pruitt (by phone October 30, 2018); Tristan Denley (by phone November 20, 2018); Hilary Pennington (by phone December 18, 2018); Bridget Burns (by phone June 18, 2018); Mark Becker (January 31, 2019); Risa Palm.

The American Association for Higher Education wound up in 2005, and the National Center for Academic Transformation in 2018. For a taste of Carol Twigg's research, see her paper "Improving Learning and Reducing Costs: New Models for Online Learning," published in *Educause Review* (September/October 2003).

On state appropriations as a proportion of higher-education funding: Data is from the Department of Education's Center for Education Statistics. By the 2015–16 academic year, public universities were receiving only 43 percent of their funding from their state.

More on Larry Abele's achievements can be found in Martin Kurzweil and Daniel Rossman's case study, "Broad-Based and Targeted: Florida State University's Efforts to Retain Every Student," Ithaka S+R, New York, April 28, 2016.

The Complete College Tennessee Act was passed in 2010, and the Tennessee Higher Education Commission now states in its mission statement that it is "relentlessly focused on increasing the number of Tennesseans with a post-secondary credential." In 2017, the Philadelphia-based group Research for Action published a study of the impact of the act and found that part-time minority and Pell-eligible students had not benefited and that full-time Pell-eligible students had progressed predominantly at community college as opposed to four-year institutions. See M. Kate Callahan, et al., "Implementation and Impact of Outcomes-Based Funding in Tennessee," Research for Action, July 2017.

Pennington's New America study, published in 2013 with co-authors Jeff

Selingo, Kevin Carey, Rachel Fishman, and Iris Palmer, is titled "The New Genera-
tion University." The other universities in the report are the University of Central
Florida, the University of California, Riverside, the University of Buffalo, and the
University of Texas at Arlington.

The University Innovation Alliance members are: Georgia State, Arizona State,
Iowa State, Ohio State, Michigan State, Purdue, Oregon State, UC Riverside, the
University of Central Florida, the University of Kansas, and the University of
Texas at Austin.

The name of the St. Louis Cardinals owner, which Patton could not recall, was
confirmed by Brian Bertow of the Cardinals press office in an email dated June 20,
2018. (Baur died in 2011.) Herman Berliner responded to Risa Palm's story in an
October 5, 2018, email. The exchange between Renick and Chris Nagel took place
at a Graduation Initiative 2025 Symposium organized by the California State University system at San Diego State on October 17, 2018. It was videoed and is available on YouTube via the CSU website.

Chapter 10: The Feeling Is Mutual

Chapter based on interviews with Drew Magliozzi (by phone July 30, 2018, by
email July 12, 2019); Kirk Daulerio (by phone July 31, 2018); Scott Burke (May 24,
2018, September 18, 2018, by phone July 26, 2019); Tim Renick (by phone September 5, 2018, by email April 25 and April 29, 2019, by phone May 23, 2019);
Kerry Heyward (by phone May 29, 2019); Lindsay Page (by phone July 9, 2018);
Jasmine Twine (by phone July 24, 2019); and Wolfgang Schloer (by phone July 12,
2019).

Some of the Georgia State data on summer melt comes from slides prepared for
Renick's regular presentations, including a presentation he gave to visiting univer-
sity administrators in Atlanta on December 7, 2018. See also Scott Jaschik, "How
Georgia State Prevents Summer Melt," *Inside Higher Ed*, October 9, 2017.

The book by Castleman and Page is *Summer Melt: Supporting Low-Income
Students Through the Transition to College* (Cambridge, MA: Harvard Education
Press, 2014). Material cited comes from pages 2–4, 44, 61–66, 98. The "five-letter
F-word" line was used by Eric Cuevas, the director of student success under Renick
and Calhoun-Brown, in a presentation to visiting university administrators, December 7, 2018. More on FAFSA can be found in Sara Goldrick-Rab's book *Paying
the Price*, 49 (she calls it "a small American bureaucratic tragedy all its own") and
in Susan Dynarski's paper, "Hope for Whom?," both cited above. One of the issues

with FAFSA verification requests, according to Renick, was that they were more likely to be triggered when applications were submitted on paper as opposed to online. A disproportionate number of lower-income students either didn't have access to the technology to file their FAFSA forms online or had problems trusting the federal government and preferred not to.

The ed tech conference where Magliozzi and Renick talked was ASU + GSV, cosponsored by Arizona State and Global Silicon Valley, an umbrella organization for investment, strategic services, and media businesses, and it ran April 18–20, 2016.

Page and Gehlbach wrote up the results of the randomized controlled trial at Georgia State in a paper for the American Educational Research Association titled "How an Artificially Intelligent Virtual Assistant Helps Students Navigate the Road to College" (December 2017).

For an example of Singularity University's output on the future of education, see Raya Bidshahri, "Reimagining Education in the Exponential Age," *Singularity-Hub*, September 20, 2018. On the concerns about Alexa, Siri, and internet privacy, see Geoffrey A. Fowler, "Alexa has been eavesdropping on you this whole time," *Washington Post*, May 6, 2019.

Chapter 11: A Hundred Years from Now

Chapter based on interviews with Mark Becker (January 31, 2019), Ceasar Mitchell (by phone May 7, 2019); Tom Lewis, Jerry Rackliffe (September 20, 2018, and by phone October 23, 2018); Lauren Adamson, Carl Patton, Jeffrey Portnoy (by phone July 25, 2019); A.J. Robinson (November 14, 2018); Bharath Parthasarathy (by phone July 18, 2019); Chris Riley, and Steve Fanczi (by phone October 17, 2018).

The account of the phone call between Mark Becker and Ceasar Mitchell is largely Becker's. Mitchell's account differed in one respect: Becker's level of overt enthusiasm about taking over Turner Field. Mitchell recalled Becker saying: "Let me give some thought to that and get back to you." Both agree, however, that Becker acted very fast on the opportunity.

Rebecca Burns's brilliant and haunting feature on the neighborhoods around Turner Field is called "The Other 284 Days" (*Atlanta*, July 2013). The construction of the east-west 20 freeway and the north-south 75/85 Atlanta Connector was accompanied by an aggressive "slum clearance" program that made room for Atlanta-Fulton County stadium, the Braves' first home, in the mid-1960s. This project was responsible for creating the asphalt eyesore that persisted through the Olympics and after. It also forced the closure of seventy-five local businesses and obliged almost one thousand families to move away without compensation. See Andrew Young, Harvey Newman, and Andrea Young, *Andrew Young and the Making of Modern Atlanta* (Macon, GA: Mercer University Press, 2016), 199.

On the other offers fielded by Mayor Reed, see Katie Leslie, "Reed says city has received multiple offers on Turner Field," *Atlanta Journal-Constitution*, April 17, 2014. Reed's quotes from the day of the sale announcement were reported in Janel Davis, "Turner Field sale becomes transformative moment for neighborhood, GSU," *Atlanta Journal-Constitution*, August 19, 2016.

The outside consultancy that initially examined the feasibility of football at Georgia State was C.H. Johnson Consulting, Inc., and the report, called "Football Program Strategy Assessment," was delivered in November 2006. On the dismal attendance at Georgia State games, see Doug Roberson, "Sun Belt ninth in attendance; Georgia State in bottom 10," *Atlanta Journal-Constitution*, June 30, 2015.

On Georgia State acquiring the bank building at 35 Broad St.: The gift was arranged by Citizens & Southern's last CEO, Bennett Brown. One executive who came into the merged bank from NCNB in North Carolina, Ken Lewis, also had an MBA from Georgia State and later, as CEO of Bank of America, donated $5 million to the nursing school, now named after his mother, Byrdine F. Lewis. A notable idiosyncrasy of the bank lobby is an empty glass Coke bottle which was left on top of a tall corner pillar during a Prohibition-era renovation and later deemed too inconvenient, or too much of a talking point, to retrieve and throw away.

On Robert Woodruff's role in pressuring the Atlanta business community to participate in a dinner to honor of King after he won the 1964 Nobel Peace Prize, see Young et al., *The Making of Modern Atlanta*, 44–46. Among the attendees of the prize dinner was Jesse Hill Jr., then vice president and chief actuary of the Atlanta Life Insurance company whose headquarters on Auburn Ave. were later turned into Centennial Hall. His wife, Ezira, had to make her own dress for the King dinner because the city's finer clothing stores were open to whites only.

Renick's influence on student housing design was immediate; Freshman Hall was designed and built in just eight months, opening in 2009. The building used for both *Spider-Man* and *The Accountant* was 55 Park Place.

For more on the opposition to Georgia State's takeover of Turner Field, see for example J. Scott Trubey, "Group takes to tents to protest Georgia State's plans for

Turner Field," *Atlanta Journal-Constitution*, April 3, 2017. Georgia State published its community engagement commitments, entitled "Anchoring Communities," later in April 2017; it is available via the Georgia State website. Carter & Associates signed a similar "Summerhill Community Investment Plan," also viewable via the Georgia State website.

The name of Carter's CEO, Scott Taylor, subsequently surfaced in email correspondence relating to the terms of a confidential settlement agreement between Mayor Reed and the former general manager of the Atlanta airport, Miguel Southwell, following Southwell's dismissal in 2016. The agreement, which was leaked to the *Atlanta Journal-Constitution*, became the subject of a federal corruption investigation because Southwell was promised money that was not part of his city severance deal and the source of the extra money was unknown. Taylor, who secured a lease with the city to build a hotel at the airport shortly after the agreement was signed, denied any knowledge of the settlement negotiations. There was no suggestion from any quarter that Georgia State had any involvement. See Dan Klepal, J. Scott Trubey, and Stephen Deere, "Secret settlement with fired airport chief new focus of federal probe," *Atlanta Journal-Constitution*, April 19, 2019.

Gratuities clause. Article 3, Section VI, Paragraph VI of the Georgia state constitution reads, in part: "The General Assembly shall not have the power to grant any donation or gratuity or to forgive any debt or obligation owing to the public."

On the success of Georgia State's Early College program in Atlanta-area high schools, see for example the university press release titled "100 Percent of First Class at Carver Early College to Graduate May 28" (May 26, 2009). The academic study cited is Tene Davis, Kalisha Woods, Cedrick Dortch, and Chloe Jackson, "The Georgia State University Early College Program: A Practice in Student Success Relevance" (presented at the National Youth At-Risk Conference, Savannah, March 4, 2015).

Crime statistics for the Atlanta Police Department's Zone 3 are available from the APD website. The stats are not an exact reflection of the impact of Georgia State on the stadium area because Zone 3 includes Grant Park, an affluent residential area to the east. Also, as Parthasarathy pointed out, correlation is not causation: multiple factors affect crime rates. But the trend is emphatically in the right direction.

Part of the story of the land acquired for the convocation center comes from emails between Steve Fanczi and Jerry Rackliffe, forwarded by Fanczi, and from an email written by Fanczi to the author on October 17, 2018.

Chapter 12: Rogue Cows

Chapter based on interviews with Hank Huckaby, Mark Becker (November 16, 2018, January 31, 2019); Jerry Rackliffe, Tim Renick (September 19, 2018); Peter Lyons (November 13, 2018, and by phone July 29, 2019); Jeffrey Portnoy, Adam Stone (by phone July 24, 2019); Carol Cohen (November 14, 2018); Scott Burke (September 18, 2018); Amanda Emery (December 5, 2018); Cary Claiborne, and Osman Saccoh (December 5, 2018).

The "abysmal leadership" line is from Jeffrey Portnoy. Rob Watts previously served as interim president of Perimeter in 2005, following the end of Jacquelyn Belcher's eleven-year tenure. Portnoy was in the forefront of faculty pushback against her, too. One of his complaints about her and Tricoli was that they failed to secure adequate board of regents funding for the Perimeter campuses, relative to their size and mission.

On Anthony Tricoli: The Georgia appeals court provided a useful summary in its final dismissal issued April 24, 2018. See *Anthony S. Tricoli v. Rob Watts, et al.*, case number A18D0406. For more on the audit, see the special board of regents' review, published on September 17, 2012. For more on the cutbacks after Rob Watts took over as interim president, see Laura Diamond, "Georgia Perimeter gains financial footing, but uncertainty remains," *Atlanta Journal-Constitution*, June 8, 2013.

The Pew Charitable Trusts analysis is Ben Wieder, "Campus Mergers Bring Big Changes but Questionable Savings," July 18, 2012.

Georgia's agriculture and mechanical arts colleges were created under Public Law 448, known as the Perry Act after state senator H.H. Perry of Gainesville. The 1906 law was an acknowledgment of the inadequacy of many schoolhouses in rural Georgia and also a throwback to the ideals of Justin Morrill, the Vermont senator who created land grant universities with the idea that "a higher and broader education should be placed in every State within the reach of those . . . who may have the courage to choose industrial vocations where the wealth of nations is produced" (per the text of a 1887 speech Morrill delivered at Massachusetts Agricultural College, now UMass Amherst). Many of these original A&M colleges either evolved or closed as Georgia's economic and educational needs changed. The state underwent a major reorganization, a precedent of sorts to Huckaby's consolidations, after the board of regents was created in the 1930s. For more, see Cameron Fincher, *Historical Development of the University System of Georgia, 1932–2002* (Athens, GA: Institute of Higher Education, University of Georgia, 2003).

The consolidations that preceded Georgia State's with Perimeter were: the University of North Georgia, Georgia Regents University in Augusta (combining Augusta State and Georgia Health Sciences), Middle Georgia State College in Macon (combining Macon State and Middle Georgia), South Georgia State College (combining Waycross and South Georgia), and Kennesaw State University in Marietta, in the northwestern Atlanta suburbs, which turned neighboring Southern Poly into its engineering and technology school. Only after the Georgia State–Perimeter merger did Huckaby undertake a consolidation of a historically black campus, Albany State, with a historically white access college, Darton State. As of 2019, the university system had twenty-six institutions, down from thirty-five when Huckaby became chancellor in 2011.

When Jerry Rackliffe attended Clarkston it was known as DeKalb College, because the three original Perimeter campuses—Clarkston, Decatur, and Dunwoody—were all in DeKalb County. Alpharetta, in northern Fulton County, and Newton, forty miles east of Atlanta near Covington, were added later; the name Georgia Perimeter College was adopted in 1997. The system also had a presence in Lawrenceville, Gwinnett County, until Georgia Gwinnett College was founded as an independent institution in 2006.

The system office press release was titled "Regents Approve Proposal to Consolidate Georgia State University and Georgia Perimeter College," dated January 6, 2015.

The salaries and reimbursed expenses of Georgia state employees are a matter of public record. See open.georgia.gov.

One significant consolidation controversy not mentioned in the text was over Perimeter's long-standing practice of admitting hundreds of English-language learners to noncredit-bearing classes each year. The Perimeter faculty argued that the program had given a chance to vulnerable students unable to enter college any other way, and a handful of them had gone on to triumph in higher education and beyond. However, the vast majority of them never progressed to degree work, and the program also turned out to be a violation of board of regents policies, which meant there was no choice but to scrap it. There was a student success component to the controversy, because English as a Second Language was subsequently offered as a "co-requisite" to credit-bearing classes across Georgia State's campuses, in line with the thinking of Tristan Denley, CCA, and others. But Renick's office had no involvement in these decisions. Lyons did his best to mitigate the pain of ending the ESL access program by guaranteeing alternative faculty positions to everyone who had taught in it. But this was one more instance where some Perimeter faculty came to feel that data—a word inextricably linked in their minds to Renick's work—was being used as a weapon against the students' best interests.

On DACA and immigration: The Georgia legislature passed a law in 2008 stipulating that noncitizens admitted to public universities must pay out-of-state rates. Two years later, an undocumented Mexican-born student at Kennesaw State, Jessica Colotl, was arrested on a traffic violation and threatened with deportation. When legislators discovered she had been paying in-state tuition fees, in violation of the 2008 law, they sought to make an example of her and threatened to ban undocumented students from Georgia public universities altogether. That didn't happen, partly because of a national outcry over Colotl and partly because the regents enacted a new policy, "splitting the baby," in Mark Becker's phrase, between a stricter policy at the five biggest schools and a laxer one elsewhere. The key paragraph in the policy, passed in 2010, is 4.1.6: "A person who is not lawfully present in the United States shall not be eligible for admission to any University System institution which, for the two most recent academic years, did not admit all academically qualified applicants (except for cases in which applicants were rejected for non-academic reasons)." Colotl later received DACA status, only to lose it temporarily after Donald Trump became president and then win it back as a result of a lawsuit brought by the American Civil Liberties Union. See Jonathan Blitzer, "The Seven-Year Saga of One Undocumented Student in Georgia," *New Yorker*, May 22, 2017. The ACLU case is *Colotl v. Kelly* (later *Colotl v. Nielsen*), case number 1:17-cv-1670-MHC, and was settled on May 25, 2018. MALDEF, the Mexican American Legal Defense and Education Fund, filed a lawsuit in September 2016 on behalf of three undocumented plaintiffs seeking to overturn the regents' policy on admitting undocumented students. Mark Becker was a named defendant along with four other university presidents and the members of the board of regents. MALDEF lost both in district court and in the Eleventh Circuit. The case is *Estrada, Alvarado and Umana v. Becker, et al.*, case number 1:16-cv-03310-TWT. In a separate case, a Georgia Superior Court judge ruled in 2016 that DACA recipients were entitled to in-state tuition rates, but he was overruled on appeal. See Elly Yu, "Ga. Supreme Court Refuses to Hear DACA In-State Tuition Case," WABE (Atlanta public radio), May 7, 2018. Meanwhile, the board of regents cleared Georgia State University as well as Augusta University to admit undocumented students in November 2016. See Elly Yu, "GSU, Augusta University to Admit Students Despite Immigration Status," WABE, November 21, 2016.

Chapter 13: Secure the Bag

Chapter based on interviews with Tim Renick (December 7, 2018, January 31, 2019); Mark Becker (January 31, 2019); Allison Calhoun-Brown (February 1, 2019); Tom Lewis (by phone January 29, 2019); Carol Cohen (November 14, 2018); State Farm executive Lonnie Smith (by phone, December 14, 2018); Terrance Rogers, Fenwick Huss (by email January 10, 2019); Tyler Mulvenna, Peter Lyons, Amanda Emery, and Bob Morse (by email November 21, 2018 and January 2, 2019), Stephanie Tran and Heather Housley (July 9, 2019). Doug Covey declined several invitations over many months to give his version of the events detailed in this chapter.

Heather Housley gave an account of her experience of new student orientation to a meeting of Tim Renick's student success managers on December 6, 2018. Amanda Emery, who had been in charge before consolidation, provided a description of how it worked previously.

The front-page *New York Times* piece was Richard Fausset, "Georgia State, Leading U.S. in Black Graduates, Is Engine of Social Mobility," May 15, 2018. Much of the data cited is from Georgia State's 2018 Complete College Georgia report, available through the university website.

More on the State Farm scholars in a May 9, 2019, Georgia State news release titled "Georgia State's Perimeter College State Farm Scholars Graduate at 2019 Spring Commencement." A wonderfully touching video of the surprise ceremony when these inaugural scholars were announced in 2017 can be viewed at success.students.gsu.edu/state-farm-scholars.

Some of the details of the housing debacle were provided by Jerry Rackliffe in an email dated December 20, 2018. See also Becca J.G. Goodwin, "400 or so GSU students to stay at Sheraton due to overbooked housing," *Atlanta Journal-Constitution*, August 17, 2017. The students could stay at the Sheraton only until September 1, because the hotel was booked thereafter for the DragonCon science fiction and fantasy convention. The press coverage largely interpreted the housing shortfall in 2017 as a symptom of Georgia State's rapid growth. The undersubscription problem in 2018 went largely unreported.

The College of Education became the College of Education & Human Development in 2015.

At the time Rogers was launching his boot camp, the business school was developing its own program, Panthers on Wall Street, which started in 2008. Fenwick

Huss, business dean at the time, had no doubt his was the superior program. He said in an email that while Rogers had done well (he went on to Harvard Business School and a flourishing career in mergers and acquisitions), he might have done better still if he'd taken what the school had to offer. Rogers responded that it wasn't about pitting one program against another. "It's about taking knowledge from beyond the horizon and bringing it back," he said. "Our goal was to put more kids on Wall Street . . . and we did that."

For more on UPS, see Kelly Yamanouchi, "UPS hiring thousands of workers for massive hub on westside of Atlanta," *Atlanta Journal-Constitution*, July 11, 2018. On Takeda's new plant in Covington, near the Newton campus, see the article "Takeda Pharmaceutical Plans Covington, Georgia, Plasma Plant," *Area Development*, March 19, 2019.

U.S. News & World Report's chief data strategist Bob Morse explained the changes in methodology for the 2019 rankings in two emails dated November 21, 2018, and January 2, 2019. In addition to the graduation criteria, Morse said: "Scores are adjusted so schools that enroll the highest percentage of low-income students get the most credit for these graduation rates." The social mobility indicators constituted 5 percent of the rankings formula. "When combined with graduation rate performance, economic diversity measures contribute to 13 percent of the Best Colleges methodology," he explained. "In addition, *U.S. News* dropped acceptance rate from the methodology this year, and reduced the weight of input measures such as expert opinion and student excellence." Morse also confirmed that Georgia State's ranking (187th) was attributable to its "strong showing" on social mobility.

The revamped new student orientation session as described was on July 9, 2019.

Chapter 14: Reproducibility

Chapter based on interviews with Tim Renick (December 7, 2018, by phone April 5, 2019, by email April 29, 2019, July 8, 2019); Allison Calhoun-Brown (by phone July 10, 2018); Fortune Onwuzuruike (September 19, 2018); Kalif Robinson (by phone August 8, 2018); Cary Claiborne, Gabriella Salinas (September 17, 2018); Austin Birchell (September 20, 2018, by phone October 30, 2018); Bridget Burns, Terri Gomez (March 4, 2019, in Pomona, CA); Teshia Roby (March 4, March 4, 2019, in Pomona, CA); Rick Sluder (by phone July 16, 2019); Mark Becker (January 31, 2019, by phone March 13, 2019, July 8, 2019), Tom Sugar, Kyle Stapleton.

Bill Gates's post and video about Georgia State, "Putting students first," appeared at his blog *GatesNotes* on October 2, 2017. Gates first summoned Renick to a private meeting at the April 2016 ASU/GSV ed tech conference in San Diego, where he talked about the opportunities that new technologies offered to education but added: "We're very much at the beginning . . . We really haven't changed the outcomes." (Video available via GSV on YouTube.) A few months later, Renick was invited to a longer session on higher education at the Gates Foundation headquarters in Seattle with about forty others.

Fortune Onwuzuruike left WellStar in 2019 for a new job with Piedmont Healthcare. The scholarship that took Robinson to Washington was a Rangel Scholar Summer Enrichment Award, and he subsequently won a Charles B. Rangel International Affairs Fellowship to see him through graduate school. Both programs were set up by the longtime New York congressman Charles Rangel in conjunction with Howard University in Washington, DC, and designed to encourage greater diversity in international service careers.

Austin Birchell's family suspects a link between his father's service in the first Gulf War—he was responsible for waving warplanes on and off the USS *Eisenhower*—and his amyotrophic lateral sclerosis, the medical name for Lou Gehrig's disease. A 2016 study conducted by the National Academies of Sciences, Engineering, and Medicine confirmed that Gulf War veterans were at higher risk of ALS than the general population. The suspicion, which the report was unable to pin down or confirm, is that the vulnerability is related to exposure to toxic substances. See Deborah A. Cory-Slechta, et al., "Gulf War and Health, Volume 10: Update of Health Effect Serving in the Gulf War" (Washington, DC: National Academies of Sciences, Engineering, and Medicine—Institute of Medicine, 2016). Among Birchell's many campus activities has been to star in a series of quirky, endearing short films highlighting aspects of life at Georgia State, entitled "Adventures with Austin," available via YouTube and the university website.

More on the reasons why students drop out of college beyond academic performance in Ed Venit's "Murky Middle" study for EAB (op. cit.). At the time of his visit to Georgia State, William Franken was vice president of student affairs at California State University, Dominguez Hills.

Terri Gomez was put in charge of student success at Cal Poly Pomona in 2016. Teshia Roby, who has a PhD from Georgia State, was appointed interim chief data officer in January 2019. The switch to the semester system was in fall 2018. The details of CSU's Graduation Initiative 2025 are at the CSU website. On the no-confidence vote at Cal State Northridge, see Hank Reichman, "CSU Northridge Faculty Senate Votes No-Confidence in CSU Chancellor White," *Academe* blog (published by the American Association of University Professors), February 19, 2019. One of the complicating factors behind the Northridge vote was that Chancellor White had championed ethnic studies and encouraged CSU campuses to hire tenured faculty to teach more of it just a couple of years earlier; now he was proposing the removal of ethnic studies from the first-year syllabus. See "Status Report on Campus Responses to Recommendations by the CSU Task Force on the Advancement of Ethnic Studies" (Long Beach, California, November 2017).

As of 2019, the University of Illinois, Chicago, had a freshman retention rate of 80 percent, eight points higher than the national average, and a six-year graduation rate of around 60 percent. The student body was 68 percent nonwhite, and more than half of its students were eligible to receive Pell grants. (Sources: UIC's Office of Institutional Research and IPEDS, the Integrated Postsecondary Education Data system.)

The data on the University of Houston is taken from its website and the data on graduation rates from the online reporting of its Office of Institutional Research. Morgan State, likewise, has extensive information on its student success programs on its website. On Indian River, see, e.g., its news release by Suzanne Seldes, "Indian River State College Named Number One in the Nation by Aspen Institute," April 2, 2019. Information on Middle Tennessee State College kindly provided by Rick Sluder.

In his new job as vice president of partnerships at EAB, Tom Sugar has established a $75 million fund to offer technical assistance to states and universities on a regional basis in exchange for a commitment to eliminate all achievement gaps within ten years.

For an example of Texas's legislative approach, see Ashley A. Smith, "Texas Requires Credit-Bearing Remediation," *Inside Higher Ed*, July 12, 2017. Texas's conservative governor, Greg Abbott, has set a goal of reaching a 60 percent college graduation rate by 2030. See also Eva-Marie Ayala, "Only about half of all Texas students graduate from college within six years," *Dallas Morning News*, September 12, 2018.

SELECTED BIBLIOGRAPHY

Books

William G. Bowen, Matthew M. Chingos, and Michael S. McPherson, *Crossing the Finish Line: Completing College at America's Public Universities* (Princeton, NJ: Princeton University Press, 2009).

Benjamin L. Castleman and Lindsay C. Page, *Summer Melt: Supporting Low-Income Students Through the Transition to College* (Cambridge, MA: Harvard Education Press, 2014).

Michael M. Crow and William B. Dabars, *Designing the New American University* (Baltimore: Johns Hopkins University Press, 2015).

William Deresiewicz, *Excellent Sheep: The Miseducation of the American Elite and the Way to a Meaningful Life* (New York: Free Press, 2014).

James J. Duderstadt, *A University for the 21st Century* (Ann Arbor, MI: University of Michigan Press, 2000).

James J. Duderstadt, Daniel E. Atkins, and Douglas Van Houweling, *Higher Education in the Digital Age* (Westport, CT: Praeger, 2002).

Claudia Goldin and Lawrence F. Katz, *The Race between Education and Technology* (Cambridge, MA: Belknap Press, 2008).

Sara Goldrick-Rab, *Paying the Price: College Costs, Financial Aid, and the Betrayal of the American Dream* (Chicago: University of Chicago Press, 2016).

Charlayne Hunter-Gault, *In My Place* (New York: Farrar, Straus and Giroux, 1992).

Martin Luther King, Jr., *Where Do We Go from Here: Chaos or Community?* (Boston: Beacon Press, 1967).

Nicholas Lemann, *The Big Test: The Secret History of the American Meritocracy* (New York: Farrar, Straus and Giroux, 2000).

Michael Lewis, *Moneyball: The Art of Winning an Unfair Game* (New York: Norton, 2003).

Merl E. Reed, *Educating the Urban New South: Atlanta and the Rise of Georgia State University, 1913–1969* (Macon, GA: Mercer University Press, 2009).

Richard V. Reeves, *Dream Hoarders: How the American Upper Middle Class Is Leaving Everyone Else in the Dust, Why That Is a Problem, and What to Do About It* (Washington, DC: Brookings Institution Press, 2017).

Timothy M. Renick, *Aquinas for Armchair Theologians* (Louisville, KY: Westminster John Knox Press, 2002).

Frank H.T. Rhodes, *The Creation of the Future: The Role of the American University* (Ithaca, NY: Cornell University Press, 2001).

Vanessa Siddle Walker, *The Lost Education of Horace Tate* (New York: The New Press, 2018).

Calvin Trillin, *An Education in Georgia: The Integration of Charlayne Hunter and Hamilton Holmes* (New York: Viking Press, 1964).

Rich Whitt, *Behind the Hedges: Big Money and Power Politics at the University of Georgia* (Montgomery, GA: New South Books, 2009).

Tom Wolfe, *A Man in Full* (New York: Farrar, Straus and Giroux, 1998).

Andrew Young, *An Easy Burden: The Civil Rights Movement and the Transformation of America* (New York: HarperCollins, 1996).

Andrew Young, Harvey Newman, and Andrea Young, *Andrew Young and the Making of Modern Atlanta* (Macon, GA: Mercer University Press, 2016).

Articles and Research Papers

Richard Adler, "Connecting the Edges: A Report of the 2012 Aspen Institute Roundtable on Institutional Innovation" (Washington, DC, Aspen Institute, 2013).

Atlanta Metro Chamber of Commerce/Accenture, "Your Talent, Your Future: 2017 Entry-Level Talent Assessment for Georgia" (Atlanta, October 24, 2017).

Liz Babiarz, "Quiet Courage," *GSU Magazine*, Fall 2009.

Steve Beschloss, "The Velocity of Change," *ASU Thrive* magazine, Vol. 20, No. 4, September 2017.

M. Kate Callahan, et al., "Implementation and Impact of Outcomes-Based Funding in Tennessee," *Research for Action*, Philadelphia, July 2017.

Elizabeth D. Capaldi, John V. Lombardi, and Victor Yellen, "Improving Graduation Rates: A Simple Method That Works," *Change: The Magazine of Higher Learning*, Vol. 38, No. 4, July–August 2006.

Anthony P. Carnevale, Nicole Smith, and Jeff Stroll, "Recovery: Job Growth and Education Requirements Through 2020," Georgetown University Center on Education and the Workforce, Washington, DC, 2013.

Complete College America, "Remediation: Higher Education's Bridge to Nowhere," Washington, DC, April 2012.

Complete College America, "Time Is the Enemy: The Surprising Truth About Why Today's College Students Aren't Graduating . . . And What Needs to Change," Washington, DC, September 2011.

Susan Dynarski, "Hope for Whom? Financial Aid for the Middle Class and Its Impact on College Attendance," *National Tax Journal*, Vol. 53, No. 3, September 2000.

Jennifer Engle and Christina Theokas, "Top Gainers: Some Public Four-Year Colleges and Universities Make Big Improvements in Minority Graduation Rates," Education Trust, January 2010.

Jennifer Engle and Christina Theokas, "Top Gap Closers: Some Public Four-Year Colleges and Universities Have Made Good Progress in Closing Graduation-Rate Gaps," Education Trust, January 2010.

Dimitrios Halikias and Richard V. Reeves, "Ladders, Labs, or Laggards? Which Public Universities Contribute Most" (Washington, DC: Brookings Institution, 2017).

Melissa Korn, "Colleges Find Micro-Grants Keep Some Student from Dropping Out," *Wall Street Journal*, October 29, 2014.

Martin Kurzweil and D. Derek Wu, "Building a Pathway to Success at Georgia State University," Ithaka S+R, April 2015.

Craig Lambert, "Twilight of the Lecture," *Harvard Magazine*, March–April 2012.

Andrew Nichols, Kimberlee Eberle Sudre, and Meredith Welch, "Rising Tide II: Do Black Students Benefit as Grad Rates Increase?" Education Trust, March 2016.

Lindsay C. Page and Hunter Gehlbach, "How an Artificially Intelligent Virtual Assistant Helps Students Navigate the Road to College," American Educational Research Association, December 12, 2017.

Michael J. Petrilli, "Pell Grants Shouldn't Pay for Remedial College," *Bloomberg Business*, April 30, 2013.

Timothy M. Renick (uncredited, on behalf of the American Academy of Religion), "The Religious Studies Major and Liberal Education," *Liberal Education*, Vol. 95, No. 2, Spring 2009.

Jenna Ashley Robinson and Duke Cheston, "Pell Grants: Where Does All the Money Go?" John William Pope Center for Higher Education Policy, June 2012.

Jeff Selingo, Kevin Carey, Hilary Pennington, Rachel Fishman, and Iris Palmer, "The New Generation University," New America Foundation, May 2013.

Jennifer H. Stephens, "Eight Themes in Strategic Planning: Reflections from a Year of Focused Learning," *Planning for Higher Education*, Vol. 45, No. 4, July–September 2017.

Carol A. Twigg, "Improving Learning and Reducing Costs: New Models for On-line Learning," *Educause Review*, September/October 2003.

Edward P. Venit, Jennifer Mason, et al., "Hardwiring Student Success: Building Disciplines for Retention and Timely Graduation," Education Advisory Board/Student Success Collaborative, 2013.

Ed Venit et al., "The Murky Middle Project—Preliminary Findings," Education Advisory Board/Student Success Initiative, 2014.

Ed Venit, "What Can Health Care Teach Us About Student Success?" EAB/Student Success Collaborative, 2016.

INDEX

AAHE (American Association of Higher Education), 169

Aaron, Hank, 200, 208

Abdelal, Ahmed, 44–45, 154, 169

Abele, Larry, 170–174, 179

Abraham Lincoln Brigade, 161

academic advising. *see also* SAC; UAC
  academic probation and, 89, 90, 98, 102–103
  chatbot and, 195
  college advising offices and, 109–112, 238–239
  data collection and, 103–105, 196
  early intervention through, 8, 9, 129–130, 132–133, 142, 250
  Education Advisory Board and, 113–120, 133, 255
  Gabriel Woods' experience of, 81, 87, 89–90, 93–94
  GradesFirst and, 103, 119
  Keep HOPE Alive and, 49
  "murky middle" and, 98, 119–120
  new student orientation and, 246
  other universities' experience of reforming, 255, 257–258, 259–260
  Panther retention grants and, 137
  Perimeter campuses and, 215, 220, 225, 228, 230
  precursors to Georgia State in reforming, 15, 64, 113, 173
  predictive analytics and, 15, 113–119, 124, 126–133
  problems with pre-2008, 87–89
  reform of, 96–133
  student-advisor ratio, 99, 107–108, 215, 277
  strategic plan and, 70
  Summer Success Academy and, 142
  University System of Georgia support for, 106–109

academic performance, as student success indicator, 51–53

academic probation, 89, 90, 98, 102–103

ACCA (Atlanta Committee for Cooperative Action), 155–156

Accountant, The (2016), 207

accounting classes, 36, 51, 83, 85–86, 131–132, 242

ACE (American Council for Education), 62

achievement gaps, 11, 69, 164, 234, 235, 256, 294n

ACT test scores, as success indicator, 54–56

Adamson, Lauren, 34, 46, 51, 52, 112, 202–203

adaptive computer learning, 51, 85, 97–98, 169, 170

admissions
  2008 financial crisis and, 32–33
  Cary Claiborne and, 123
  chatbot and, 184–188, 194–195
  meta majors and, 142
  Perimeter campuses and, 225
  programs with extra requirements, 83–85, 130–131
  Scott Burke and, 184–185
  segregation era and, 155–159
  selectivity in, 182
  test scores and, 37–38, 54–57

AdmitHub, 184–185, 188–195, 255
advising. *see* academic advising; SAC;
    UAC
Advisory Board Company. *see* Education
    Advisory Board
Affleck, Ben, 207
African American student performance at
    Georgia State, 11–12, 132, 271n
African American Studies program,
    153–154
agricultural and mechanical arts colleges,
    216, 288n
Albany State University, 162–163, 282n,
    289n
Alberto, Paul, 27, 61–65, 147
Alpharetta campus, Perimeter College,
    219
American Association of Higher Education
    (AAHE), 169
American Council for Education (ACE),
    62
American Recovery and Reinvestment Act,
    30–31
Andrew Young School of Policy Studies
    background on, 67–68, 160, 166
    firing of Dean Hildreth, 66–67
Apple Inc. "think different" ad, 20
Aquinas, Thomas, 42–43
Arizona State University
    academic advising and, 113
    in New America report, 177
    pioneering work of, 14, 63–65
    strategic planning committee's visit to,
        63–65
    University Innovation Alliance and,
        177, 178
    U.S. News & World Report and, 245
Arrington, Bob, 44
artificial intelligence in higher education,
    see chatbot; AdmitHub
Ashmore, Henry, 162
Association of Public Land Grant
    Universities, 198

Atlanta, GA
    1992 unrest following Rodney King
        trial, 153
    1996 Olympics, 67, 152, 164–166,
        199–200
    2011 snowstorm, 93
    Atlanta Connector interstate, 16, 120,
        122, 203, 207, 210
    Broad Street, 204, 286n
    Buckhead, 36–37, 154, 161, 285–286n
    Castleberry Hill, 6
    civil rights movement and, 16–17,
        154–160
    Downtown, 16, 36–37, 151, 152, 154,
        164–166, 198, 199, 203–208, 218,
        230, 235, 245
    economic dynamism of, 10, 22, 26,
        27, 67–68, 147, 160, 216, 220, 239,
        242–243, 260
    Fairlie-Poplar, 203–204
    Georgia State's role in diversifying and
        internationalizing, 10, 16, 106
    Hartsfield-Jackson International
        Airport, 93, 245, 287n
    Lithonia, 90, 91
    Midtown, 16, 36
    state capitol, 30, 198, 205, 211–212, 240
    Summerhill, Mechanicsville and
        Peoplestown, 198–212
    Sweet Auburn, 16, 204
    Woodruff Park, 119, 166, 204, 206,
        207
Atlanta Braves baseball team, 179, 198,
    200, 208, 285
Atlanta Committee for Cooperative Action
    (ACCA). *see* ACCA
Atlanta Falcons football team, 12, 199, 202
Atlanta Life Insurance company, 205–206
Atlanta Metropolitan State College, 5, 89,
    122, 123
Atlanta Technical College, 5
Atlanta University Center, 92, 165. *see also*
    Clark; Spelman; Morehouse

Austin Peay State University, Clarksville, TN, 174–175

B-52s, 10
Baby Driver (2017), 207
Banner (Georgia State student database), 102, 104, 105, 118, 128, 226
Barr, Pamela, 61–65, 74
Baur, Drew, 179
Beane, Billy, 117
Becker, Mark
    2008 recession and, 27, 31
    2015 pay increase, 224–225
    academic advising and, 106–109, 110–112
    admissions policy and, 32–33, 37, 54–57
    Arizona State University visit, 63–65
    background, 21–26
    belief in Atlanta, 22, 27, 106, 199, 203
    career services and, 240
    convocation center land acquisition, 211–212
    data warehouse and, 103–106
    firing Dean Hildreth, 66–68
    Huss's relationship with, 111, 149
    interviewing for president position, 26–27
    misgivings about, 19–21, 61–62, 64–65, 68
    Palm's relationship with, 33–34, 37, 56, 57, 58, 60, 67, 147–148
    Panther retention grants and, 134, 136
    Perimeter consolidation and, 215, 217, 219, 223
    philosophy and leadership style of, 3, 15, 22–24, 25–26, 32, 34, 37, 60–61, 117, 138, 147, 235–237, 244–245, 263
    Renick's relationship with, 53–57, 99–100, 104, 105, 133, 240
    strategic plan and, 58–73
    student affairs division and, 233–234, 235–237
    Turner Field acquisition, 198–201, 203, 208–210, 285
    University Innovation Alliance and, 177

University System of Georgia and, 106–109
Berkeley. *see* University of California, Berkeley
Berliner, Herman, 181
Bernhardt, Ken, 58–60, 68, 71, 162
Big Test, The (Lemann), 55
Bill & Melinda Gates Foundation. *see* Gates Foundation
Birchell, Austin, 252–254
Birchell, Brent, 254
Blair, J.D., 156
board of regents, 30, 106, 152, 157, 170, 203, 213–215, 225, 226, 256, 279n, 282n, 288n, 289n, 290n
Boggs, Grace Lee, vii
bridge programs, for low test score admission applicants, 140–141
Brown v. Board of Education, 155
Brunswick, GA, 76–78, 80, 93
Buckhead, Atlanta, 36–37, 154, 161
budget cuts, Georgia State, 27–31, 56, 66, 108, 134
Burke, Scott, 184–185, 187–188
Burns, Bridget, 178–179, 255
Burns, Rebecca, 200, 285
business school (Robinson College of Business, Georgia State). *see also* accounting
    academic advising and, 111
    Citizens & Southern National Bank building and, 204
    failure rate at, 84–86, 131–132
    predictive analytics and, 127–128, 130–131
    professional training, 240–241, 291–292n
    resistance to student success project, 53, 54, 56, 70–71, 84, 111, 140, 148–150, 236, 254
    strategic plan and, 61, 68, 70–71
    "swirler" problem and, 83–84
    view of student quality, 35–36, 56, 84–86

Cal State Northridge, 257

Calhoun-Brown, Allison, 21, 51–53, 61–65, 69, 70, 87, 98, 101–103, 112, 115–116, 132, 141–142, 238–239, 251, 256

California State Polytechnic, Pomona, 256–258

campus expansion, Georgia State, 165–167, 198–212

Campus tracking software (since relaunched as Navigate), 118–120, 125, 126–129. see also academic advising; data

campus unions, 258

Capaldi, Betty, 113–114, 278

career services, 149, 236, 239–243, 247, 291–292n

Carter & Associates, 201

Carver, Duane, 78, 90–91

Castleman, Benjamin, 185–187

Catch-22 (Joseph Heller), 137, 279n

CCA (Complete College America), 107, 173–174, 176–177, 180–181, 271

Central Atlanta Progress, 204–205

chatbot, 15, 183–196, 228, 234, 253–254

Cheek, Brianna, 49–50

City University of New York, 174

Claiborne, Cary, 120–125, 126, 219, 229–231, 247, 250

Clark Atlanta University, 92, 153, 155

Clarkston campus, Perimeter College, 217, 220, 289n

Clinton, Bill, 163

Coastal Orchestra of Georgia, 78

Coca-Cola Company, 37, 58, 204

Cohen, Carol, 100–103, 119, 126, 130

Coley, Soraya, 256

College of Arts and Sciences, 15, 34, 44, 46, 51, 69, 112, 154, 169

College of Education (renamed College of Education & Human Development in 2015), 61, 82, 104, 147, 209, 237, 257

Colotl, Jessica, 290n

"community benefit agreement," with Atlanta Braves, 208

community colleges, Atlanta. see Perimeter

Complete College America (CCA), 107, 173–174

Complete College Georgia, 107–109

computer learning, adaptive, 51, 85, 97–98, 169, 170

consolidation (of campuses within University System of Georgia), 215–231, 232, 234–235, 289n

convocation center, 210–212

Cotter, Maury, 62, 74

Covey, Doug, 233, 235–237, 239, 291n

Crow, Michael, 63–65, 67, 113, 177, 178

DACA (Deferred Action for Childhood Arrivals) program, 226, 290n

Dartmouth College, Hanover, NH, 39–41

data, 11, 15, 53, 54–55, 70, 97–98, 99, 101, 103–105, 106, 116–117, 118–120, 125–133, 135, 140, 143, 170–172, 178, 179, 180–181, 184, 194–96, 220–221, 225–226, 228, 234, 235–236, 237–239, 244, 255, 257–258, 260–261

academic advising and, 96–134

baseball, use of and lessons for higher ed, 117, 260–261, 279n

cultural challenges of, 118–120, 125–126, 131

development of data technologies, 116–117, 260–261

developing reliable data warehouse at Georgia State, 103–105

early university reform and, 170–172, 173–175

Perimeter consolidation and, 220–221, 225–226, 228, 234–235

privacy and dystopian concerns surrounding, 110, 115, 194–196

questioning of, 180–181

Renick's use of, 15, 45, 47–48, 53, 54–55, 97–98, 126–129, 130–131, 132–133, 135, 237–239
  on reliability of standardized testing, 54–55
  story-telling power and purpose of, 54, 108–9, 179, 234
  student affairs division resistance to, 235–236
Daulerio, Kirk, 182–184, 187–188, 193
Davis, Erroll, 27, 28–29, 66, 106
Deal, Nathan, 106, 107, 207
Death by Meeting (Patrick Lencioni), 280n
Decatur campus, Perimeter College, 219, 243, 289n
Deferred Action for Childhood Arrivals (DACA) program, 226, 243, 290n
Dell Foundation, 195, 196
Denley, Tristan, 175
discrimination. *see* race and racial discrimination
Downtown Atlanta, 16, 36–37, 151, 152, 154, 165–166, 199, 203–208, 245, 260
Dream Hoarders (Reeves), 13
Driesell, Lefty, 166
drop-out rates, 47–49, 98–99, 128, 135, 140–141, 173–174, 254, 293n
Duderstadt, James, vii, 25
Dunwoody campus, Perimeter College, 219, 220, 243

EAB (Education Advisory Board), 115, 116, 117–120, 125, 127, 133, 175, 228, 238, 242, 255, 260, 261, 278n
Ebenezer Baptist Church, 16
Education Trust, 69, 276n
Emory University, Atlanta, 11, 23
Eriksen, Michael, 20, 33–34, 61–65, 147

FAFSA (Free Application for Federal Student Aid), 187, 193–194
Fanczi, Steve, 212

Family Educational Rights and Privacy Act (FERPA), 111
financial aid office, challenges with Perimeter consolidation, 226–228
financial need, 5, 7, 12, 35–36, 51, 84, 87, 135–138, 144–147, 163–164, 170, 186, 207, 227, 250–251
first-generation students, 15, 33, 44, 84–86, 88, 89, 120, 172, 182–183, 184–185, 194, 209, 259
flipped model, 169. *see also* adaptive computer learning
Florida, Richard, 22
Florida State University, Tallahassee, 170–172
football at Georgia State, 12, 199, 201–203, 208, 209, 211, 246
Forte-Reid, Lynette, 123
Franken, William, 256
Free Application for Federal Student Aid (FAFSA), 187, 193–194
freshman learning communities. *see* learning communities
freshman no-shows. *see* summer melt
freshmen orientation. *see* new student orientation Fulton County, GA summer melt study, 185
funding, government. *see* American Recovery and Investment Act; Pell grants; HOPE scholarships
funding, student. *see* HOPE scholarships; Keep HOPE Alive; Panther retention grants; Pell grants; State Farm Insurance scholarship

Gainesville State College, GA, 216
Gates, Bill, 248–249, 254, 293n
Gates Foundation, 107, 176, 177, 248–249
Gehlbach, Hunter, 189
Georgia Building Authority, 211, 212
Georgia Institute of Technology. *see* Georgia Tech

Georgia Perimeter College. *see* Perimeter College

Georgia state legislature, 10, 28–30, 31, 66, 106–107, 202, 205, 212, 223, 262, 282n, 290n

Georgia State College of Business Administration (former name of Georgia State), 156

Georgia State University, Atlanta. *see also* achievement gaps; Georgia State University buildings; graduation rates, Georgia State; presidents, Georgia State; student stories; student success programs; University Innovation Alliance

2008 recession and, 28–33, 55, 56

2011 strategic plan, 58–75

2018, class of, 3–10

academic advising reform, 87–89, 96–133

campus expansion, 198–212

civil rights legacy and, 16–17, 151–167

employer of alumni, 243

foundation, 49, 134, 151, 170, 225, 276n

graduation ceremonies, 3, 12, 94, 179, 210–212

history of, 27–28, 151–167, 168–170, 179–181, 201–208

Perimeter consolidation, 213–232

reputation of, 7, 10, 11, 18, 26, 30, 33–34

research at, 19, 22–23, 27–28, 60, 62, 64, 68, 72, 147, 148, 149–150, 152, 166, 209, 215, 223

teaching at, 23, 36, 41–44, 50–51, 52, 62, 70, 84–86, 169, 220, 221, 222–223, 245, 255

U.S. News & World Report rankings, 35–36, 62, 245

versus the Ivy League, 7, 14, 39, 41

Georgia State University buildings

55 Park Place, 206, 286n

Aderhold Learning Center, 166

Buckhead Center, 36–37

Centennial Hall, 205–206, 208, 286n

Citizens & Southern National Bank building (35 Broad Street), 204, 286n

Citizens Trust building (75 Piedmont), 237

Commons, The, 165, 167, 205, 207, 208

Dahlberg Hall, 153

Kell Hall (old parking garage), 166

Langdale Hall (formerly General Classroom Building), 92, 277n

law school, 207, 271

library, 91, 92, 93, 166

parking decks, 199, 206

Patton Hall (formerly Freshman Hall), 207

Petit Science Center, 166, 167

Rialto theater, 166, 204

student center, 19, 53, 228, 246

SunTrust building (25 Park Place), 119

University Lofts, 166

Georgia Tech (Georgia Institute of Technology), Atlanta, 12, 23, 30, 91, 156, 159, 165, 211, 212, 224, 273n

Gindhart, Maria, 79

Gomez, Terri, 257–258

government funding

American Recovery and Reinvestment Act, 30

HOPE scholarship, 48–50, 78, 106, 107, 135, 137, 139, 142–143, 144–145, 163–164, 250, 253, 283n

Pell grants, 6, 8, 14, 234, 245, 271n, 283n

Zell Miller scholarship, 253

GradesFirst student tracking system, 103, 119

graduation rates, Georgia State, 9–12, 23, 28, 36, 55, 62, 73, 86, 106, 107, 108, 113, 132, 137, 148, 149, 218, 234, 235, 240, 249

Great Gatsby, The (F. Scott Fitzgerald), 39

Griffin, Marvin, 156
Gwinnett College (now Georgia Gwinnett
    College), 120–121, 231, 289n

Hall, Annette Lucille, 159
Harvard University, Cambridge MA, 7, 45,
    86, 150, 182, 241, 292n
Havre de Grace, MD, 24
HBCUs (historically black colleges and
    universities), 92, 153, 162, 165, 216,
    259, 289n
Helping Outstanding Pupils Educationally.
    see HOPE scholarship
Henry, Ron, 38, 46–47, 69, 85, 87, 97, 141,
    147, 168–173
High Velocity Culture Change (Pritchett
    and Pound), 63–64
Hildreth, Bart, 66–67, 275–276n
Hill, Jesse, 155–156, 158–159, 286n
Hill, Ezira, 286n
Hinton, Matt, 43
Hispanic students. *see* Latino student
    performance at Georgia State
historically black colleges and universities.
    see HBCUs
Holmes, Hamilton, 159
"HOPE-mobiles," 164
HOPE scholarship, 48–50, 78, 106, 107,
    135, 137, 139, 142–143, 144–145,
    163–164, 250, 253, 283n
housing, campus, 120, 164–166, 187,
    201, 207–208, 235, 246, 286n,
    291n
Housley, Heather, 232–233, 246–247
Huckaby, Hank, 106–109, 137–138, 163,
    214–218, 224–225, 289n
Hudson, Hugh, 34–35, 74, 273n
Hunt, Barbara, 157
Hunter, Charlayne (later Charlayne
    Hunter-Gault), 159, 281n
Huss, Fenwick, 36–37, 46, 53, 54, 56, 68,
    70–71, 84–86, 111, 130–131, 140,
    148–150, 236, 240, 254

Indian River State College, FL, 259
Isakson, Johnny, 138, 279–280n
Iskander, John, 45
Ivory, Mo, 271–272n
Ivy League, 13, 14, 39, 40, 62, 174

Jarrett, Elisha, 87, 88–89, 100, 120, 124
Jobs, Steve, 20
Johnson, Larry Felton, 7
Jones, Dennis, 215, 230–231
Jones, Stan, 173–174

Kaminshine, Steve, 61
Keep HOPE Alive, 48–50, 70, 157, 204
King, Martin Luther, Jr., 16
King, Rodney, 152
Kings Point, NY, 39–40

"land for children" swap, 205
Langdale, Noah, 152, 158, 160–162,
    164–165, 166, 282n
Latino student performance at Georgia
    State, 11, 132, 234
learning communities, 47, 97, 124, 141,
    142, 147, 168, 170, 173, 215, 228–229,
    236, 246
legal affairs department, 111, 189–190, 196,
    209, 219, 233, 277–278n
Lemann, Nicholas, 55
Lewis, Michael, 117, 132, 279n
Lewis, Tom, 29–30, 67–68, 75, 166,
    201–203, 205, 211–212, 273n
lottery, to fund HOPE scholarship, 163–164
lower-income students, 8, 11, 14, 15, 22, 31,
    33, 39, 48, 57, 63, 70, 80, 83, 99, 108,
    134–140, 164–165, 169, 172, 173,
    175, 185, 207–208, 213, 224–225,
    234–235, 239–240, 243, 245, 254,
    256, 271n, 284–285n
Ludacris, 10, 271–272n
Lyons, Matt, 43
Lyons, Peter, 73–74, 104–105, 148,
    218–220, 222, 226–227, 243

Magliozzi, Andrew, 182–184, 187–193, 195, 196

MALDEF (Mexican American Legal Defense and Education Fund), 290

Martinez-Vasquez, Jorge, 61, 64, 65, 67, 69, 149–150, 160, 161

math department, 50, 81, 84–86, 97–98

Mauriello, Ken, 117

merger of colleges. *see* consolidation

meta majors, 142, 174, 228, 236, 246, 262, 280n

Mexican American Legal Defense and Education Fund (MALDEF), 290

Middle Tennessee State University, Nashville, 259–260

Miller, Zell, 106, 163–164, 205

Mitchell, Ceasar, 198–199, 201, 203, 207, 210, 285n

Mitchell, Crystal, 89–90, 93–95, 96, 97, 99, 119, 120, 125, 145, 201, 240

Moneyball (Lewis), 117, 132, 279n

Morehouse College, Atlanta, 92, 155

Morgan State University, Baltimore, 259

Morrill, Justin, 288n

Morse, Bob, 292n

movie industry, Atlanta, 22, 206–207

Mulvenna, Tyler, 143–147, 241–242

"murky middle," 98–99, 108, 116, 119–120, 125, 130–131

Murphy, Tom, 205

music department, Georgia State, 76, 79–82, 90, 92–93, 204

Myers Middle School, Savannah, 94

NACADA (National Association of Academic Advising), 99, 277

National Association of Student Financial Aid Administration, 227–228

National Center for Education Statistics, 13

National Center for Higher Education Management Systems, 215–216

NCAT (National Center for Academic Transformation), 169

Nelson, Bill, 51

Nelson, Princeton, 3–7, 137

New America foundation report, 177–178

New Orleans Saints football team, 20, 21

new student orientation, 8, 232–234, 236, 246–247

Newman, Harvey, 161

Newnan, GA, 144, 146

Newton campus, Perimeter College, 220

North Georgia State University, 216

Oakland A's baseball team, 117, 260–261

Obama, Barack, 108, 126, 138, 226, 280n

Office of Institutional Research, 271n

Okinola-King, Joshua, 96

Oli the Owl (chatbot), 183–184, 189. *see also* Pounce

Olympics (1996) in Atlanta, 67, 152, 164–166, 167, 199, 200

Onwuzuruike, Fortune, 249–250, 254

orientation. *see* new student orientation

Page, Lindsay, 185–189, 193

Paige, Jovan, 86

Palm, Risa, 33–38, 46, 53, 54–57, 58–63, 67, 68–69, 73, 105, 110, 112, 131–132, 140, 141, 143, 147–148, 149, 180–181, 237, 241, 254, 273n, 280n

Panther Excellence Program, 144

Panther retention grants, 134–140, 145–147, 170, 228, 251, 252, 262, 279–280n

Parthasarathy, Bharath, 209–210, 287n

Pastides, Harris, 22, 26, 65

Patton, Carl, 27–28, 30, 34, 147, 151–154, 162, 164–167, 170, 179, 201–202, 204, 209

Patton Hall. *see* Georgia State University buildings

peer instruction. *see* supplemental instruction

Pell grants, 6, 8, 14, 234, 245, 271n, 283n

Pennington, Hilary, 176–179
Perimeter College (formerly Georgia
     Perimeter College), 121, 213–231
Peterson, Bud, 224
Petro, Anthony, 43–44
Phi Beta Sigma fraternity, 153
philosophy department, Georgia State,
     41–42, 44–46, 97, 161
Pi Kappa Alpha fraternity, 153, 154
Portch, Stephen, 163
Portnoy, Jeffrey, 203, 218, 221–222
Pounce (chatbot), 189, 191–192, 194–196,
     253–254. see also Oli the Owl
presidents, Georgia State. see also Becker,
     Mark
  Bill Suttles, 152, 160–161, 282n
  Carl Patton, 27–30, 151–154, 164–167,
     170, 179, 201–202
  George Sparks, 156
  Noah Langdale, 152, 158, 160–162,
     164–165
Princeton University, NJ, 40, 41, 44, 45, 55,
     150, 164, 245
probation, academic, 82, 90, 98, 102–103,
     121
Prothero, Stephen, 42, 44
Pruitt, Dennis, 176, 237

Race and racial discrimination, 11–12, 17,
     63, 78, 81, 123, 132, 147, 152–154,
     154–160, 162–163, 199–200,
     203–204, 216, 234, 240–241, 254,
     271n, 281n, 289n
Rackliffe, Jerry, 30–31, 55–56, 107–110,
     136–137, 202, 204–208, 211–212,
     217, 237, 273n, 279n
Rainbolt, George, 45
recession (2008), 10–11, 15, 22, 27, 28–33,
     55, 56, 66, 73–74, 99, 106–107, 110,
     113, 134, 144, 173, 176, 205, 206,
     213, 239, 250, 261, 273n
Reed, Kasim, 201
Reeves, Dan, 202

Reeves, Richard, 13
religious studies, 15, 37, 40–45, 161
R.E.M., 10
Renick, Tim
  academic advising reform and, 96–133
  adaptive computer learning and, 50–51,
     85
  background pre–Georgia State, 39–40
  Becker's relationship with, 53–57,
     99–100, 104, 105, 133, 240
  Bill Gates visit and, 248
  Calhoun-Brown's relationship with
     51–53
  career as religious studies professor,
     41–46
  career services and, 239–240, 242–243
  chatbot and, 190, 193–194
  Complete College America, touring
     with, 174
  data privacy and, 196
  housing and, 207, 235–236, 286n
  Keep HOPE Alive and, 47–50
  moral imperative driving, 15–16
  Palm's relationship with, 37–38,
     147–148
  Panther retention grants and,
     134–138
  Perimeter consolidation and, 213,
     217–219, 220–221, 223, 225–228,
     234
  public speaking presentations, 109, 178,
     180–181, 256, 279n
  reproducing the Georgia State model,
     ideas on, 258–262
  Ron Henry's recruitment of, 46–47
  SAT and ACT test, views, 37–38,
     54–57
  strategic plan and, 61, 69, 70, 71, 72,
     74–75, 180
  student affairs division and, 232–234,
     236–237
  "summer melt" and, 185, 187
  Summer Success Academy and, 140–143

Renick, Tim (*cont.*)
  supplemental instruction and, 50
  "swirlers" and, 83–84
  University Innovation Alliance and,
    177–178
  unmet student need insights, 51
  weed-out teaching, views on, 85, 86
  weekly managers' meeting, 237–239
  working style, 45–46, 75, 244
reproducibility, of the Georgia State model,
  254–263
residential housing, campus. *see* housing,
  campus
retention grants. *see* Panther retention
  grants
retirement separation policy, 30–31
return on investment. *see* student success
  programs, cost-effectiveness of
Rhodes, Frank, 25–26
Rialto theater, 166, 204
Richardson, Glenn, 282n
Riley, Chris, 207, 211–212
Roberts, Julia, 10
Robinson, A.J., 204
Robinson, Kalif, 250–251, 254
Robinson College of Business, Georgia
  State. *see* business school, Georgia
  State
Rogers, Terrance, 86, 240–241

SAC (Student Advisement Center). *see
  also* UAC, 87–89, 97–105, 118–120,
  123–124
Saccoh, Osman, 229–230
Salinas, Gabriella, 251–252, 254
Sample, Sharon, 138–140
SAT tests, 35–38, 54–56, 140–143
Schloer, Wolfgang, 196–197
scholarships. *see* funding, student
Schumpeter, Joseph, 63
segregation era, 152, 154–159, 160
SEO (Sponsors for Educational
  Opportunity), 241

Shenzhen, 20
SignalVine service, 188
sit-in (1992), 153–154
Sluder, Rick, 259–260
Smith, Bob, 28–30, 66, 273
Southern Association of Colleges and
  Schools, 60
Sparks, George, 156
Spelman College, Atlanta, 89, 92
Spider-Man 2: Homecoming (2017), 206–207
Sponsors for Educational Opportunity
  (SEO), 241
Staley, Rich, 118
Stapleton, Kyle, 86, 167, 263
Starfish software company, 115
State Farm Insurance
  Georgia State relationship with, 243
  scholarships, 230
Stone, Adam, 219, 222
strategic planning committee, 58–75
Student Advisement Center (SAC). *see*
  SAC
student affairs division, 232–239
student housing. *see* housing, campus
student stories
  Anthony Petro, 43–44
  Austin Birchell, 252–254
  Brianna Cheek, 49–50
  Cary Claiborne, 120–125
  Fortune Onwuzuruike, 249–250,
    254
  Gabriel Woods, 76–82, 89–95
  Gabriella Salinas, 251–252, 254
  Greyson Walldorff, 8, 271
  Jasmine Twine, 194, 195
  Joshua Okinola-King, 96
  Jovan Paige, 86
  Kalif Robinson, 250–251, 254
  Kyle Stapleton, 86, 167, 263
  Larry Felton Johnson, 8
  Matt Hinton, 43
  Osman Saccoh, 229–230
  Princeton Nelson, 3–8, 137

Savannah Torrance, 8, 129–130

Sharon Sample, 138–140

Stephanie Tran, 142–143, 243

Terrance Rogers, 86, 240–241

Tyler Mulvenna, 143–147, 241–242

student success programs. *see* academic advising; chatbot; data; funding, student; Keep HOPE Alive, Panther retention grants; Summer Success Academy; supplemental instruction; student stories

accomplishments of students presented to Bill Gates, 248–254

cost effectiveness, of, 137–138, 262, 279n

implementation at Perimeter, 213–215

Panther Excellence Program, 144–145

reproducibility at other institutions of Georgia State's, 254–263

strategic planning committee implementation of, 69–75

Sugar, Tom, 173–174, 180, 261

"summer melt," 185–188, 189, 192, 193, 195, 254

Summer Success Academy, 140–143, 243, 247, 249, 251

supplemental instruction, 47, 50, 97, 124, 142, 176, 215, 228, 229, 243

Suttles, Bill, 160–161, 282

Sweet Auburn (Atlanta neighborhood), 16, 204

"swirlers," students as, 83–85, 130–131

Tai, P.C., 69

Takeda Pharmaceutical, Atlanta, 243

texting, as communication with students, 187–188

Torbert, Edgar, 202

Torrance, Savannah, 7, 129–130, 271

Tran, Stephanie, 142–143, 243

Tricoli, Anthony, 214, 223

Turner Field, Georgia State acquisition of, 198–201, 203, 208–210

Twigg, Carol, 169

Twine, Jasmine, 194, 195

UAC (University Advisement Center), 119–120, 126–133, 238–239

unions, campus, 258

United Parcel Service, Atlanta, 243–244

University Advisement Center (UAC). *see* UAC

University Innovation Alliance (UIA), 177–178

University of California, Berkeley, 11, 32, 151–152

University of California, Riverside, 177–178

University of Central Florida, Orlando, 178

University of Georgia, Athens, 10, 30, 63, 94, 106, 109, 118, 121, 154, 156, 159, 164, 211

University of Houston, TX, 259

University of Illinois, Chicago, 258, 294n

University of Iowa, Iowa City, 26

University of North Carolina, Chapel Hill, 32, 33

University of North Georgia, Dahlonega, 216

University of Pittsburgh, PA, 187

University of South Carolina, Columbia, 21, 26, 59, 176, 217, 222, 237

U.S. News & World Report rankings, 32, 35–36, 56, 57, 62, 245, 292

University System of Georgia, 44, 66, 106, 107–109, 138, 157, 159, 163, 203, 213–218, 220, 224–225, 227, 262. *see also* agricultural and mechanical arts colleges

University System of Georgia Board of Regents. *see* board of regents

Vandiver, Ernest, 157–159

Venit, Ed, 113–116, 133, 277

Walldorff, Greyson, 7
Ward, David, 62–63
Ward, Horace, 154–162
Warner, Mary Belle Reynolds, 160
Watts, Rob, 214
Woods, Gabriel, 76–79, 80–82, 89–95

Wolfe, Tom, 36
"World House, The" (King, Jr.), 16

Young, Andrew, 17, 67–68, 165–166

Zell Miller scholarship, 253

ABOUT THE AUTHOR

Andrew Gumbel is a British-born journalist, based in Los Angeles, who has won awards for his work as an investigative reporter, political columnist, and feature writer. For more than twenty years he worked as a foreign correspondent, covering stories in Europe, the Middle East, and the Americas, and he still writes regularly for *The Guardian* on a broad range of subjects including immigration, voting rights, and counterterrorism. While he has taught in a variety of settings—both to university students and to lower-income high schoolers—this is his first extensive foray into researching and writing about education. His other books include *Oklahoma City*, about the 1995 bombing; *Down for the Count*, about America's tattered democratic history; and, as co-editor with David W. Orr, Bakari Kitwana, and William S. Becker, and as a contributor, *Democracy Unchained*. The two latter titles are also from The New Press

PUBLISHING IN THE
PUBLIC INTEREST

Thank you for reading this book published by The New Press. The New Press is a nonprofit, public interest publisher. New Press books and authors play a crucial role in sparking conversations about the key political and social issues of our day.

We hope you enjoyed this book and that you will stay in touch with The New Press. Here are a few ways to stay up to date with our books, events, and the issues we cover:

- Sign up at www.thenewpress.com/subscribe to receive updates on New Press authors and issues and to be notified about local events
- Like us on Facebook: www.facebook.com/new pressbooks
- Follow us on Twitter: www.twitter.com/thenewpress

Please consider buying New Press books for yourself; for friends and family; or to donate to schools, libraries, community centers, prison libraries, and other organizations involved with the issues our authors write about.

The New Press is a 501(c)(3) nonprofit organization. You can also support our work with a tax-deductible gift by visiting www.thenewpress.com/donate.